Abraham R Horne

Das Leben und Wirken von Vater Josua Jäger

Evangelisch-Lutherischem Prediger

Abraham R Horne

Das Leben und Wirken von Vater Josua Jäger
Evangelisch-Lutherischem Prediger

ISBN/EAN: 9783741169502

Manufactured in Europe, USA, Canada, Australia, Japa

Cover: Foto ©Lupo / pixelio.de

Manufactured and distributed by brebook publishing software (www.brebook.com)

Abraham R Horne

Das Leben und Wirken von Vater Josua Jäger

Joshua Yeager.

Das Leben und Wirken

von

Vater Josua Jäger,

Evangelisch-Lutherischem Prediger;

wie auch

Ein Verzeichniß seiner Amtsgeschäfte.

"Gedenket an eure Lehrer, die euch das Wort Gottes gesagt haben, welcher Ende schauet an, und folget ihrem Glauben nach. Jesus Christus gestern und heute, und Derselbe auch in Ewigkeit."—Eb. 13: 7, 8.

ALLENTOWN, PA.:
PUBLISHED AT THE OFFICE OF THE NATIONAL EDUCATOR.
1889.

Seinen Gemeinden gewidmet von
seinem Nachfolger.

APOLOGY.

These Memoirs are necessarily brief. Much more could have been written of a life so long and useful, but it was feared that to do so might make too bulky a volume. The desire was found to prevail everywhere among his people that the book should contain a register of the most important *acta ministeriales* of their former pastor to which reference can be had. Besides, it was deemed necessary to let the biographical sketch appear both in German and English, from the fact that the older people in the congregations neither read nor understand English, while many of the younger portion cannot read German. For this reason, too, the record of deaths appears in German, while that of marriages and confirmations is given in English.

I.

Vater Jäger's Eltern.

Die Großeltern Vater Jäger's kamen von Deutschland. Er wußte aber ganz wenig von denselben. In seines Vaters Familie sah er öfters ein Buch, in welchem ein schönes Gebet geschrieben war, das sein Großvater wahrscheinlich verfaßt hatte. Von seinen Eltern lernte er auch, daß sein Großvater mit seiner Haushaltung dem Gott seiner Väter diente und seine Familie in der Zucht und dem Gehorsam des Herrn zu erziehen suchte.

Der Ehrwürdige Johann Conrad Jäger, Vater von Josua Jäger, wurde in York County, Pennsylvanien, in der Nähe der Stadt York, geboren. Desgleichen auch seine Mutter, die eine geborne Schmidt war.

Johann Conrad Jäger war seines Handwerks ein Cigarrenmacher und hatte einen kleinen Tabaksladen in der Stadt York. Sie hatten schon drei Kinder, als er sich entschied, sich dem christlichen Predigtamt zu widmen, und zwar unter folgenden Umständen und Veranlassungen: Als er eines Tages an seiner Handwerksbank saß, beschäftigt mit Cigarrenmachen, kam sein Pastor, der Ehrw. Dr. Göhring, zu ihm. Dr. Göhring bediente die Lutherische Gemeinde zu York. Vater Conrad Jäger war ein treues Mitglied dieser Gemeinde und ein fleißiger Kirchenbesucher. Dr. Göhring hatte schon eine geraume Zeit lang Herrn Jäger im Augenmerk und glaubte, daß er für das heilige Amt bestimmt sei.

Vielleicht war der Gedanke Herrn Jäger auch nicht fremd, obschon er sich niemals darüber äußerte, aus der Ursache, daß er keine Möglichkeit sah, solchen Wunsch auszuführen. Dr. Göhring benutzte diese Gelegenheit, indem er zu Herrn Jäger trat, ihm über die Schulter blickte und sagte: „Johann, ich lade dich ein, in mein Haus zu kommen; du hast Gaben für Besseres als Cigarrenmachen. Du solltest ein Prediger des Evangeliums werden." Herr Jäger hatte eine ordentliche Schulbildung in seiner Jugend genossen und durch fleißiges Studiren sich solche Kenntnisse erworben, wie sie die Schulen jener Zeit gewährten.

Mit solchen unvollkommenen Vorbereitungskenntnissen kam er zu Dr. Göhring und fing seine Studien für das Predigtamt an. Unter andern unternahm er auch die griechische Sprache zu studiren, welches mit großer Schwierigkeit verbunden ist. In dieser Sprache studirte er in späteren Jahren die Texte seiner Predigten. Nachdem er ein Jahr unter Dr. Göhring studirt hatte, und zur selben Zeit auch sein kleines Geschäft fortführte zum Unterhalt seiner Familie, ging er auf Empfehlung von Dr. Göhring nach Philadelphia.

Damals war es Gebrauch der Candidaten für das Predigtamt, unter den Stadtpastoren zu studiren, wo sie Unterricht und Anleitung erhielten, so viel als möglich, in Verbindung mit der Pastoral=Arbeit ihrer Lehrer. Conrad Jäger wurde Student der Doktoren Schmidt, Schäffer und Helmuth. Der Unterricht war gründlich und praktisch, obschon sehr eingeschränkt. Da Herr Jäger ein fleißiger

Student war, hatte er am Ende eines Jahres solche Fortschritte gemacht, daß seine Lehrer ihn der Synode zur Examination vorstellten, und er auch tüchtig vorbereitet erfunden ward, in das Predigtamt aufgenommen zu werden. Er wurde daher von dem Evangelisch-Lutherischen Ministerium von Pennsylvanien lizensirt.

Nach seiner Aufnahme in die Synode erhielt er einen Ruf von drei kleinen Gemeinden in New Jersey, unweit Easton, Pa. Die alte, sogenannte Stroh=Kirche in Greenwich Township, Warren County, war eine seiner Gemeinden. Als er der Prediger dieser Gemeinde war, kam er eines Tages nach Easton, um in Herrn Herschter's Store einige nothwendige Artikel zu kaufen. Herr Herrschter wußte von Pastor Jäger und hatte manches Günstige von ihm gehört. Pastor Jäger war arm und daher schlecht gekleidet. Herr Herrschter betrachtete seine abgetragenen Kleider und erkundigte sich über seine Umstände. „Ich sehe manches hier, das ich brauche," sagte Jäger, „und wovon meine Familie benöthigt ist, aber ich habe kein Geld es zu kaufen und muß daher ohne dasselbe vorlieb nehmen." Herr Herrschter sagte zu seinem Gehilfen: „Gehe hin und schneide Herrn Jäger Tuch ab für einen Anzug, messe ihm einen Hut an und schneide ihm auch ein Kleid für seine Frau; wiege zwanzig Pfund Zucker, etwas Kaffee und gieb ihm andere nöthige Artikel für seine Familie." „Nehmen Sie dies mit nach Haus," sagte Herr H., „und lassen Sie sich einen Anzug verfertigen, allererst für sich selbst, so daß Sie auch ein ordentliches Aussehen haben wenn Sie unter Fremde gehen." „Ja wohl," sagte Pastor Jäger, „aber ich habe kein Geld um für diese Artikel zu bezahlen." "Das ist einerlei, nur ganz zufrieden," sagte Herr H. "Sie können in einigen Jahren kommen, wenn Sie einmal Geld haben und dafür bezahlen."

Daß diese Ueberraschung die Herzen der Familie von Pastor Jäger hoch erfreute, läßt sich denken. Hier war ein Freund in der Noth ein Freund in der That. Als einige Jahre vorbeigerollt, obschon Pastor Jäger's Arbeit mit Segen gekrönt war, war er aber immer noch in dürftigen Umständen und auch nicht vermögend, seine Schuld zu bezahlen. Als er aber eines Tages zu seinem Wohlthäter kam, um einen Theil seiner Schuld abzutragen, frug ihn dieser: "Wie geht's jetzt bei Ihnen?" "Recht gut," antwortete Pastor J., "und ich bin gekommen, einen Theil meiner Schuld abzutragen, obschon ich noch zu arm bin um das Ganze zu entrichten." "Gieb ihm eine Quittung für das Ganze," sagte Herr H. "Ich höre so manches Gute von Ihnen, daß ich bereit bin, Ihnen die ganze Schuld zu entlassen; ich bin völlig befriedigt." Herr Jäger ging, wie zu erwarten, mit leichtem Herzen heim.

Vater Conrad Jäger's zweite Pfarrstelle war Williams Township, Northampton Co., und Saucon (Friedensville), Lecha Co. Er gründete die Saucon-Gemeinde. Er predigte einige Zeit lang in Herrn Morey's Scheune, da die Kirche im Bauen begriffen war. Dies war im Jahre 1793.

In späteren Jahren bekam er auch noch die Trockenland (Hecktown), Hanover (Schönersville) und Allentown Gemeinden. Während dieser Zeit wohnte er in Williams Township. Nun aber zog er nach Hanover, woselbst er

HOMESTEAD OF REV. J. YEAGER.

eine Bauerei von 236 Acker gekauft hatte. Hier wurde sein Sohn Josua, dessen Lebensgeschichte wir hier schreiben, geboren. Ehrw. J. Conrad Jäger arbeitete in diesem Feld, mit Segen und Erfolg, bis zum Ende seines Lebens, welches in 1832 stattfand.

II.

Pastor Josua Jäger's Jugend.

Josua Jäger, das jüngste Glied einer Familie von neun Söhnen und zwei Töchtern, erblickte das Licht der Welt am 23. September, im Jahre unseres Herrn 1802. Es wurde für ihn gesorgt, daß er in seiner zarten Kindheit dem Dreieinigen Gott in der heiligen Taufe geweiht werde. In spätern Jahren wurde er von seinem Vater in den Heilswahrheiten unserer heiligen Religion gründlich unterrichtet, konfirmirt und als Glied der Evangelisch=Lutherischen Kirche in die Christus=Gemeinde zu Schönersville aufgenommen.

Im elterlichen Hause wurde regelmäßig vom Familienhaupt an Wochentag Abenden Unterricht im Lesen, Schreiben und Rechnen ertheilt. Im Vergleich mit jetziger Zeit war die Gelegenheit Unterricht zu bekommen äußerst gering. Was aber in weltlicher Lehre fehlte, wurde völlig aufgemacht in Religions=Unterricht, wie derselbe im Elternhause ertheilt wurde. Religions=Unterricht wurde damals als Hauptsache betrachtet, etwas welches leider heutzutage in manchen Familien zu viel und oftmals beinahe gänzlich vernachläſſigt wird. Die frommen Väter jener Zeit folgten dem göttlichem Befehle: „Trachtet am erſten nach dem Reich Gottes und ſeiner Gerechtigkeit," indem ſie ſuchten Eindrücke auf das Herz und Leben der Jugend zu machen, durch Unterricht in den großen Heilswahrheiten des göttlichen Wortes. Eine ſo hochwichtige Sache dem einſtündigen Sonntagſchul-Unterricht zu überlaſſen, wo, nebenbei geſagt, es noch oftmals ſehr unvollkommen geſchieht; oder ſogar ſich auf die Wochenſchule zu verlaſſen, wo Religions-Unterricht nicht gelitten wird, das würden die frommen Väter jener alten Zeiten mit heiligem Schauder und gerechtem Abſcheu angeſehen haben, indem ſie die große Verantwortlichkeit, das Prieſteramt in ihren Familien zu verwalten, hehr und heilig hielten.

Bibelleſen und nachher niederzuſchreiben was im Gedächtniß behalten wurde, wenigſtens ein Bogen Schreibpapier voll täglich, darin beſtand ein Theil des Familien-Schulunterrichts im Hauſe des ältern Vater Jäger's. Der Sohn Joſua genoß freilich dieſen Unterricht, der zwar ſehr gründlich, aber doch im Vergleich mit dem Schulunterricht heutigen Tags ſehr beſchränkt war. Nachdem er das Alter erreichte, wo er ſich brauchbar auf der Bauerei machen konnte, beſtand ſeine tägliche Beſchäftigung in Arbeit auf einer 236 Acker großen Bauerei, und es blieb ihm nur wenig Zeit zum Studiren oder zur Erholung übrig. Als er eines Sommertages mit Pflügen beſchäftigt war, kam ſein Vater hinaus in das Feld, und begleitete ihn bis an das Ende des Feldes. Joſua konnte ſich kaum dieſen ungewöhnlichen Vorfall erklären. Als aber das Ende der

Furche erreicht war, sagte der Vater zu ihm: „Warte ein wenig. Ich habe dir etwas zu sagen. Es ist mein Wunsch, daß du, mit Gottes Hilfe, ein Prediger werden mögest." Dieser unerwartete Vorschlag erfüllte den jungen Jäger mit Furcht. „Komm auf mein Zimmer morgen früh," fuhr Vater Jäger fort, „verlasse deinen Pflug, es sind Andere welche diese Arbeit besorgen können. Ich wünsche dir eine dreimonatliche Probe zu geben, um zu entscheiden, ob du Talent hast fürs Predigtamt; wenn so, so sollst du deine Studien fortsetzen, wenn nicht, so werde ich's dir sagen."

Der Vater überreichte dem Sohn eine lateinische Grammatik mit der Bemerkung: „Dies ist ein verhältnißmäßig leichtes Studium, aber du wirst daraus einen Begriff von der Grammatik überhaupt bekommen, welches sehr nothwendig ist beim Studium der Sprachen. Studire zwei Stunden darin, und frage mich dann über alles was du verstehst und nicht verstehst. Nachher komm in den Garten und arbeite so viel du willst. Des Abends studire wieder zwei Stunden, und fahre also fort." Auf diese Weise studirte Josua Jäger nun. Sein Vater war ein meisterhafter Lehrer und Zuchtmeister. Auf das Betragen seines Sohnes war er besonders aufmerksam. Er suchte Eindrücke auf ihn zu machen in Bezug auf die Wichtigkeit und Verantwortlichkeit seines Unternehmens. Er ermahnte ihn, sich stets so zu betragen wie es einem Candidaten fürs heilige Predigtamt geziemt und wie man es vor Gott und Menschen verantworten kann.

Diese Erziehung, die so oft gering geschätzt wird von denen, welche junge Männer für das Predigtamt vorbe=

reiten, die aber höchst nothwendig ist um den rechten Grund
zu dem Charakter eines Predigers des Herrn Jesu Christi zu
legen, machte einen tiefen und bleibenden Eindruck auf das
Gemüth des jungen Jäger. Diesem mehr als irgend etwas
sonst muß die Gemüthsstimmung, sowie der Ernst und der
Eifer, welchen Josua Jäger in seiner Amtsverwaltung von
beinahe sechzig Jahren bewies, zugeschrieben werden. Dies
machte ihn auch so beliebt bei denen, die er so lang versorgte
und die ihn stets so gern hatten.

Als die drei Monate verflossen waren, erhielt Josua die
Aufmunterung, welche ihm so freudig gegeben wurde von
seinem Vater, fortzufahren mit seinen Studien, denn er
hatte durch Fleiß und Fortschritte Beweise geliefert, daß sein
Vater sich nicht geirrt hatte ihn auszusondern als denjenigen,
auf den sein Mantel einmal fallen sollte. Die Brüder ver=
richteten die Arbeit auf der Bauerei, und Josua setzte seine
Studien vier Jahre lang mit Fleiß fort.

Diese vier Jahre bei der Seite seines Vaters und in
seiner Nähe, unter beständiger Uebung und der Aufsicht seines
Vaters, im Studiren seiner Schulbücher, von alten und
modernen Sprachen, Dogmatik, Kirchengeschichte, Homiletik,
Exegese 2c., welche alle gründlich bemeistert werden mußten
unter seines Vaters tief eingreifenden Fragemethoden, und
die damit verbundene praktische Katechetik und Pastoral=
Theologie waren ihm, wie er selbst zu sagen pflegte, viel=
leicht so viel werth, als zweimal vier Jahre in einem theo=
logischen Seminar.

Der Unterricht wurde nach der katechetischen Methode,
mit Fragen und Antworten ertheilt. Die Fragen waren
keineswegs solche deren Antworten aus den Büchern ge=

lernt werden konnten. Dieselben erstreckten sich über ein
weites Feld des Nachforschens und Nachdenkens und erforderten daher nicht nur das Studiren eines Lehrbuches, sondern oft von ein halb Dutzend und mehr, und viel Nachsuchen
nebenbei. Dieses Lehrsystem des alten Vaters ist hoch anzuempfehlen und wird von den besten Lehrern befolgt. Es
weckt zum Nachdenken und beantwortet nicht die Frage für
den Studenten, sondern ist ihm ein Leitfaden und eine Hilfe
in seinen Forschungen Geheimnisse zu enthüllen. So zog sich
der junge Jäger gar oft in sein Zimmer zurück mit unbeantworteten Fragen und Aufgaben, die ihm seine Gedanken
in Anspruch nahmen in den stillen Stunden der Nacht,
während er auch des Tages über beständiglich mit Nachdenken
und Ueberlegungen der Gegenstände seiner verschiedenen
Studien beschäftigt war.

III.

Vater Jäger's Amtsthätigkeit.

Bei der Jahres=Versammlung des Evangelisch=Lutherischen Ministeriums von Pennsylvanien, gehalten während
der Woche anfangend mit Trinitatis=Sonntag 1827, wurde
Josua Jäger mit zwei anderen Candidaten geprüft, um ins
Predigtamt aufgenommen zu werden. Ehrw. Dr. F. W.
Geissenhainer, von der Stadt New York, war Vorsitzer
des Examinations=Committees. Er wurde einem gründlichen

Examen unterworfen. Vater Jäger erinnerte sich besonders noch in seinem hohen Alter, wie er über die morgenländische Literatur examinirt wurde, und als es von ihm gefordert wurde die Beschreibung der Verklärung Christi, in Matth. xvii, aus dem Griechischen ins Deutsche zu übersetzen, schien Dr. Geissenhainer sehr gut zufrieden uz sein mit der Ueberseßung, bis das griechische Zeitwort Προσχυνειν erreicht wurde. Er wurde sehr aufgeregt, beinahe erzürnt über Jäger's Ueberseßung, da er es las, „sie beugten sich und schienen anzubeten." Dr. Geissenhainer rief mit Donnerstimme, „Was, nicht sie schienen es zu thun, es war so," und fügte hinzu, „man kann sehen bei wem er studirt hat." Die drei Candidaten machten ein befriedigendes Examen und wurden in die Synode aufgenommen.

Bei der Synode des folgenden Jahres, 1828, die sich in Reading versammelte, wird berichtet, wie in den Verhandlungen zu sehen ist: „Herrn Jäger's Papiere sind sehr gut." Bei dieser Gelegenheit predigte er am letzten Abend der Synode, Dienstag den 3. Juli, über den Text: 1 Tim. iv, 12—16.

Von 1827 bis 1831 war er Gehilfe seines Vaters in den vier Gemeinden Friedensville, Allentown, Schönersville und Hecktown. In 1831 gab ihm sein Vater die Friedensville und Allentown Gemeinden und behielt Schönersville und Hecktown für sich. Nach seines Vaters Tod, in 1832, wurde er auch als Pastor und Nachfolger seines Vaters in diesen Gemeinden gewählt. Bei der Leiche von Johann Conrad Jäger hielten die Prediger der Bethlehem Brüder-Gemeinde, mit welchen er immer auf sehr freundlichem Fuße war, die Reden im Leichenhause, und die Trombonen wurden am Grabe und auf dem Weg nach dem Gotteshaus geblasen. Pastoren Wertman und Probst, von der Lutherischen Kirche, hielten den Leichengottesdienst; ersterer die Predigt und zweiter den Altargottesdienst in der alten Schönersville Kirche, auf deren Gottesacker er begraben ist.

Die verschiedenen Gemeinden, welche Josua Jäger mehr als ein halbes Jahrhundert lang bediente, erstreckten sich zuerst über ein großes Gebiet. Die Schönersville, Friedensville und Allentown Gemeinden umfaßten das ganze Territorium von Centre Valley über Bethlehem bis nach Howertown und Bath, der Monocacy entlang und über die Lecha nach Whitehall und zurück bis nach Allentown. Während seiner langen Amtsthätigkeit erlebte es Vater Jäger, daß ein ganzes Dutzend Gemeinden aus diesen drei Muttergemeinden entstanden. Die Appel's Kirche, die Hellertown Kirche, die Süd=Bethlehem, Bethlehem, West=Bethlehem, Salzburg (Jerusalem), Altona, Rittersville, Catasauqua, Howertown, Bath, St. Paulus, St. Michael's, St. John's (englisch) und St. Peter's Kirche in Allentown sind entweder ganz oder größtentheils aus diesen drei Gemeinden entstanden, und in andern Kirchen der Umgegend befinden sich noch Viele, die in Vater Jäger's Pfarrstelle ins Reich Gottes aufgenommen worden sind.

Die Allentown St. Paulus=Gemeinde, welche 1763 gegründet wurde, und in welcher Johann Joseph Roth, Jakob Van Buskirk, Johann Christian Leps, Joseph Wichterman, George Friederich Ellisen Pastoren waren, wurde Anno 1799 von Johann Conrad Jäger übernommen und sein Sohn Josua wurde sein Nachfolger in 1831. Nachdem er hier gewählt war, machte er Allentown zu seiner Heimath und wohnte sodann auch hier bis zum Tag seines Todes. Sobald er sein Amt hier antrat, fing ein neues Leben an in der Gemeinde zu herrschen. Er hielt alsobald jede zwei Wochen Gottesdienst und auch an Wochentag Abenden. In 1834 wurde auch eine Sonntagschule in Verbindung mit der Gemeinde gegründet, welche ihr Entstehen der Thätigkeit Vater Jäger's zu verdanken hatte; denn er machte es sich zur Aufgabe von Haus zu Haus zu gehen, um die Eltern zu ermuntern, ihre Kinder zu schicken. Er blieb der Pastor dieser Gemeinde zweiundzwanzig Jahre lang, bis 1853. Er war stets hoch geachtet und sehr beliebt in dieser Gemeinde, nicht allein bei den Gemeindegliedern, sondern auch bei den Einwohnern Allentown's überhaupt, so daß wenn es in spätern Jahren angezeigt wurde, daß Vater Jäger in einer der Kirchen Allentown's predige, er immer eine von Zuhörern gedrängte Kirche hatte. Pastor Schmauk sagte bei seiner Leichenpredigt: „Wie hast du dich nicht gefreut, St. Michael's=Gemeinde, wenn es hieß, Vater Jäger wird hier predigen!"

Vater Jäger resignirte seine Allentown Gemeinde, da die Stadt so an Bevölkerung zugenommen hatte, daß es unumgänglich nothwendig wurde, jeden Sonntag Gottesdienst zu halten und auch die englische Sprache beim Gottesdienst einzuführen, und ihm dadurch nur die Wahl übrig blieb, entweder seine Landgemeinden aufzugeben, oder die Stadt=gemeinde. Er zog vor, seine Landgemeinden zu behalten, weil es ihm immer doch am liebsten bei den Landgemeinden war, und auch der deutschen Sprache wegen, welche seine Muttersprache war. Obschon er auch zuweilen in Englisch

Amtspflichten verrichtete, fühlte er sich doch am meisten daheim in der deutschen Sprache.

Verschiedene Bewegungen in der Allentown Gemeinde, während der Amtsverwaltung Vater Jäger's, verursachten mehr oder weniger Störung, aber seine Standhaftigkeit und Amtstreue beseitigten dieselben und der Sieg blieb immer auf seiner Seite.

So war ein gewisser Ginal, von Philadelphia, eine Zeitlang beschäftigt, eine sogenannte Vernunft-Gemeinde hier ins Leben zu rufen. Zuerst schien die Sache Aufsehen zu erregen, und eine „freie Kirche" wurde gebaut, aber es ging nach Vater Jäger's eigenen Worten: „es fing klein an und endete klein." Während dieser Zeit hielt Vater Jäger manche Lehr- und Bekenntniß-Predigten, welche ihm und seiner Kirche und der Sache Jesu Christi viel Ehre machten.

Zu einer andern Zeit machte ein Prediger, der in seinen Gemeinden Streitigkeiten hatte und deswegen dieselben verließ, den Versuch Eingriffe in die Allentown Gemeinde zu machen. Ein Kirchenrath für eine neue Oppositionsgemeinde wurde gewählt und Confirmations-Unterricht angefangen. Nur fünf Personen meldeten sich. Vater Jäger fing auch an mit Unterricht, und es meldeten sich schon beim ersten Male sechsundfünfzig. Das neue Unternehmen wurde alsbald aufgegeben.

Drei Morale hierüber in Vater Jäger's eigenen Worten:

1. Freie Vernunft-Gemeinden haben ein kurzes Bestehen.

2. "Side shows" haben kein Wachsthum wo ein Pastor treulich seine Pflichten erfüllt.

3. Ein kluger Seelsorger, welcher sein Amt treulich verwaltet, kann sehr oft Spaltungen verhüten und Friede und Einigkeit herstellen.

Ungeachtet der Bekenntnißtreue Vater Jäger's hatte er aber doch stets sehr brüderlichen Umgang mit seinen Amtsbrüdern von andern Gemeinschaften, nicht nur in Allentown, sondern auch in benachbarten Städten und in seinen Landgemeinden. Mit seinen Reformirten Collegen, wie Dr. Dubbs, Dr. Becker, Vater Zellers und auch den jüngern Brüdern, mit welchen er gemeinschaftlich in seinen Kirchen wirkte, stand er immer auf freundlichem Fuß.

Der Bischof der Episcopal=Kirche machte das Ersuchen, in der St. Paulus=Kirche in Allentown an „leeren Sonntagen" zu predigen, welches ihm gestattet wurde.

In den Jahren da Vater Jäger Allentown bediente wurde er öfters nach Bethlehem gerufen und hatte sehr vertrauten Umgang daselbst mit den Predigern der Brüder=Gemeinde. Die Ehrw. Seidel, Ebermann, Jacobson und besonders Bischof Schulz waren seine intimen Freunde, mit welchen er auch zuweilen Kanzeln wechselte. Freilich geschah dies nur mit solchen, die im Geist einverstanden waren mit seinem Glaubensbekenntniß.

Während seiner Amtsverwaltung in der St. Paulus=Kirche schaffte sich dieselbe eine große Orgel an, wozu Vater Jäger seinen Gehalt eines ganzen Jahres gab. Die Gemeinde bezahlte ihm zuerst $100 das Jahr, und nachher, als er öfters predigte, $175. Die Synode versammelte sich verschiedene Male in Allentown, während er Pastor daselbst war. Als sich dieselbe das erste Mal hier versammelte zählte sie blos 48 Mitglieder. Jetzt sind es sechs mal so

INTERIOR OF FRIEDENSVILLE CHURCH.
(FATHER YEAGER IN THE PULPIT ON HIS 85TH BIRTHDAY.)

viel. Bei dieser Synode wurde die erste deutsche Kirchenzeitung ins Dasein gerufen, unter Pastor F. Schmidt, zu deren Gründung Vater Jäger auch seine $100 gab. Jetzt sind es über fünfzig deutsche und ebensoviel englische, sowie auch noch ungefähr dieselbe Zahl in Schwedisch, Norwegisch und anderen Sprachen herausgegebene. Diesen großen, erfreulichen Wachsthum seiner Kirche wurde es Vater Jäger zu erleben gestattet.

Unter seinen vielen persönlichen Freunden in Allentown rechnete Vater Jäger besonders den achtbaren Robert E. Wright, einen der hervorragendsten Advokaten und Schriftsteller, der im selben Jahre in Allentown sich niederließ, und zwei Jahre ihm voran in die Ewigkeit ging. Vater Jäger's letzter öffentlicher Auftritt war bei der Leiche seines alten Freundes Wright, woselbst er das Gebet hielt.

Die Friedens=Gemeinde zu Friedensville, in Upper Saucon, Lecha Co., wurde am allerlängsten von Vater Jäger bedient, denn er trat sein Amt als regelmäßiger Pastor am 22. Mai 1831 in derselben an, und resignirte auf Trinitatis 1885, nach einer Amtsverwaltung von 54 Jahren. Aber als Gehilfe seines Vaters, der die Gemeinde gegründet, wie schon gemeldet, kann man sagen, daß er für dieselbe predigte von 1827 bis 1885, also 58 Jahre. Hier wurde im September 1882 ein Fest gefeiert, zum Andenken an seine 55jährige Arbeit in der Gemeinde, auf seinen 80. Geburtstag, wobei ihm die Gemeinde ein schönes, werthvolles Geschenk machte. Manche seiner Amtsbrüder betheiligten sich an dieser Festlichkeit. Die erste Kirche hier wurde gebaut in 1793, vergrößert in 1817, und die jetzige in 1839.

Die Christus=Gemeinde zu Schönersville, Lecha Co., bediente er nur einige Jahre weniger als Pastor, aber in Verbindung mit seinem Vater doch eben so lang. Hier wurde er als Nachfolger seines Vaters gewählt, Dezember 1832, und verwaltete sein Amt bis Trinitatis 1885, zwischen 52 und 53 Jahren. Diese Gemeinde wurde Anno 1780 von Ehrw. Johann Faust mit 24 Gliedern gegründet. Eine kleine Block=Kirche wurde in demselben Jahre gebaut, dann eine steinerne Kirche in 1819 und die jetzige schöne backsteinerne in 1872, welche $17,000 gekostet hat. Die Pastoren dieser Gemeinde vor Jäger's Zeiten waren Johann Faust und George Joseph Wichtermann.

Die Lecha=Kirche in Nieder=Macungie, Lecha Co., zuerst die Heilige Dreieinigkeits=Kirche und nachher die Zions= Kirche genannt, bediente Vater Jäger vom 21. August 1842 bis Trinitatis 1885, 43 Jahre lang. Diese Gemeinde wurde in 1745 organisirt und die erste Kirche gebaut in 1750, unter Philip Heinrich Rapp. Hier war der Wohnort der lutherischen Prediger jener frühen Zeit, welche die umliegenden Gemeinden bedienten. Die zweite Kirche wurde gebaut in 1785, da Jakob Van Buskirk Pastor war, ein steinernes Gebäude. In 1843 wurde diese Kirche inwendig verändert, und blieb also so lange Vater Jäger daselbst predigte. Die Prediger vor ihm waren Schertlein, Wießner, Obenhausen, Geissenhainer, Heyse, Stecher, V. German und J. Schindel.

Die Rittersville= (St. Petrus) Kirche wurde in 1842 gebaut. Die Gemeinde war vorher ein Theil der Christus= Gemeinde zu Schönersville. Vater Jäger war Pastor daselbst von der Zeit da die Gemeinde organisirt wurde bis er die letzte Predigt seines Lebens daselbst hielt, auf Himmelfahrt 1885,—eine Leichenpredigt, die der Ehegattin von Charles Schmoyer, hielt er einige Wochen nachher in der Lecha-Kirche.

Neben diesen Kirchen bediente er auch die folgenden drei eine Zeit lang:

Die Jerusalems-Kirche in Salzburg, von 1843 bis 1883. Vor mehr als hundert Jahren war hier eine Kirche, die aber in Verfall gerathen war und deren Gliederschaft sich zerstreut hatte, bis Vater Jäger sie wiederum sammelte und ihnen behilflich war eine Kirche zu bauen.

Die Salomons-Kirche in dem Städtchen Macungie, früher Millerstown, von 1856 bis 1867.

Die Hecktown-Kirche, von 1832 bis 1842.

Uebersicht seiner Amts-Verwaltung.

Aufnahme in die Synode, Trinitatis-Sonntag 1827.

Kinder getauft, 6,859.

Confirmirt, 3,875.

Das Abendmahl gereicht, 50,000.

Beerdigt, 2,763.

Copulirt, 2,000.

Pastor der Allentown St. Paulus-Gemeinde vom 10. April 1831 bis 1853—22 Jahre.

Der Schönersville Christus-Gemeinde von Dezember 1832 bis Trinitatis 1885—53 Jahre.

Friedens-Gemeinde, Friedensville, vom 22. Mai 1831 bis Trinitatis 1885—54 Jahre.

Lecha Zions-Kirche, vom 21. August 1842 bis Trinitatis 1885—43 Jahre.

Rittersville St. Petrus=Kirche, vom 2. Oktober 1842 bis Trinitatis 1885—43 Jahre.

Millerstown (Macungie) Solomons=Kirche, vom 17. Februar 1856 bis 1867—11 Jahre.

Salzburg Jerusalems=Kirche, von 1846 bis 1883—37 Jahre.

―――――――

IV.

Charakterzüge aus dem Leben Josua Jäger's.

1. Fleiß und Thätigkeit.

Von seiner frühesten Jugend an schwere Arbeit gewöhnt, war Josua Jäger keine Aufgabe zu schwierig. Er war kein Weichling. Dem Leibe nach rüstig, stark gebaut, von großer Postur, Kopf und Schultern über manche seiner Mitarbeiter erhaben, konnte er Arbeit verrichten, vor welcher es Manchem bang gewesen wäre. Als fleißiger Student zeichnete er sich in seinen Vorbereitungen für die Kanzel aus. Er studirte seine Texte stets in der Ursprache. Seine Predigten waren daher belehrend und praktisch,—immer frisch. Obschon er in seiner langen Amtsthätigkeit öfters über dieselben Schriftstellen predigte, so hielt er doch nie wieder, selbst nicht an weit von einander entfernten Orten, dieselbe Predigt, ausgenommen in Nothfällen. Seine Vorträge waren daher frisch und man hörte ihn immer gern. Montag Morgens hatte er sich zur Regel gemacht, seinen Text zu wählen für die Predigt des folgenden Sonn=

tags, und die ganze Woche hindurch war er beschäftigt im Sammeln der Gedanken für die Predigt und im Ausarbeiten derselben.

Ebenso fleißig war er im Confirmanden=Unterricht und im Krankenbesuch. Der Confirmanden=Unterricht war sehr gründlich und wußte er auch immer die Jugend anzuziehen. Die Kranken besuchte er mit gewissenhafter Treue, wenn es ihm kund gethan wurde, daß man seine Besuche wünschte. Selbst in seinem hohen Alter versäumte er keinen Kranken. Es wurde zuweilen von Solchen, die da meinten er sollte sein Amt niederlegen, bemerkt, daß er seinen Amtspflichten nicht mehr nachkommen könnte. Es muß aber von ihm gesagt werden, daß er immer kam, wenn er gerufen wurde oder eine Bestellung hatte. Er versäumte keine einzige Bestellung oder Einladung und war auch immer pünktlich zur bestimmten Zeit an Ort und Stelle.

II. Seine Gesundheit.

Nie hörte man, daß Vater Jäger krank sei. Kaum ein einziges Mal während seiner mehr als halbjahrhundertlangen Thätigkeit verfehlte er, Krankheit wegen, eine Bestellung. Daß er so gute Gesundheit und körperliche Stärke genoß, war, mit Gottes Hilfe, seiner Beobachtung der Gesundheitsregeln zuzuschreiben. In seiner Jugend wohnte er den Vorträgen eines berühmten Arztes bei, welcher seinen Zuhörern anrieth, jeden Abend den ganzen Körper zu baden und dann mit einem rauhen Handtuche trocken zu reiben. Diese Sanitätsregel befolgte er viele Jahre bis ins hohe Alter und genoß dadurch stete Gesundheit. Nebenbei war er sehr mäßig im Essen und Trinken, und obwohl er stets

aß „was ihm vorgetragen wurde und nichts forschte," so
hielt er, daß man zu viel essen sowohl als zu viel trinken
könne und daß beides, unmäßiges Essen und Trinken, sünd=
haft sei. So war er auch, wenn möglich, sehr regelmäßig
in seinen Gebräuchen. Sein heiterer Sinn und seine Ge=
müthlichkeit trugen sehr viel zur Bewahrung seiner Gesund=
heit bei. Auch war er sehr besorgt in seiner Kleidung und
vermied es, sich unnöthig der Nässe und Kälte auszusetzen.

III. Seine Ernsthaftigkeit.

Obschon Vater Jäger stets heiteren Sinnes war und oft=
mals scherzte, war er aber dennoch eingedenk der Wichtigkeit
und Verantwortlichkeit seines Amtes, und erlaubte sich und
auch keinem Andern in seiner Gegenwart, ohne ihn zu be=
strafen, mit heiligen Dingen Leichtfertigkeit oder Scherz zu
treiben.

Dieses bewies er besonders im Umgang mit seinen Amts=
brüdern. Als er noch, zum Beispiel, ein verhältnißmäßig
junger Mann war, befand er sich einmal in Gesellschaft
einer Anzahl Prediger, woselbst einer dieser Herrn durch
Anführen von Schriftstellen sich lustig machte und Andere
zum Lachen anzuregen suchte. Jäger saß unbewegt, aber
offenbar mit Mißfallen im Herzen da, denn er benutzte
nachher die Gelegenheit zu diesem Amtsbruder zu
sagen: „Bruder, Sie haben diesen Abend den Namen
Gottes mißbraucht." Dieser Mann kam am nächsten
Morgen in der Frühe in Jäger's Haus und machte sein
Bekenntniß. „Lieber Bruder," sagte er, „ich habe nicht
gut geschlafen letzte Nacht; ich habe Unrecht gethan und
werde nie den gerechten Verweis, welchen Sie mir gegeben

haben, vergessen." Es ist leider zu oft der Fall, daß
geschwiegen wird, wenn so etwas sich zuträgt. Vater
Jäger wollte durchaus nicht sich Anderer Sünden theilhaftig
machen, und nicht nur Prediger, sondern alle können hierin
von seinem schönen Beispiel lernen.

IV. Vater Jäger als Prediger.

Ernsthaftigkeit war auch ein besonderer Charakterzug in
Vater Jäger's Predigten. Er blieb stets der Thatsache
eingedenk, daß er zwischen Gott und Menschen stand, wenn
er auftrat zu predigen. Wer ihn jemals auf der Kanzel
sah, wird sein ernsthaftes Benehmen und seine tiefeingrei=
fenden Reden nicht vergessen. Seinen Finger auf die
Stirne legend und mit heller Stimme ausrufend: „Merkt!"
redete er als Wächter auf Zion's Mauern, predigte er mit
tiefer Rührung und außerordentlich eindrucksvoll. Ach,
wie oft stand er mit von Thränen erfüllten Augen da, so daß
er mit schluchzenden Worten ausrief: „Lasset euch mit Gott
versöhnen." Halb pietistisch, aber doch streng lutherisch,
predigte er im Geiste Franke's und Spener's, Luther's und
Melanchthon's. Für erweckte Seelen war er besonders be=
sorgt und eine seiner eindrucksvollsten Predigten hielt er über
diesen Gegenstand, wovon wir hier das Konzept folgen
lassen:

Skizze einer Predigt gehalten im Jahr 1840
von Vater Josua Jäger.

Wie soll sich der Prediger verhalten in Zeiten der Er=
weckung?

I. Wie gegen die Erweckung überhaupt?

1. Nicht gleichgültig.—Er sehe sie an als die vorlaufende und vorbereitende Gnade zur Bekehrung.

2. Doch schenke er nicht einer jeden Erweckung gleiches Zutrauen,—denn es giebt wahre und falsche Erweckungen.

3. Woran kann man aber eine wahre von einer falschen Erweckung erkennen?

II. Wie in seinen Predigten in solchen Zeiten?

1. Er übergehe in denselben den Gegenstand nicht stillschweigend,—sondern suche seine Zuhörer darüber zu belehren.

2. Er wähle solche Texte, die ihm Veranlassung geben, auf die Ordnung des Heils hinzuweisen und vergesse nicht, daß auch seine Leute der Erweckung höchst benöthigt sind, um sich gründlich zu bekehren.

3. Am allerwenigsten trete er in Opposition gegen die Sache auf,—doch erlaube er sich, Irrthümer anzugreifen und zu berichtigen, die in der Gemeinde darüber obwalten.

Er rede mit Ernst und Würde von der Erweckung und Bekehrung, so daß seine Zuhörer es ihm ansehen und anhören können, wie ihm ihr Seelenheil so nahe am Herzen liege.

III. Wie im Umgang mit einzelnen erweckten Personen in seiner Gemeinde?

1. Wenn sie seine besondere Mitwirkung begehren, so weigere er sich nicht, ihnen behilflich zu sein.—In einem solchen Fall kann er manchmal mehr wirken, als durch seine Predigten.

2. Er vergesse nicht, daß es leichter ist mit einem Bekehrten als mit einem Erweckten umzugehen,—die letzteren nehmen gerne eine falsche Richtung ein.

3. Wenn andere Gemeindeglieder einen Anstoß, wie es oft der Fall ist, daran nehmen, daß sich der Prediger mit den einzelnen Erweckten besonders beschäftige, so muß er sich dadurch nicht davon abhalten lassen, eingedenk seines Seelsorgeramtes.

4. Sollten sie eine Neigung aussprechen, ihre Kirche zu verlassen und zu einer andern überzugehen, in der Meinung, sie könnten da ihr Vorhaben leichter und besser ausführen, so sage man ihnen: nicht die Benennung, sondern das Wort Gottes, welches ja in seiner Kirche ist und gepredigt wird, muß das Werk anfangen und vollenden.

5. Er sage ihnen und suche es ihnen klar zu machen, daß die durch den heiligen Geist im Wort gewirkte Erweckung sich im Glauben an Jesum Christum vollenden müsse.

Seine Predigten waren immer kurz und zwar aus dem Grunde, weil er dieselben wohl zubereitet hatte. Er predigte ganz systematisch und war besorgt für jedes Pünktlein, so daß Alles richtig nach Einordnung und Ausdruck sein mußte. Er hatte deshalb die Gewohnheit, auch bis in sein hohes Alter, sein Konzept vor sich in der Bibel zu haben.

V. Vater Jäger als Lehrer.

Sein Confirmations=Unterricht, sowie seine Predigten, mußten stets sehr gründlich sein. Er drang darauf, daß viele Bibel=Beweissprüche auswendig gelernt werden muß= ten. Er hielt seinen Unterricht oftmals Vor= und Nach= mittags mit derselben Klasse, und auch etliche Mal die Woche während der Unterrichtszeit. Unvergeßlich bleibt seinen zwei Tausend Confirmanden die Treue, mit welcher

Vater Jäger sie zur Buße und zum Glauben an Jesum Christum ermahnte in den Stunden des Unterrichts. Wie Manche, die wir besuchen, besonders die auf Krankenbetten, vermögen heute noch, nach Verlauf von einem halben Jahrhundert, die schönen Bibel- und Katechismus-Sprüche und Liederverse herzusagen zu ihrem Troste und erinnern sich mit Dankbarkeit seiner Ermahnungen.

"Gelobet seist du, Jesu Christ, daß du der Sünder Heiland bist," war eins der Lieblingslieder bei seinem Unterricht, und viele Hunderte seiner Confirmanden erquicken sich in stillen Stunden an solchen kernhaften Liedern, die ihnen ins Gedächtniß eingeprägt wurden von ihrem geliebten Seelsorger.

Vater Jäger war aber auch Lehrer in einem andern Sinne, denn er bereitete verschiedene Studenten fürs Predigtamt vor. Der selige Samuel K. Brobst war eine Zeitlang sein Student und hatte seine Heimath bei Vater Jäger. Noch ehe er im Amt war, gründete er Sonntagschulen, unter Aufsicht Vater Jäger's, in verschiedenen Theilen von Lecha und Northampton Counties.

Der Ehrw. O. Leopold war ebenfalls vier Jahre lang sein Student. Er bestand ein sehr gutes Examen als er in die Synode aufgenommen wurde, ein Beweis, daß sein Meister ihm gründlichen theologischen Unterricht ertheilt hatte. Als Pastor hat derselbe auch in seiner nun schon dreißig Jahre langen Thätigkeit sich seines Lehrmeisters würdig gezeigt und ihm das schöne Zeugniß beigelegt, daß er einen tüchtigen Präceptor hatte.

VI. Seine Rechtgläubigkeit.

Vater Jäger war beides, recht = gläubig und recht gläubig. Von einem Zeitalter herstammend wo der Rationalismus im Schwunge ging, waren viele der Prediger mit der Vernunft=Lehre mehr oder weniger angesteckt. Niemals aber, obschon große Versuchung dazu vorhanden war, erlaubte Vater Jäger sich auch nur einen Finger breit von Gottes Offenbarung abzuweichen. Sein Lieblingslied:

> „Ich habe nun den Grund gefunden,
> Der meinen Anker ewig hält;
> Wo anders als in Jesu Wunden,
> Da lag er vor der Zeit der Welt,
> Der Grund der unbeweglich steht,
> Wann Erd und Himmel untergeht."

erklärte in diesen schönen Worten seinen Glaubensgrund. „Niemals," sagte er in seinem fünfundachtzigsten Lebensjahre, „habe ich auch den geringsten Zweifel gehabt an der Gottheit Jesu Christi und an Seinem vollgültigen Versöhnungsopfer." Er predigte stets Christum, den Gekreuzigten, mit allem Ernste, und wies Sünder hin auf Sein für sie am Kreuze vergossenes Blut, durch welches allein Gnade und Seligkeit zu finden ist. Im Blute Jesu hatte er Vergebung gefunden, daran glaubte er, darauf vertraute er. Es hieß bei ihm:

> „Ach, Vater, deck all meine Sünde
> Mit dem Verdienste Jesu zu;
> Auf daß ich hier Vergebung finde
> Und dort die langgewünschte Ruh.
> Mein Gott, ich bitt durch Christi Blut,
> Mach's nur mit meinem Ende gut."

Wie beim Predigen, so auch beim Krankenbesuch, lenkte er immer, in seinem Umgang mit den Kranken, ihre ganze Aufmerksamkeit auf den Heiland, und tröstete sie nur allein mit Ihm. Jesus Christus gestern, heute und auch in Ewigkeit.

VII. Friedliches Ende. Seliger Tod.

Vater Jäger's später Lebensabend war, wie sein Arbeitstag, friedlich. In seiner langzeitigen Seelsorger-Arbeit lebte er stets im Frieden mit den Seinigen. Nicht daß er sagte, Friede, Friede, wo kein Friede war; denn er eiferte unabläßig gegen die Sünde, und kämpfte bis aufs Blut und Leben mit dem Seelen-Feind. Damit hielt er feurig an, war's auch Tag und Nacht gethan. Aber niemals, in seiner beinahe sechzigjährigen Amtsverwaltung, hatte er Streit in seinen Gemeinden, oder erlaubte er, daß Unfriede zwischen ihm und den Seinigen herrschte. Wenn es zuweilen Mißverständnisse gab, so ruhte er nicht bis dieselben ins Reine gebracht waren. So nahm man denn auch seinen väterlichen Rath immer mit friedlicher Ergebung an. Das dauerte fort bis zum Tag da er Altersschwäche wegen sein Amt niederlegen mußte. Man betrauerte allgemein das Unvermeidliche, seinen Abschied von seinen Gemeinden, welche er so lange bedient und so innig geliebt hatte.

Von Trinitatis 1885 bis zum Tage seines seligen Todes, am 1. August 1888, hatte er sich von aller Arbeit zurückgezogen und in die Ruhe begeben. Seine Gemeinden waren ihm aber immer noch sehr angelegen. Er begleitete seinen Nachfolger öfters, so lange er konnte, Sonntags zu dem Gottesdienste. Es war seine größte Freude, seine vielen früheren Gemeindeglieder zu begrüßen. Montag Morgens, wenn er am vorhergehenden Tag nicht mitgehen konnte, war er aber immer begierig zu hören, wie es bei seinen lieben Freunden stände.

Etliche Jahre vor seinem Tode wurde er vom Schlag gerührt; er erholte sich aber bald wieder, so daß er besser als vorher war. Am Gräberschmückungstag 1888 aber, als er an seinem Lieblingsfenster saß, hatte er einen so heftigen Schlaganfall, daß er auf der einen Seite seines Körpers gänzlich gelähmt wurde. Bald folgten andere Anfälle, bis er ganz hilflos geworden war. Obschon er nicht mehr genau ein Jedes kannte, so wurde er doch erst bewußtlos kurz vor seinem Ende. Er gab immer kund, daß es ihm lieb war, wenn man ihn besuchte, und besonders gern hörte er von seinen Gemeinden. Auch war er sehr erfreut, als man ihm vorschlug, das heilige Abendmahl zu reichen. Die Doktoren Spieker, Repaß und Horne verwalteten sodann auf sein ganz gewisses Verlangen hin diese heilige Stiftung. Allmählich wurde er schwächer, und am 1. August 1888 ließ der Herr Seinen Diener in Frieden dahin fahren, indem er es bis zu einem Alter von 85 Jahren, 10 Monaten und 8 Tagen brachte.

Zu seinem Leichengottesdienste, welcher am Donnerstag nach seinem Ableben in der St. Michael's Lutherischen Kirche in Allentown stattfand, hatte sich eine große Anzahl seiner alten Freunde und früheren Gemeindemitglieder aus der Nähe und Ferne eingefunden, und auch dreißig seiner Amtsbrüder waren zugegen. Auf des Verstorbenen Ersuchen leitete Dr. S. A. Repaß, Pastor der St. Johannis

Englisch=Lutherischen Kirche von Allentown, den Leichen=
gottesdienst im Sterbehause. In der Kirche hielt Pastor
B. W. Schmauk, ehemaliger Pastor der St. Michael's=
Kirche, die deutsche und Dr. G. J. Spieker, jetziger Pastor
genannter Kirche, die englische Rede. Die Personalien
verlas Dr. A. R. Horne, Nachfolger in des Dahingeschie=
denen Gemeinden. Auch verrichtete Dr. Horne die Be=
erdigungs=Ceremonie auf dem Fair View Friedhof von
Allentown, woselbst seine entseelte Hülle neben der ihm
vorangegangenen Ehegattin und seinem Sohne, Dr. Theo=
dore C. Jäger, bestattet wurde.

Er hinterließ einen Sohn, Robert J. Jäger, von Allen=
town, und eine Tochter, Anna Maria, Ehegattin von J. B.
Reeme, Esq., von Chicago. Seine Gattin, Maria, ge=
borene Grimm, Tochter von Jakob und Maria Grimm,
von Friedensville, ging ihm 11 Jahre voran in die
Ewigkeit. Auch ein Sohn, Dr. Theodore C., und zwei
Töchter, Amanda, erste Gattin von J. C. Reeme, und
Sarah W., starben vor Jahren zurück. Er hinterließ sechs
Kindeskinder: Minnie W. und Norton, Kinder von Dr.
Theodore; Albert und Andrew, Söhne von Robert J.;
und Effie B. und Annetta, Töchter von J. B. Reeme.

„Er redet noch, wiewohl er gestorben ist."

Beerdigte

während 50 Jahre, 1834—1885.

Erklärung. — Die den verschiedenen Amtshandlungen beige=
setzten Buchstaben beziehen sich auf die verschiedenen Gemeinden, an
denen der Verstorbene amtirte.

So steht A. für die Gemeinde zu Allentown.
    S.   "   "   " Saucon (Friedensville).
    H.   "   "   " Hanover (Schönersville).
    R.   "   "   " Rittersville.
    M.   "   "   " Macungie (Lecha=Kirche).
  Salz.   "   "   " Salzburg (Jerusalems=Kirche).
  Mac.   "   "   " Macungie Boro'.
    T.   "   "   " Trockenland (Hecktown).
    N.   "   "   " Nieder=Saucon.
   Ob.   "   "   " Ober=Saucon.

Nur Erwachsene werden angegeben.

Jahr 1834.

	Wann beerdigt.	Name.	Alter.		
			Jahr	Monat	Tag
T.	Juni	1, Abraham Vogel	54	11	5
A.	"	3, Michael Gebel	49		
A.	"	7, Hanna Minnich	23	11	5
S.	Juli	21, Margaretha Stumpf	62	8	12
R.	Aug.	21, Leonhardt Frankenfield	74	10	22
G.	"	25, Margaretha Jünger	76	2	8
S.	Sept.	14, Rosina Jacoby	73		
A.	"	24, Jakob Horn	53	1	12
S.	Okt.	5, Katharina Hoffert	47	8	15
A.	Nov.	21, Samuel Küchlein	37	4	20
A.	Dez.	5, Wilhelm Weldon	35	4	4
H.	"	23, Barbara Frey	39	9	24

1835.

				Jahr	Monat	Tag
A.	Jan.	3, Maria Vogel	23	7	3
A.	"	7, Nikolaus Säger	75	7	21
N.	"	26, Johann Schmidt	76	5	3
A.	Febr.	6, Salomon Jarret	38	5	20
H.	"	12, Katharina Fatzinger	71	2	24
H.	"	14, Johann Schneider	60	5	24
N.	"	14, Katharina Ritter	69	8	24
A.	März	15, Maria Hoffmann	83	2	4
A.	"	20, Daniel Krämer	40	9	1
A.	April	4, Abraham Sterner	85		
H.	"	4, Heinrich Fatzinger	82	5	4
N.	"	11, Anna Maria Gratwohl	16	11	13
S.	"	14, Katharina Ruhf	27	7	7
A.	"	15, Deborah Ruhr	21	6	20
S.	Mai	15, Jakob Bauer	17	2	3
A.	"	18, Christian Giltner	72		
A.	Juli	16, Eva Straßburger	87	10	15
A.	Aug.	15, Jakob Sprandel	46		
A.	"	18, Johann Lehr	63	7	8
H.	"	24, Georg Frey	75		
A.	Sept.	3, Joh. Quier	28	4	29
A.	"	20, Sarah Reip	36		
H.	Okt.	11, Nikolaus Miller	40	6	10
A.	"	31, Katharina Barbara Herz	82	5	14
S.	Nov.	15, Elisabeth Gernert	81		14
H.	"	20, Elisabeth Kleber	52		23
A.	Dez.	1, Friedrich W. Ibach	26		28
A.	"	24, Merin Sevitz	77	2	9
H.	"	26, Jos. Jonathan Hauer	74	3	18

1836.

A.	Jan.	5, Peter Waldman	56	10	27
A.	"	12, Maria Magdalena Litzenberger	44	11	23
A.	"	23, Christian Dieter	73	10	7
H.	"	23, Maria Magdalena Goßler	29	2	26

				Jahr	Monat	Tag
H.	Febr.	16,	Georg Höle	69	7	26
T.	"	24,	Johann Klees	78	2	9
A.	März	10,	Maria Anna Sterner	20	1	20
A.	April	1,	Julianna Diefendörfer	26	2	10
A.	Mai	11,	Rebekka Eschenbach	82	7	3
H.	Aug.	6,	David Trexler	27		28
A.	"	29,	Daniel Ritter	78		25
A.	Sept.	6,	Christine Barbara Ludwig	72	11	7
H.	"	17,	Peter Boyern	21	5	
S.	"	24,	Christina Hoffmann	68	10	22
A.	Okt.	24,	Anna N. Krämer	76	7	10
A.	Nov.	18,	Joh. Oßmann	38	10	20
S.	"	22,	Heinrich Röber	40	9	23
A.	Dez.	7,	Anna Maria Gratwohl	73	10	5
A.	"	14,	Sarah Tetten	34	9	16
A.	"	16,	Nikolaus Krämer	69	1	3

1837.

				Jahr	Monat	Tag
H.	Jan.	1,	Heinrich Hoch	50	9	3
N.	März	17,	Maria Magdalena Fuchs	55	8	23
A.	"	31,	Katharina Meßer	51	5	16
H.	April	7,	Elisabeth Keim	86	11	25
S.	"	16,	Peter Weber	88	1	24
H.	"	20,	Elisabeth Zellner	85	8	3
A.	"	24,	Georg Litzenberger	49	3	19
S.	"	28,	Katharina Zerlein	82	2	28
A.	Juni	15,	Joseph Reider	43	7	3
H.	"	18,	Heinrich Fogelmann	64	3	8
A.	Juli	13,	Gertraud Rinker	81		
A.	"	14,	Georg Kleck	56	5	1
A.	Aug.	28,	Wilhelm Gangewer	30	2	7
A.	Sept.	9,	David Leibensperger	87		21
A.	Okt.	8,	Anna Katharina Franz	80	2	26
A.	Dez.	3,	Jakob Nagel	55	8	7
N.	"	14,	Katharina Gloeß	16		10

1838.

				Jahr	Monat	Tag
A.	Jan.	3, Heinrich Fried	33	11	16
Db.	"	11, Magdalena Kämmer	70	3	24
S.	"	20, Peter Steinberger	40	1	25
A.	"	30, Georg Duier	73	11	17
H.	Febr.	5, Christoph Jörg	72		
S.	"	16, Margaretha Martin	61	6	13
S.	"	17, Katharina Sander	69	9	21
S.	März	31, Sarah Moyer	24	7	27
H.	April	5, Konrad Rau	48	6	18
A.	"	12, Anna Schmidt	24	9	21
S.	"	29, Joh. Kleckner	43	2	7
A.	Mai	4, Katharina Brechall	27		6
S.	"	5, Katharina Bachman	44	5	9
A.	"	15, Elisabeth Musgenug	53		
A.	"	19, Joh. Heinrich Bacher	51	6	13
S.	"	28, Anna Margaretha Buchecker	93	2	21
S.	Juni	23, Daniel Duier	49		28
A.	Juli	5, Katharina März	73		5
R.	"	9, Maria Kath. Klees	77	4	21
H.	"	14, Jakob Keim	49	6	13
H.	"	18, Maria Breinig	41		7
A.	Aug.	4, Anna Margaretha Ritter	86	6	23
A.	"	10, Maria Charlotta Ginkinger	75	11	27
H.	"	13, Jesse Daniel	26	9	14
H.	"	16, Susanna Eberhardt	73	9	28
A.	Sept.	9, Susanna Eckert	58	2	18
A.	"	15, Ruben Stein	17	8	19
Bath.	Okt.	7, Joh. Wind	52	8	29
S.	"	10, Joh. Moritz	46	1	20
A.	"	18, Elisabeth Moyer	21	10	17
H.	Nov.	19, Elisabeth Meyer	68	2	14

1839.

A.	Jan.	3, Sarah Egge	48	9	13
S.	"	23, Anna Sibilla Derr	86	5	19

				Jahr	Monat	Tag
S.	Jan.	24,	Maria Schäffer	31	11	16
A.	"	26,	Heinrich Gaumer	25		22
A.	März	21,	Lisetta Edelmann	23	6	3
H.	"	23,	Barbara Sterner	78	3	24
H.	Mai	5,	Elisabeth Klöckner	71	6	6
A.	"	23,	Nikolaus Horn	87		
H.	Juni	16,	Maria Magdalena Bernz	77		
S.	Aug.	31,	Georg Bilgar	45	4	17
H.	Sept.	20,	Elisabeth Hey	32	10	12
H.	Okt.	6,	Sarah Huber	53	5	6
S.	"	13,	Salome Miller	81	4	6
A.	"	23,	Eliza Gumpert	41	5	9
A.	Nov.	3,	Barbara Gebel	82		
N.	"	29,	Johann Schweitzer	84	3	22
H.	Dez.	26,	Katharina Elisabeth Schöner	65	5	8
A.	"	27,	Magdalena Winder	64		

1840.

				Jahr	Monat	Tag
N.	März	2,	Elisabeth Gangewer	25		21
A.	"	16,	Mathias Groß	63	10	
A.	"	21,	Eliza D. Wagner	42	1	26
A.	April	2,	Maria Katharina Deyly	79	1	24
Db.	"	11,	Maria M. Weikel	76	3	25
S.	"	13,	Heinrich Weber	39	2	24
S.	"	13,	Katharina Frey	48	1	16
A.	Mai	2,	Anna Maria Eberhardt	63	10	12
A.	Juni	3,	Sarah März	52	5	23
A.	"	19,	Joh. August Hartman	51	5	7
H.	Juli	6,	Lovina Ritter	26	4	17
A.	"	15,	Kath. Maria Henrietta Ruhe	85	10	16
A.	"	29,	Maria Anna Boeder	23	6	29
S.	Sept.	16,	Rebekka Flexer	21	8	20
A.	"	17,	Gottlieb Bender	40	6	11
A.	Okt.	8,	Sarah Hend	27	3	22
A.	"	8,	Daniel Miller	73	2	13
H.	"	16,	Maria Magdalena Daniel	83	7	5

				Jahr	Monat	Tag
S.	Okt.	30,	Katharina Schwander	43	9	28
A.	Nov.	2,	Peter Fertig	28		1
A.	"	11,	Peter Schäfer	21	4	5
S.	"	23,	Joh. Georg Gieß	75	5	22

1841.

				Jahr	Monat	Tag
A.	Feb.	17,	Joh. Georg Helfrich	55	4	20
A.	März	10,	Sarah Heimbach	27	11	21
A.	Mai	28,	Joseph Duier	52	6	3
A.	"	30,	Maria Edelmann	77	8	22
H.	Aug.	17,	Wilhelm Stuber	Etwa 47 Jahre.		
A.	"	25,	David Reck	47	10	5
H.	"	27,	Katharina Stuber	42	9	1
A.	Sept.	10,	Nathan Säger	29	7	13
A.	"	20,	Peter Transu	64	4	27
A.	"	24,	Franklin Säger	18	5	11
H.	Okt.	4,	Barbara Faust	66	7	24
Db.	"	12,	Wilhelm Wasser	19	2	
A.	"	20,	Michael Helfrich	81	6	
A.	Nov.	4,	Abigail Heß	25	4	14
S.	"	8,	Joh. Philip Wind	82	3	29
H.	"	17,	Obilia Dillinger	81		
S.	Dez.	10,	Susanna Ihrig	70	9	14

1842.

				Jahr	Monat	Tag
H.	Jan.	20,	Michael Reichert	85	2	12
S.	Feb.	8,	Joh. H. Wind	62	10	23
S.	"	14,	Samuel Lein	34	2	9
A.	"	27,	Jakob Stein	70	5	14
A.	März	6,	Katharina Heinrich	55	11	28
H.	"	10,	Heinrich Hillman	41	1	23
S.	"	17,	Joh. Michael Herlein	84	2	20
A.	April	14,	Martin Kunsmann	30	6	25
Db.	"	26,	Katharine Borz	26	5	
Db.	Mai	2,	Eva Reinhard	77	1	17
S.	"	11,	Maria Hofmann	48	7	9

39

				Jahr	Monat	Tag
R.	Mai	27,	Carolina Stuber	17	9	7
S.	Juni	12,	Katharina Elisabeth Gauff . .	71	2	8
A.	Juli	29,	Anna Margaretha Frankenfield .	57	8	15
M.	Aug.	24,	Eva Maria Christman . . .	71		10
H.	"	27,	Jakob Hauer	80	4	14
A.	Sept.	8,	Joh. Jakob Edelmann	61	8	13
T.	"	14,	Margaretha Mack	63	4	5
S.	"	25,	Maria Margaretha Kop	64	10	
M.	Okt.	11,	Jakob Schmeier	68	3	16
S.	"	10,	Sabina Buchel	77	1	
S.	"	13,	Maria Wind	28	4	15
H.	"	17,	Michael Jung	45	1	24
A.	"	19,	Emilie Ruhe	18	6	12
A.	"	19,	James Walter Stein	17	5	29
S.	"	19,	Johannes Hoffert	76	4	5
H.	"	24,	Jakob Meyer	30	7	9
A.	"	26,	Wilhelm Heinrich Kuhns	17		16
A.	"	30,	Johann Danner	39	11	30

1843.

M.	Jan.	9,	Katharina Barbara Schmeier .	86	9	6
M.	"	23,	Magdalena Haas	62	5	28
A.	Feb.	4,	Maria Nunemacher . . . . . ,	58	4	5
S.	"	27,	Israel L. Thomas	32	11	16
A.	März	9,	Katharina Miller	72		
S.	"	9,	Maria Barbara Mory	83	11	27
H.	"	17,	Joh. Sterner	82	4	5
A.	Mai	3,	Anna Maria Knauß	20	8	16
S.	"	5,	Mathilde Ziegenfuß	27	11	2
H.	"	5,	Kath. Magd. H. Keim	50	5	7
A.	"	15,	Joh. Kratzer	17	3	14
Db.	Juli	1,	Johann Robenberger	65	6	14
A.	"	30,	Joh. Michael Meßer	67	11	24
A.	Sept.	12,	Therese Miller	29	11	9
H.	"		Joh. Busch	76	4	11
S.	Okt.	10,	Joh. Philip Gieß	82	6	15

				Jahr	Monat	Tag
H.	Nov.	8,	David Neuhardt	24	10	7
S.	"	14,	Peter Fatzinger	24	2	6
A.	Dez.	1,	Friedrich Kämmerer	86	9	7

1844.

				Jahr	Monat	Tag
S.	Jan.	1,	Franz Theobald Olb	26	2	6
H.	"	9,	Thomas Kibb	49	10	3
A.	"	13,	Heinrich C. Kneip	15	7	
H.	"	19,	Joseph Adam Kibb	18	7	14
M.	Feb.	1,	Heinrich Boyer	73	11	28
M.	"	1,	Jonathan Muth	18	1	4
S.	"	9,	Jakob Ziegler	57		2
H.	"	13,	Elisabeth Deily	17	7	26
S.	"	16,	Jakob Mohr	59	4	20
H.	"	19,	Salome Kibb	48	3	
H.	"	24,	Thomas Deily	20		23
A.	März	5,	Friederich Deliuß	83		
M.	"	12,	Margaretha Hein	57	3	9
M.	"	13,	Margaretha Danner	77	3	
A.	"	16,	Elisabeth Frey	22	8	11
A.	"	22,	Elisabeth Wieser	79	8	3
H.	"	28,	Anna Kratzer	45	1	26
S.	April	9,	Alexander Moritz	26	5	15
Salzb.	"	14,	Maria Magd. Kämmerer	71	4	19
A.	"	20,	Samuel Young	21	6	21
Mac.	"	22,	David Gorr	32	6	27
S.	Mai	4,	Susanna Rath	40	3	13
A.	"	31,	Dr. Carl H. Martin	62	5	4
S.	Juni	26,	Katharina Weber	51	10	6
S.	"	30,	Katharina Scherer	48	5	20
A.	Juli	11,	Andreas Gangwer	96	9	26
M.	"	24,	Elisabeth Walbert	70	11	29
H.	Aug.	7,	Esther Ott	22	6	13
H.	"	24,	Katharina Neuhardt	29	9	6
T.	Sept.	1,	Andreas Vogel	70	4	17
M.	"	16,	Johann Wetzel	78	5	12

				Jahr	Monat	Tag
A.	Sept.	19,	Adam Seip	63	7	29
H.	"	21,	Katharina Schurz	55	11	18
R.	"	24,	Katharina Sendel	82	11	25
A.	"	29,	Maria Elisabeth Martin	22	4	17
A.	Okt.	2,	Karl Meßer	38	5	19
M.	"	8,	Maria Wünsch	30	9	27
A.	"	13,	Hanna Rhoads	39	5	4
H.	"	23,	Katharina Daniel	16	8	16
A.	"	24,	Joh. Schiffer	64		29
H.	"	25,	Heinrich Reim	16	9	22
A.	Nov.	21,	Georg Schmidt	44	8	13
A.	"	22,	Kath. Lester	68		
A.	"	23,	Maria Magd. Nagel	33	8	11
A.	"	26,	Abraham Ibach	26	6	18
M.	"	26,	Stephan Reiß	21	3	7
S.	Dez.	19,	Heinrich Stahl	85	7	11
S.	"	21,	Katharina Miller	56	3	4

1845.

A.	Jan.	4,	Maria Anna Hollman	15	9	5
H.	"	14,	Philip Klöckner	83	4	19
H.	"	20,	Barbara Duier	61		
S.	"	23,	Jakob Hartmann	74	4	
H.	"	28,	Lorenz Minich	66	4	10
H.	Febr.	1,	Jakob Daniel	43	7	20
S.	"	2,	Maria Bernts	52	11	12
H.	"	19,	Anna Maria Hauer	78		
H.	März	3,	Elisabeth Lazarus	41	4	4
H.	"	16,	Maria Magd. Herbst	28	2	16
A.	"	30,	Margaretha Hagenbuch	80	10	22
H.	April	1,	Joh. Leibert	37	6	2
A.	Mai	28,	Christina Philippina Kneller	39	5	23
S.	Juni	27,	Katharina Stuber	64		
S.	Juli	4,	Johann Jakob Stöhr	39	8	12
R.	"	20,	Hanna Kiefer	77		2
H.	"	30,	Samuel Ritter	28	11	5

				Jahr	Monat	Tag
A.	Aug.	6,	Joh. Nunemacher	66	4	23
S.	Sept.	9,	Susanne Wambold	41	6	4
S.	"	16,	Susanne Hoffert	69	4	10
S.	"	16,	Maria Brecht	31	2	19
M.	Nov.	16,	Friederich Salomon Keck	23	2	11
A.	Dez.	16,	Katharina Reinschmidt	74	2	15

1846.

H.	Jan.	17,	Henriette Scheimer	18	9	29
A.	"	19,	Karl Fatzinger	42	4	29
A.	Febr.	16,	Louisa Knaus	29	2	15
A.	"	27,	Tobias Hoffert	38	9	16
A.	März	4,	Joh. Miller	83		
R.	"	11,	Simon Schneider	38	7	7
A.	"	12,	Mathilda Melvina Nunemacher	24	3	18
A.	April	16,	Joh. Jos. Jost	71	4	3
M.	Mai	7,	Heinrich Gunner	66	2	27
H.	Juni	29,	Heinrich Jörg	29	8	26
A.	Juli	13,	Anna Maria Worman	72		26
S.	"	15,	Georg Detterer	52	3	24
S.	Aug.	6,	Elisabeth Noth	70	1	24
A.	"	19,	Anna B. Schmauck	57	10	12
A.	Sept.	6,	Abraham Wormann	75		
H.	"	7,	Oliver Harzer Perry Schneider	32	10	28
S.	Okt.	2,	Elisabeth Benner	42		
A.	Nov.	1,	Abraham Gangwer	39	1	4
A.	"	10,	Wilhelm Sterner	19	10	8
A.	"	19,	Nathan Schmidt	24	5	7
S.	"	20,	Julia Jacoby	30	4	7
S.	Dez.	22,	Dianna Fatzinger	16	10	17
S.	"	23,	Johannes Mory	49	9	8
S.	"	26,	Maria Fatzinger	52	7	24

1847.

S.	Jan.	27,	Georg Weber	57	10	17
Salz.	Febr.	12,	Eva Härzel	87	6	11

				Jahr	Monat	Tag
S.	Febr.	26,	Johann Fatzinger	31		14
A.	März	4,	Peter Lehr	70	1	16
H.	Mai	7,	Katharina Herwig	55	6	11
H.	"	10,	Adam Daniels	29		2
H.	Juni	11,	Judith Simon	33	10	8
A.	"	18,	Katharina Wagner	80	4	23
A.	"	22,	Joh. Adam Lautenschläger	77	1	4
S.	"	28,	Joh. Moritz	87	2	13
H.	Juli	5,	Kath. Margaretha Zehner	88	7	21
H.	"	14,	Anna Margaretha Flores	53	6	16
S.	"	19,	Esther Knepply	89	3	17
H.	Aug.	5,	Christian Scherer,	Alter zw. 59 u. 60		
H.	"	21,	David Schweitzer	24	5	16
A.	"	22,	Johann Seitz	61	7	6
A.	Sept.	6,	Anna Barbara Krämer	80	3	24
Salz.	"	12,	Dianna Deily	16	7	13
A.	"	29,	Kath. Stettler	69	10	
A.	Okt.	10,	Lovina Hittel	29		29
A.	"	21,	Aaron John	29		1
S.	Nov.	29,	Augustus Groß	32	8	21
H.	Dez.	3,	Katharine Biery	75	4	5
M.	"	10,	Susanna Wagner	72	2	

1848.

H.	Jan.	2,	Georg Heinrich Jung	64	7	18
S.	"	10,	Urias Schmidt	25	9	26
S.	"	11,	Tobias Gangwer	54	6	2
R.	"	18,	Joh. Thomas Diehm	47	8	19
S.	"	30,	Andreas Martin	80	1	4
S.	Febr.	8,	Sarah Schmidt	30	8	
H.	"	10,	Joseph Roth	48	4	14
H.	"	14,	Maria Frey	76		
H.	"	20,	Matthäus Tron	67	11	16
Sa.	März	22,	Libia Linn	35	11	24
M.	April	3,	Elisabeth Rappenberger	42	8	
A.	"	4,	Elisabeth Hildebeitel	38	7	26

				Jahr	Monat	Tag
A.	Mai	28,	Ludwig Kuntz	47	9	6
A.	Juni	22,	Thomas M. Hopkins	41	2	28
M.	"	23,	Jakob Romich	28	11	20
S.	"	30,	Maria Gernet	64	3	10
S.	Juli	10,	Anna Katharina Diehl	59		16
M.	"	13,	Johann Gorr	44	10	8
M.	"	21,	Georg Mattern	76	6	20
A.	Aug.	24,	Joseph Saeger	61	3	6
A.	"	31,	William Ginkinger	57	4	8
A.	Sept.	3,	Joh. Abraham Harlacher . . .	67	9	23
A.	"	10,	Leonhard Weiß	85	5	29
A.	"	11,	Maria Totten	82	1	2
H.	"	17,	Sarah Deily	57	5	17
A.	"	22,	Elisabeth Christina Walz . . .	43	9	20
M.	"	24,	Johann Mattern	74		13
S.	"	28,	Lovina Siegfried	24	6	7
H.	Okt.	3,	Katharina Emilie Kibb	17	1	
H.	"	6,	Elisabeth Miller	38	10	17
A.	"	29,	Jakob John	58	1	
A.	Nov.	4,	Johann Joseph Schmidt . .	63	4	10
M.	"	4,	Anna Elisabeth Breinig	81		
A.	"	11,	Ruben Schwentzer	28		
A.	Dez.	11,	David Deschler	48	2	27
A.	"	14,	Kath. Evert	43	3	8
S.	"	17,	Philip Jhrig	39	2	8

1849.

M.	Jan.	2,	Karl Gangewer	28	8	7
A.	"	15,	Benjamin Owen Halbach . . .	19	8	22
H.	Feb.	12,	Elisabeth Seider, ...	44		2
A.	"	15,	Margaretha Hunsberger	62		28
A.	"	20,	Georg Weiß	82	2	20
S.	"	21,	Eliza Romig	31	6	6
S.	März	11,	Elisabeth Schneider	34	11	23
Sal.	"	21,	Friedrich Stuber	68	5	9
A.	"	23,	Maria Albrecht	69		18

				Jahr	Monat	Tag
H.	April	12,	Joh. Heinrich Ritter	71	3	28
H.	"	17,	Johann Hellmann	72	10	6
A.	"	21,	Jakob Wagner	83	9	12
Sal.	"	22,	Hetty Johnson	79		
S.	Juli	6,	Maria Jüngling	43	5	21
A.	"	17,	Katharina Dorothea Knepply	74	5	2
Sal.	"	30,	Andreas Ulmer	68	10	
H.	Aug.	5,	Christian Ludwig Knobloch	47	2	27
A.	"	9,	Wilhelm Heinz	25	1	4
S.	"	13,	Melchior Knepply	79	4	17
A.	Sept.	8,	Augustus A. Gaßler	17	3	20
H.	Okt.	29,	Jonathan Rood	24	3	17
A.	Nov.	14,	David Landes	37		24
S.	"	30,	David Bilger	42		4
A.	Dez.	11,	Maria Abellona Bauer	56	10	6
M.	"	16,	Maria Elisabeth Muth	70	5	22
S.	"	20,	Elisabeth Miller	58	11	7
A.	"	23,	Katharina John	55	10	7
S.	"	25,	Eliza Lehr	36		29

1850.

A.	Jan.	27,	Christian Gangwer	75	3	27
A.	März	4,	Hanna Dennhart	49	4	14
A.	"	9,	Maria A. Serfaß	36	10	1
A.	"	10,	Wilhelmina Kath. Witte	22	4	7
A.	"	19,	Anna Ludwig	76	7	11
A.	"	21,	Jakob W. Albrecht	44	2	21
Sa.	"	27,	Abbelina Ohl	23	10	9
A.	"	31,	Samuel Roth	29	5	7
H.	"	31,	Eduard Saylor	20	7	26
M.	April	10,	Peter Schmeier	71	8	22
S.	Mai	2,	Adam Ueberroth	39	8	26
A.	"	15,	Johann Klecner	43	11	
A.	Juni	15,	Elisa Egge	36	9	24
H.	"	20,	Margaretha Vogelmann	72	5	20
S.	Juli	17,	Anna M. Blank	73	5	

46

				Jahr	Monat	Tag
H.	Aug.	28,	Anna Elisabeth Ritter	69	8	8
A.	Sept.	16,	Charlotte Wendel	42	11	21
A.	"	27,	Joel Krauß	48	11	24
A.	Okt.	21,	Heinrich Nagel	49	8	18
A.	"	26,	Daniel Ludwig	51	8	15
S.	Nov.	9,	Katharina Herwy	81	1	23
H.	"	23,	Daniel Quier	64	10	10
A.	Dez.	5,	Friedrich Scharth	41	10	4
S.	"	15,	Sarah Ann Harres	17	4	27
S.	"	21,	Jakob Knepply	68	7	25
A.	"	24,	Katharina Gutekunst	81	9	13
S.	"	26,	Lucy Ann Harmony	16	7	8

1851.

H.	Jan.	5,	Sarah Elisabeth Schneider	16	2	11
A.	"	12,	Johann Edelmann	81		
R.	"	19,	Calvin Cahoon	33	9	2
A.	"	21,	Susanna Sterner	88	8	29
M.	"	22,	Caroline Boyer	40	1	12
M.	"	27,	Maria Heinly	82	2	12
H.	Feb.	9,	Lisette Daniel	42	1	8
Sal.	"	21,	Johann Kämmerer	85	2	27
R.	"	25,	William Nagel	31	8	20
M.	März	16,	Philipp Knappenberger	75		9
H.	"	18,	Anna Fatzinger	56	11	3
A.	"	19,	Heinrich Preisch	65	9	19
M.	Mai	12,	Susanna Schmeier	56	6	22
A.	"	30,	Heinrich Daubert	67	6	14
H.	Juni	4,	Margaretha Huber	42	1	28
Sal.	Aug.	21,	Joh. Emrich	17	5	26
A.	"	27,	Johann Schönebruch	79	2	15
H.	Sept.	2,	Katharina Kichlein	69	6	12
A.	"	8,	Thomas Ginkinger	52	2	4
H.	"	14,	Johann Schweitzer	66	8	13
M.	"	18,	Lorenz Gorr	81	9	21
H.	Nov.	16,	Jonas Michael	47		20

			Jahr	Monat	Tag
A.	Nov.	28, Maria Weber	24		
A.	"	29, Franklin Gangwer	30	7	10
M.	Dez.	29, Maria Ruth	49	11	18

1852.

			Jahr	Monat	Tag
H.	Jan.	18, William Fatzinger	27	9	22
S.	"	20, Maria Seusloff	77		8
Sal.	"	29, Salomon Gieß	37	6	
A.	Feb.	4, Elisabeth Jarret	70	11	8
H.	"	6, Susanna Fatzinger	19	2	27
A.	"	10, Lea Reichard	27	10	9
S.	April	4, Mathilda Ziegenfuß	16	7	26
H.	"	7, Joh. Reichard	56	1	29
H.	"	21, Joh. Kaspar Meyer	84	6	26
M.	"	22, Katharina Schmeier	78	3	7
A.	Mai	14, Joh. Wenner	57	7	21
Sal.	Juni	24, Karl Happer	49	9	19
S.	Aug.	17, Lea Emig	34	2	2
S.	"	30, Elisabeth Ellen	79	4	12
A.	"	25, Heinrich Reichard	23	9	29
A.	Okt.	4, Magdalena Wolf	64	2	28
S.	"	4, Philip Buchecker	75	11	20
Sal.	"	20, Werner Schrumpf	34	11	20
M.	Nov.	1, Jakob Trexler	37	6	3
A.	"	13, Thomas Rickert	47	2	
A.	"	20, Maria Gangwer	61	9	24
S.	"	25, Charlotte Heckman	51	2	14
H.	Dez.	30, Elisabeth Bender	79	5	7

1853.

			Jahr	Monat	Tag
M.	Jan.	14, Judith Romig	61	1	
H.	"	15, Julianna Kuns	43	3	1
A.	"	18, Georg H. Lautenschläger	18	1	28
S.	Febr.	21, Johann Blank	49	8	1
M.	"	22, Isaak Schmeier	19	10	4

			Jahr	Monat	Tag
M.	März	4, Isaak Schmeier	65	2	
M.	"	5, Anna Maria Ruth	77	8	24
R.	"	19, Johann Heinrich Kremser	28	9	14
S.	April	3, Thomas Reinbold	40	6	26
A.	"	20, Peter Albrecht	82	8	2
A.	Mai	5, Georg Sterner	21	3	8
S.	Juni	3, Elisabeth Bilgert	52	5	18
Sal.	Juli	6, Eva Duier	62	2	26
A.	"	17, Sarah Rau	43	9	7
H.	"	18, Katharina Schoeneberger	31	10	4
H.	"	28, Susanna Kleier	69	4	3
A.	Aug.	11, Maria Albert	77		28
Sal.	"	17, James Leibensperger	18	8	7
A.	"	26, Maria Magd. Hecker	67	11	17
M.	Sept.	1, Katharina Mattern	78	11	28
S.	"	16, Rebekka Rincker	51	10	23
S.	Okt.	3, J. Yeager	26	1	21
Sal.	"	6, William Stuber	85	1	17
Sal.	"	8, Elisabeth Jaeger	19	6	5
S.	Nov.	10, Joh. Georg Blank	77		25
M.	Dez.	5, Maria Wendling	88	9	25
A.	"	14, Elovina Schweitzer	21		6
R.	"	26, Peter Linn	89	10	6
S.	"	30, Joseph Bilgert	45		3
H.	"	31, Elisabeth Schneider	81		

1854.

			Jahr	Monat	Tag
M.	Jan.	27, Anna Maria Breinig	20	3	14
S.	Febr.	6, Johann Ihrig	62	6	25
A.	"	12, Thomas Krämer	54	3	25
H.	März	2, Karl Wind	20		16
R.	"	14, Michael Ritter	71	10	29
S.	"	24, Jakob Reis	64	4	19
S.	"	27, Peter Knepply	81	6	
M.	April	19, Barbara Knappenberger	76	10	1
R.	"	29, Peter Ihrig	16	7	4

				Jahr	Monat	Tag
S.	Mai	4,	Philip Fleger	88	5	18
M.	"	23,	Heinrich Schmeier	45	10	7
H.	"	29,	Susanna Heller	44	4	20
R.	Juni	5,	Heinrich Heiwig	61	1	10
R.	"	15,	Karolina Ehret	31	7	22
S.	"	17,	Hanna Zeisloff	80	4	9
A.	"	17,	Katharina Eckspellen	70		
R.	"	19,	Elisabeth Sterner	26	8	7
R.	Juli	4,	Sarah Ann Sterner	17	10	3
H.	"	7,	Michael Zoellner	42	4	23
A.	"	23,	Joh. Jakob Laury	64	10	5
A.	"	27,	Susanna Steinberger . . .	60		26
R.	Aug.	2,	Cecilia Hoehle	33	5	28
R.	Sept.	7,	Anna Maria Diehm	46		
Sa.	"	7,	Daniel Deily	45	10	27
H.	"	8,	Joseph Frey	69	8	16
Sa.	"	10,	Lorenz Sagemeister	43	11	14
M.	"	17,	William Romig	37	7	1
S.	"	27,	Katharina Senty	55	8	7
A.	Okt.	17,	David Hauck	61	5	23
A.	"	21,	Peter Haltemann	48	6	21
H.	"	29,	Anna Barbara Thron . . .	78	9	28
S.	"	31,	Jakob Detterer	54	3	5
A.	Nov.	8,	Anna Eliza Heimbach . . .	15	8	6
A.	"	12,	Katharina Jung	52	11	21
H.	"	15,	Heinrich Schneider	84	8	12
	"	20,	Peter Miller (Armenhaus) . . .	52	9	24
R.	Dez.	18,	Heinrich Reichenbach	21	5	7

1855.

A.	März	5,	Joh. Heinrich Dewald	15	6	25
S.	"	14,	Johann Jacoby	76	11	17
S.	"	18,	Philipp Senty	50	5	9
Sal.	"	28,	Sarah Ann Werner	40	2	17
S.	"	30,	Katharina Jacoby	71	3	16
Sa.	April	1,	William Abbott	41		22

3

			Jahr	Monat	Tag
M.	April	4, Georg Wagner	84	9	23
H.	Mai	12, William Hummel	81	10	9
S.	Juni	6, Maria Soladay	57	7	26
H.	Sept.	8, Elisabeth Heckman	27	9	30
H.	"	29, Maria Schneider	52	2	9
S.	Okt.	18, Hanna Benner	81	6	7
Sa.	Nov.	1, Christian Deile	66		
M.	Dez.	28, Joh. Georg Ludwig	66	1	13

1856.

A.	Jan.	12, Joh. Steinberger	47		
S.	"	31, Israel Harres	28	4	21
S.	"	31, Hanna Hoffert	95	4	29
S.	Febr.	6, Ruben Benner	21	7	22
M.	"	27, Aaron Schmeier	29	3	3
A.	April	2, Daniel Gangwer	91		
A.	"	2, Salome Dankel	70	1	17
A.	"	6, Christina Friederich	56	2	1
H.	"	12, Peter Schneider	91	1	8
H.	Mai	20, Kath. Anna Reibenauer	20	8	2
M.	Juli	7, Daniel Friederich	49	9	14
S.	"	28, Adam Miller	73		
N.	Aug.	1, Francis Hill	42		
S.	"	14, Johann Senty	59	6	12
Mill.	Sept.	17, Jonas Baer	28	2	28
Sal.	Okt.	29, Norah Quier	44	1	28
S.	"	30, Christian Clewell	71	11	14
S.	Dez.	9, Georg Martin	47		27
S.	"	23, Ahlum Milton	87	2	28
S.	"	28, Clomeine Diehl	27	4	22

1857.

S.	Jan.	2, Johann Weil	50	3	15
S.	"	4, Anna Reichard	56	4	10
S.	"	14, Theresia Zellener	53	5	4

				Jahr	Monat	Tag
Mill.	Jan.	16,	Elisabeth März	66	3	3
S.	"	21,	Johann Diehl	29	11	5
	Febr.	9,	Salome Lehr (Armenhaus)	64	9	7
H.	"	17,	Hanna Torn	51	7	28
M.	"	24,	Sarah E. Masteller	24	9	13
H.	März	23,	Christian Ritter	64	5	6
M.	"	23,	Libia Karolina Trexler	18	5	19
Sal.	"	24,	Gottlieb Petzhold	54		
A.	"	24,	Kasper Kleckner	77		
R.	April	5,	Heinrich Frey	77	6	28
M.	Mai	5,	Salomon Fogel	71	5	24
S.	"	26,	Ulrich Leichty	65	10	12
Sal.	Juni	12,	Hetty Emrich	26	4	7
S.	Aug.	9,	Regina Eppler	29	5	28
Sal.	"	21,	Jesse Gieß	44	5	5
S.	Okt.	5,	Joel Benner	38		19
M.	"	24,	Elisabeth Gorr	83	7	15
H.	"	28,	Anna Maria Zöllner	81	2	15
H.	Nov.	5,	Daniel Lazarus	89	6	25
H.	"	7,	Elisabeth Ritter	72	7	3
A.	"	8,	Charles Fetzer	82		18
A.	"	15,	Mathilda Gangwer	27	6	5
H.	"	26,	Michael Huber	79		4
Mill.	"	30,	Johann Peter Muth	70	4	26
S.	Dez.	12,	Adam Urffur	17	11	23
H.	"	13,	Thomas Reichard	25	11	5
Sal.	"	24,	James Kingate	62	2	2

1858.

S.	Jan.	26,	Johann Wint	56	8	10
A.	"	26,	Amanda L. Hunter	36	11	13
H.	Febr.	21,	Peter Meyer	50	11	3
Mill.	März	7,	Katharina Siegfried	73	1	17
Mill.	"	14,	Joseph Haman	80	9	27
A.	"	24,	Maria Anna Knerr	21	2	20
M.	April	11,	Sarah A. Haman	15	3	16

				Jahr	Monat	Tag
A.	April	25,	Elisabeth Nunemacher	18	6	17
H.	Mai	3,	Abraham Rohn	55	11	17
H.	"	3,	Joh. Michael Kunsman	76	1	23
H.	"	6,	Sophia Schneider	32	8	22
M.	"	12,	Susanna Albrecht	67		
M.	"	15,	Johann Albrecht	68	6	10
A.	"	16,	Elisabeth Kratzer	62	4	22
M.	"	19,	Daniel Schankweiler	69	3	18
S.	"	24,	Jakob Allen	89	5	
Mac.	Juni	17,	Elisabeth Titlow	42	3	27
S.	"	24,	Susanna Hoffert	86	4	20
A.	Juli	20,	Sarah Holman	63	1	9
M.	"	21,	Maria Anna Christman	38	9	27
S.	"	28,	Jakob Weber	27	1	8
M.	Aug.	11,	Heinrich Knappenberger	47	3	8
S.	"	16,	Rebekka Gernet	43	6	14
M.	"	17,	Libia Heinly	20	5	14
M.	"	17,	Heinrich Miller	41	9	
A.	"	19,	Salomon Gangwer	78	11	12
S.	"	31,	Anna Christine Reinhart	51	4	25
R.	Sept.	4,	Anna Minnich	67	6	29
A.	"	12,	Louise Woodring	30	6	9
A.	"	20,	Daniel März	76	7	3
A.	"	20,	Joel W. Venkerk	17	5	2
A.	"	28,	Elenora Bohlen	100	7	
M.	Okt.	9,	Susanna Friederich	38	4	19
Salz.	"	11,	Elisa Daniel	29	9	7
M.	Nov.	1,	Franklin Tretzler	28	7	8
Salz.	"	26,	Joseph Lein	74	9	26
"	Dez.	9,	Johann Ihrig	64	1	29
A.	"	30,	Magdalena Neuhard	71	11	12
Salz.	"	31,	Jacob Ruf	23	11	19

1859.

A.	Jan.	5,	Elisabeth Gutekunst	73	10	5
M.	"	9,	David Desch	25		4

53

				Jahr	Monat	Tag
M.	Jan.	15,	Libia Schmeier	47	7	26
A.	"	16,	Johann Georg Steinberger	26	1	8
R.	"	21,	Elisabeth Roth	78	8	10
M.	"	25,	Ruben Desch	21	6	20
H.	"	27,	Sarah Elisabeth Sanden	23	4	22
M.	"	28,	Maria Acker	65	11	1
M.	"	31,	Peter Desch	22	8	3
M.	Feb.	8,	Margaretha Romig	56	3	8
R.	"	11,	Margaretha Ritter	72		
H.	März	18,	Elisabeth Daniel	23	6	28
R.	"	25,	Elisabeth Frey	80	2	15
R.	April	4,	Sarah Frey	52		1
A.	Mai	1,	Johann Fahlstich	61	1	25
M.	"	1,	Salomon Ohl	88	10	3
Mac.	"	25,	Elisabeth Schmeier	21	3	7
S.	Juni	18,	David Lerch	54	8	10
H.	Juli	7,	Anna Rosina Groß	58	5	25
T.	Sept.	2,	Salomon Diefendörfer	25	6	25
R.	"	26,	Stephan Lutz	51	9	28
S.	Okt.	17,	―― Hartman	19	8	13
Flat-land.	Nov.	16,	Katharina Hoffert	63		5

1860.

H.	Jan.	2,	Heinrich Schneider	59	3	27
H.	"	4,	Francis Tiron	18	7	21
M.	"	14,	Karolina Bortz	25	9	28
S.	"	18,	John Laury	52	10	12
S.	Feb.	10,	William Hohle	84	11	15
M.	"	15,	Salomon Schaefer	81	8	18
M.	"	28,	Annjaline Schaub	18	9	1
Cat.	März	2,	Maria Panisch	17	9	2
B.	"	15,	Johann Adamy	75		1
A.	"	24,	Joh. Georg Steinberger	65	1	13
H.	April	1,	Georg Schorz	79	2	9
S.	"	6,	Heinrich Martin Reinbold	18		8

54

				Jahr	Monat	Tag
M.	April	11,	Andreas Knebler	72	10	4
M.	"	16,	Margaretha Nagel	62	11	8
S.	Mai	27,	Fanette Kinkabe	23	7	2
A.	"	28,	Maria Nunemacher	78	1	20
Mac.	Juli	24,	Stephan Frieberich	22	8	27
S.	Sept.	16,	William H. Hartman	23	7	25
S.	"	19,	Christina Ueberroth	71	8	16
S.	Okt.	1,	Maria Keck	70	10	26
H.	"	10,	Joh. A. Dech	34		9
S.	Nov.	27,	Jakob Nath	59	8	2
S.	"	28,	Ruben Mohr	30	3	12
H.	Dez.	3,	Joseph Daniel	68	7	2

1861.

R.	Jan.	10,	Karl Heinrich Höhle	47		19
S.	"	14,	Anna M. Scholl	27	10	12
H.	Feb.	4,	Elisabeth Koch	65	5	9
M.	"	13,	Daniel Stettler	70	10	12
M.	"	23,	Dr. David D. Moffer	38	10	9
M.	März	2,	Ruben Kienly	69		12
M.	"	3,	David Heinle	62	4	23
A.	"	15,	Sarah Knappenberger	70	1	24
M.	"	29,	Charlotte Rudolph	69	6	
A.	April	3,	Charles F. Uebach	29	7	26
	"	29,	Sarah Kercher (Armenhaus)	86		
A.	Mai	15,	Charles W. Colver	21	5	18
S.	Juli	7,	Georg Onkel	77	6	23
C.	"	22,	Lewis Beitler	23	1	15
M.	"	22,	Heinrich März	75	3	19
A.	"	28,	Katharina Hall	67	9	23
C.	Aug.	24,	Johann Beitler	64	11	11
M.	Sept.	10,	Johann Heinly	84		14
S.	"	12,	Johann Schleider	64		8
A.	"	18,	James Kleckner	50	2	11
A.	"	22,	Barbara Kleckner	89	7	
M.	"	27,	Katharina Schankweiler	87	6	7

				Jahr	Monat	Tag
S.	Okt.	1,	Johann Mohr	74	7	4
A.	"	18,	Heinrich Reichert	70		19
M.	"	26,	Joseph Haman	48	11	18
A.	Nov.	4,	Amandes Hopper	27	5	4
A.	"	26,	James Hall	88	3	3
M.	"	28,	Joel Friederich	37	2	11
M.	Dez.	6,	Salome Bender	39	8	27
R.	"	13,	Charles Henry Merz	42	8	21
R.	"	19,	Rosina Hoehle	75	9	14

1862.

				Jahr	Monat	Tag
S.	Jan.	12,	Allavesta Robney	25	4	4
Sal.	"	22,	Jonas David Gieß	21	10	12
Sal.	"	29,	Helena Kath. Moritz	95	10	2
S.	Febr.	4,	Georg Weber	87	5	9
S.	"	4,	Jakob Ueberroth	75	9	27
Sal.	"	22,	Maria Emmerich	54	4	13
S.	März	12,	Johann Gilbert	60	9	13
Sal.	"	16,	Joseph Kincaid	23		27
S.	"	17,	Margaretha Ziegenfuß	85	10	17
M.	April	5,	Francis Harrison Romig	16	10	23
M.	Mai	2,	E. E. E. Fegely	18		6
R.	"	30,	Jakob Bast	82	3	10
H.	Juni	26,	Georg Steinmetz	47	3	15
S.	Juli	10,	Samuel Urffer	58	7	21
R.	"	11,	Daniel Keiper	68	3	24
H.	"	28,	Amanda Elisabeth Reichert	17		25
Sal.	"	29,	Elisabeth Leim	70	7	22
S.	Aug.	13,	Anna Maria Magd. Hellener	35	1	6
R.	Sept.	8,	Dianna Albrecht	32	9	21
A.	"	18,	Sarah Clewell	60	1	4
H.	Okt.	9,	Katharina Huber	48		12
H.	"	21,	Sarah Kidd	59	7	18
S.	Nov.	2,	Maria Gernet	50		5
S.	Dez.	16,	Maria Barbara Mory	75	7	8
M.	"	27,	Magdalena Foegely	76	5	23

1863.

			Jahr	Monat	Tag
M.	Jan.	3, Johann Friederich 28	10	5
Sal.	"	17, Jakob A. Wimmer 58	10	11
S.	Febr.	9, Salomon Ihrig 62	2	13
M.	März	25, David Romig 50	10	12
H.	April	8, Sarah Moll 54	3	17
M.	Mai	7, Johann Joseph Jarret . . . 24	2	13
M.	"	26, Christina Gaumer 70	11	20
H.	Juni	26, Georg Schreh 48	1	5
S.	Aug.	23, Elisabeth Stein 29	8	16
S.	Sept.	6, Sarah Ihrig 33	10	11
S.	"	20, Magdalena Wittman 83	1	28
M.	"	21, Heinrich Knappenberger . . . 56	11	19
R.	"	21, Dianna Ritter 57	3	5
S.	Okt.	9, Katharina Salisa Diehl . . . 25	6	1
Sal.	"	19, David Schlosser 18	3	12
S.	"	20, Friederich Binder 24	11	28
S.	Nov.	2, Jonathan Rümfeld 56	5	4
M.	"	23, Heinrich U. Schankweiler . . . 15	8	7
Sal.	"	27, Jakob Leibensperger 52	7	4
S.	"	30, Paulina Schneider 28	4	
M.	Dez.	13, Lidia Trexler 80	8	23
S.	"	20, Nathan Jost 71	10	29
Salz.	"	24, Maria Reichenbach 72		3
Salz.	"	30, Lidia Herbst 59	6	19
S.	"	30, Christian Schäffer 92		18
H.	"	31, Sarah Frey 56		

1864.

H.	Jan.	2, Elisabeth Petterson 70	11	28
S.	"	4, Anni Amanda Gangwer 24	8	13
Sal.	"	10, Heinrich Deily 27	4	5
M.	"	20, Sarah A. Wieder 27	2	7
H.	"	24, Michael Kunsman 33	9	29
A.	"	25, Katharina Jung 79	6	2
S.	Febr.	14, Elisabeth Schaerer 17	7	25

				Jahr	Monat	Tag
Salz.	Febr.	17,	Katharina Ihrig	64	4	8
S.	"	17,	Heinrich Ueberroth	55	3	25
S.	"	20,	Katharina Ueberroth	74	4	4
H.	März	2,	Tilghman Dixon	24	2	9
Sal.	"	4,	Anna Julina Ueberroth	29		21
Jordan	"	6,	Hanna Leopold	78	6	21
Sal.	"	9,	David Ueberroth	47	11	1
Hellerstown	"	24,	Elisabeth Schaeffer	70	9	4
S.	"	29,	Jakob J. Harres	85	1	28
Sal.	April	6,	Sarah Reise	92	2	16
R.	"	22,	Katharina Götz	61	4	4
H.	"	24,	Oliver Buß	18	10	24
S.	Juni	8,	Sarah A. Merz	19	10	16
R.	Aug.	10,	Elisabeth Beitler	59	9	6
S.	"	13,	Edwin Pflueger	28		4
S.	Sept.	2,	Susanna Strunk	77	1	12
M.	"	24,	William Goer	32		17
Salz.	"	28,	Mary Elisabeth Ueberroth	22	2	20
M.	Okt.	17,	Maria M. Boyer	82	1	7
S.	Nov.	9,	Jakob J. Schleiter	27	11	19
Salz.	"	14,	Johann Miller	65	9	27
M.	"	24,	Sarah C. Rebekka Marsteller	33	6	14
M.	"	29,	Lidia Marsteller	62	9	28

1865.

S.	Jan.	2,	Fayette Ihrig	19	7	9
R.	"	11,	Philip Nagel	76		
S.	"	21,	Sarah M. Duier	24	4	14
S.	"	27,	Philip Wind	78	9	2
M.	"	27,	Karolina Miller	30	5	24
M.	Febr.	19,	Jesse Breinig	68	2	24
Salz.	"	23,	Elisabeth Barbara Kram	60	2	14
A.	März	11,	Charles F. L. Weber	30	11	3
H.	"	24,	Heinrich Schneider	69	4	11
A.	"	26,	Robert Eschenbach	22		12

				Jahr	Monat	Tag
A.	Mai	1,	Benjamin F. Siegfried	23	10	25
S.	Juni	10,	Peter Weber	95	10	21
Salz.	"	21,	Sarah Abbott	58	11	28
S.	"	25,	Margaretha Hornung	55	6	25
H.	"	30,	Andreas Frankenfield	52	7	
M.			Margaretha Miller	88		
S.	Juli	10,	Johann Georg Gernet	85	1	28
R.	Aug.	9,	Fayette Meyer	33	5	14
S.	Sept.	10,	Katharina Schlebenbecker	34	9	
M.	"	13,	Lucinda Reinhart	38	4	27
S.	"	17,	Susanna Keßler	22	8	5
S.	Okt.	3,	David E. Lerch	28	7	
Salz.	"	17,	Susanna Deily	71		
Salz.	"	22,	Katharina Ruhf	88	5	14
H.	"	25,	Barbara Jörg	85	6	14
Salz.	"	26,	Magdalena Ulmer	73		
S.	Nov.	9,	Johannes Dotterer	67	6	19
A.	"	12,	Francis Oliver Schmetzer	42	9	11
H.	"	18,	Edwin Daniel Fogelmann	26	6	18
R.	Dez.	15,	Leah Reichard	52	7	7
M.	"	17,	Libia Singmeister	86	6	3

1866.

M.	Jan.	14,	James Heinley	56	11	8
A.	Febr.	5,	Walter Peter Fetzer	22	11	8
S.	"	23,	Johann Friedrich Pflüger	64	10	1
S.	"	24,	Daniel Bilger	23	8	3
Salz.	"	26,	Joseph Nagel	71	2	12
M.	März	5,	Johann Schmeier	86	7	15
H.	"	8,	Rahel Hummel	87	2	5
S.	"	16,	Anna Margaretha Heerlein	85	7	14
S.	"	24,	Johann Martin Stotz	51		
Salz.	April	10,	Charles Bauer	23	4	14
H.	"	30,	Konrad Scheimer	68	4	23
A.	Mai	6,	Jakob Bitz	80	6	12
Salz.	"	23,	Tobias Schmidt	60	10	1

				Jahr	Monat	Tag
Salz.	Juni	5,	Rebekka Louise Deily	50	4	17
Salz.	"	9,	Maria Jost	78	5	14
R.	"	20,	Joseph Laubach	68		28
R.	"	20,	Maria Laubach	89	8	2
M.	"	20,	David Foegely	87	2	
S.	Juli	5,	Maria Rosetta Jost	60		12
A.	"	29,	Eugene Daniel Jung	16	6	2
S.	Aug.	7,	Jakob Hillegaß	53	7	11
H.	"	13,	Julianna Ott	47	10	26
M.	Sept.	9,	Katharina Dankel	74	8	4
H.	"	20,	Heinrich Hummel	63	10	17
S.	Okt.	3,	Alfred Wint	25	11	15
H.	Nov.	26,	Karolina Long	54		24

1867.

Salz.	Jan.	5,	Johann Miller	76	9	13
M.	"	9,	James Friederich	26		10
H.	"	12,	Barbara Bräber	69	6	15
M.	"	13,	Eliza Schmeier	43		12
A.	"	14,	Jakob S. Long	69	11	19
A.	"	15,	Daniel Jung	74		
S.	März	6,	Owen Herwy	34	4	13
S.	April	2,	Susanna Heller	72	10	12
H.	"	6,	Daniel Zellner	60		28
A.	"	11,	Jakob Scholl	65	3	13
H.	"	24,	Michael Lazarus	64		24
A.	"	27,	Elisabeth Runemacher	61	3	27
A.	Mai	27,	Gustav D. Hoffmann	43	6	25
S.	"	28,	Abalina Sarah Ann Stern	24	8	13
S.	"	29,	Sarah Ann Herwy	25	4	4
S.	Juni	4,	Moses Gangwer	71	4	5
Salz.	"	7,	Milton Ruhf	28	3	4
S.	"	10,	Maria Baun	51		7
Salz.	"	10,	Johann M. Baier	40	7	22
S.	Aug.	9,	Elisabeth Herwy	29	8	12
M.	"	19,	Christian Weber	81	4	7

				Jahr	Monat	Tag
S.	Okt.	24,	Joh. Friederich Wirth	41	2	9
H.	"	26,	Johann Ritter	85	8	1
Raths:
Kirche	Nov.	2,	Salome Walter	56		22
M.	"	22,	Benneville Friederich	23	7	26
H.	"	30,	Joseph Kidd	68	1	2
A.	Dez.	3,	Mary Ann Fetzer	88	5	25
A.	"	6,	Susanna Sellers	83		
S.	"	24,	Joh. Jakob Mory	84	10	17
S.	"	24,	James Wint	22	1	10

1868.

				Jahr	Monat	Tag
Salz.	Jan.	6,	Allenspacher Mory	34	4	21
R.	"	17,	Anna M. S. Knoll	29	5	1
S.	"	29,	Virginia Katharina Weidner	16	5	7
H.	Febr.	2,	Susanna Minnich	70		3
H.	März	3,	Sarah Frankenfield	54		24
M.	"	6,	Susanna Fegely	90		27
S.	"	11,	Franklin Benner	22	9	
A.	"	19,	Susanna Jane Brong	25		3
R.	"	29,	Samuel Knauß	65	11	12
M.	April	9,	Anna Maria Weiler	81	6	
S.	"	16,	Addison Laury	26	7	
M.	"	25,	Ruben Schmeier	61	4	8
Bl. K.	Mai	4,	Salomon Greenewald	64	11	22
S.	"	5,	Isaak Benner	55	8	28
S.	"	10,	Bernhard Zentner	47	6	13
Salz.	Juni	3,	Maria Kath. Gebhart	75	11	23
M.	"	18,	Ellen Jane Warmkessel	15	10	9
A.	"	19,	Christina Geißer	82	4	4
R.	"	25,	Emilia Paulina Reichard	35	6	2
Salz.	Juli	1,	John Edwards	27		
Salz.	"	3,	Ambros H. Gieß	22	4	6
S.	"	12,	Jakob Ueberroth	46	3	20
A.	"	12,	Reuben Guth	54	6	24
H.	"	18,	Elisabeth C. Odenwälder	21		14

				Jahr	Monat	Tag
S.	Juli	23,	James P. Fischer	52	6	4
S.	Aug.	28,	Johannes Gangwer	68	11	16
Salz.	Sept.	9,	Adam A. Leibensperger	35	8	5
H.	"	15,	Isaak Huber	61	9	14
A.	Okt.	27,	Amilia C. Ruhf	60		19
Salz.	Nov.	11,	Johann Jakob David Weil	39	11	25
S.	"	27,	Louisa Roth	23	3	3
H.	"	30,	Michael Bauer	87	1	
S.	Dez.	4,	Benjamin F. Merz	43	3	19
S.	"	19,	Felix Seipert	56	11	15

1869.

				Jahr	Monat	Tag
A.	Febr.	20,	Nancy Hoffert	71	6	5
S.	März	16,	Franz Joseph Moser	43	9	19
H.	"	27,	Karoline R. Miller	40	1	5
A.	April	2,	Jakob Egge	87	2	19
H.	Juni	17,	Karoline Dickson	20	10	7
M.	"	26,	Johann Schmeier	72	4	16
S.	"	27,	Johann W. Hittinger	47	4	5
A.	Aug.	7,	Philip L. Belling	71	1	20
A.	"	8,	Christiana F. Schütz	51	8	26
S.	"	27,	Susanna Merz	65	5	12
A.	Sept.	[2,	Marg. Woodring	82	4	
A.	"	16,	Christian F. Beitel	89	7	23
A.	"	26,	Salome Schäffer	92	5	23
A.	Nov.	3,	Oliver A. Ritter	35	1	3
H.	"	8,	Georg Edwin Hoch	19	4	20
S.	Dez.	3,	Maria Kath. Ihrig	72	8	9
H.	"	20,	Alina Elisabeth Kuhn	21	6	22
Ziegelf.	"	20,	Susanna Lichtenwallner	76	3	27

1870.

				Jahr	Monat	Tag
S.	Jan.	1,	Johann Knepply	94	5	23
M.	"	31,	Sarah Friederich	33	9	21
R.	Febr.	2,	Maria Kath. Keiper	86		25

62

				Jahr	Monat	Tag
A.	Febr.	21,	Katharina Dutt	27	1	9
S.	März	6,	Johann Trapp	81	5	3
A.	"	18,	Jakob Hagenbuch	73	1	21
H.	April	3,	Elisabeth Kunsman	56	7	16
A.	"	4,	William Fatzinger	65	5	22
A.	"	17,	Bernhard Nagel	81	10	17
S.	Mai	12,	Lewis C. Quier	53	10	26
Salz.	Juni	1,	Gottlieb Holzward	46	8	8
S.	"	7,	David Blank	57	9	17
S.	"	20,	Katharina Mohr	80	4	5
S.	"	22,	William H. Weierbach	55	2	20
S.	"	28,	John Merz	85	9	29
Salz.	Juli	16,	Louisa Ueberroth	56		18
H.	"	18,	John Moyer	75	4	20
M.	"	31,	David Dengler	44	5	23
H.	Aug.	8,	Sarah Illick	56	4	
S.	"	12,	Levi Weber	45	7	20
R.	"	30,	Heinrich Fatzinger	77	5	11
S.	Sept.	14,	Katharina Weber	72		
S.	"	27,	Gottlieb F. Leibfried	79	10	26
S.	Nov.	12,	William Ohl	74	8	8
H.	"	18,	Sabina Frankenfield	25		24
S.	"	20,	Aaron Frey	68	4	8
H.	"	21,	Georg Deily	89	4	24
A.	"	22,	Nathan Schaefer	52	7	9
S.	Dez.	2,	Alles Berger	18	5	
M.	"	11,	Elisabeth Breinig	65	8	10
M.	"	13,	Lovina Schmeyer	53	2	9
S.	"	29,	William Taylor	72	7	22

1871.

M.	Jan.	31,	George Gorr	61	7	30
M.	Feb.	19,	Lowina Layton	31	7	4
Salz.	"	28,	Joseph Benner	67	10	29
A.	März	16,	Anna Oppermiller	24		
A.	"	27,	Susanna Knerr	82	11	1

				Jahr	Monat	Tag
S.	März	27,	Stephan H. Diehl	31	5	2
A.	April	3,	James L. Pflüger	49	1	24
S.	"	4,	Katharina März	78	3	17
S.	Mai	2,	Anna M. Geyer	20	8	26
S.	"	6,	Heinrich Miller	19	10	4
A.	"	6,	Barbara Trogel	83	2	18
A.	"	12,	Sarah Ann Fink	22	10	29
Salz.	"	19,	Joel Schaeffer	61	10	6
S.	"	20,	Sarah A. C. Reiß	22	5	
A.	"	28,	Heinrich Lautenschläger	80	7	
Salz.	Juni	19,	Friedrich Aubend	77	3	11
M.	"	21,	Josua Schmeier	75	2	27
Salz.	Juli	10,	Konrad Weil	76	4	4
H.	"	22,	Lidia Gräber	52	10	
A.	Aug.	10,	Eduard Schnerr	60	6	10
M.	"	16,	Susanna Stein	43	1	12
M.	Sept.	5,	Johann A. Gaumer	81	1	29
H.	"	19,	Anna Maria Schorz	55	4	
A.	"	24,	Edmund J. Balliet	50	6	20
H.	"	24,	Thomas Lazarus	61	9	20
S.	Okt.	3,	Anna Christina Quier	82	8	1
A.	"	7,	Anthony Gangwer	87	10	
A.	"	14,	Salomon Jüngling	68	4	3
H.	Nov.	3,	Jakob Huber	76	3	
S.	"	4,	David Weil	62	7	5
A.	"	6,	Harriette Richard	18	6	22
A.	"	14,	Ruben Wuchter	40	9	5
M.	Dez.	22,	John W. Wetzel	27	6	28
S.	"	30,	Adam Merkel	42		7

1872.

S.	Jan.	4,	Jonas Herwy	42	4	17
S.	"	14,	Charles Moritz	59	10	11
S.	"	20,	Marg. Doll	49		
S.	März	3,	Adam Fleger	38	5	16
Salz.	"	8,	Sarah Amanda Sterner	25	11	26

				Jahr	Monat	Tag
M.	März	3,	Maria M. Romig	80	1	12
Salz.	"	9,	Josua S. Nagel	25	5	11
M.	"	11,	Maria Elisabeth Schankweiler	49	3	26
Salz.	"	18,	Elisabeth Dony	75	1	9
"	"	19,	Samuel A. Nagel	27		10
R.	April	7,	Diana R. Ihrig	40	3	15
M.	"	12,	Ida V. Mosser	17	3	25
R.	"	17,	Joseph Richlein	56		18
H.	"	19,	Annie M. Huber	30	11	3
A.	"	21,	James N. Kramer	42	6	21
S.	Mai	4,	John Allen	24		
Salz.	"	21,	George Ruhf	73	2	17
A.	Juni	3,	Maria M. Nunemacher	95	4	25
M.	"	4,	Salomon Ahner	68	9	22
A.	"	8,	Daniel Fritz	49	7	27
S.	"	17,	John Yost	74	7	26
H.	Juli	24,	Salomon Deily	44	5	15
M.	"	28,	Christian Seiberling	87	3	28
A.	Aug.	4,	William Edelmann	61	3	
M.	"	8,	Karoline Breinig	46	11	14
R.	"	10,	Elisabeth Hilles	26	5	29
S.	"	11,	Rudolph E. Kern	32	3	30
M.	"	27,	Maria Ann Breinig	70	8	
S.	Sept.	13,	Sinclare Snyder	64		
M.	"	15,	Philipp Friederich	74	11	28
A.	"	21,	Joseph Gangwer	61	2	6
A.	Okt.	14,	Walter J. Getter	33	8	7
M.	"	14,	Jonathan Knappenberger	36	1	19
A.	"	20,	William Miller	81	9	11
H.	"	26,	Jakob Ribb	73	3	10
Salz.	Nov.	3,	Marg. Olpp	28	10	15
A.	"	24,	Katharina Fenstermacher	79	7	16
A.	Dez.	5,	Susanna Fried	69	3	6
S.	"	8,	Susanna Kunsman	56	6	28
R.	"	23,	Elisa A. Weaver	23	8	4
S.	"	25,	Esther Schneider	62	4	24

1873.

				Jahr	Monat	Tag
R.	Jan.	23, Katharina Osenbach	89	4	12
S.	"	27, Eliza Mory	54	1	1
M.	Febr.	6, Katharina Klein	67	7	29
S.	"	18, William H. M. Leible	17	6	22
R.	"	26, Mary Zellner	66	2	7
M.	März	1, Peter Bickel	70	10	4
H.	"	31, Martin C. Illick	21	7	23
A.	April	3, Eliza A. Steidinger	43		30
M.	"	12, Georg Klauß	73	7	28
S.	"	16, Jakob Thron	67	6	3
Salz.	"	27, William H. Torns	18	3	17
Salz.	Mai	5, Mary M. Barner	50	2	22
S.	"	28, Adam Zeck	62	4	29
H.	"	28, Elisabeth Zöllner	72	5	13
S.	Juni	16, John Braun	81	2	20
H.	"	19, William Rohn	70	6	4
Salz.	"	20, William Merkel	80	6	28
S.	"	29, Heinrich Bilgart	39	1	8
S.	Juli	20, Andreas Wint	69		26
S.	"	21, William Hottenstein	39	6	19
A.	"	23, John Geißer	75	9	16
S.	Sept.	5, Johann Philip Herlein	79	6	10
H.	"	11, Maria S. Kunzman	85	5	14
S.	"	20, Levi Miller	68		6
R.	Okt.	12, Peter Osenbach	89	8	8
R.	"	16, Katharina Fatzinger	90	8	
H.	Nov.	12, Annie Miller	71	7	26
H.	"	11, Georg Pier	54	4	17
R.	"	16, Katharina Sterner	70	8	8

1874.

S.	Jan.	26, Wilhelmina Schmidt	48		
H.	"	28, Anna Bickert	69		
M.	"	28, Karolina Stettler	58	6	12
H.	Febr.	2, Maria Huber	70	4	21

				Jahr	Monat	Tag
S.	Febr.	27,	Thomas Weber	76	1	
H.	"	28,	John Bickert	79	8	7
	März	5,	Samuel Boyer (Armenhaus) . .	45	6	16
H.	"	28,	Ruben Hagenbuch	48	8	14
S.	April	5,	Christina Klein	70	5	11
Salz.	"	14,	Georg R. Bauer	73	11	18
M.	"	30,	Hanna Schuler	71	2	3
Salz.	Mai	19,	Katharina C. Leibensperger . .	35	4	9
H.	"	24,	Monroe A. Reichard	20	2	9
A.	"	27,	Margaretha Mory	78	10	25
R.	Juni	12,	John Acker	29	10	23
S.	"	14,	Maria Gangwer	72	6	26
S.	Juli	9,	Wilhelmina Wenger	40		
S.	"	12,	Benjamin Billigard	28	3	11
M.	"	14,	Katharina M. Bickel	29	2	21
S.	"	21,	Maria Hermany	71	4	18
R.	"	29,	Amalia L. Roller	47	7	2
Salz.	Aug.	8,	Theophilus Reice	67	5	14
S.	"	12,	Abraham Mohr	43	4	2
Salz.	"	27,	Jonas Emrich	64	11	3
A.	Sept.	26,	Gottlieb Fritz	49	10	29
M.	Okt.	8,	Elisabeth Schmeier	80	8	14
R.	"	30,	William D. Ritter	55	3	6
H.	Dez.	4,	Charles Schneider	62	5	7

1875.

H.	Febr.	1,	Jakob Fogelmann	76	10	17
R.	"	5,	Rebekka Frey	54	11	27
Sal.	"	11,	Katharina D. Schneider	41	8	19
S.	"	12,	Joseph Frank	81	10	13
A.	"	16,	Salomon Boyer	55	11	3
H.	"	18,	Daniel Neuhart	77	6	6
S.	"	22,	Frau Franz Weisbecker	86		
H.	März	18,	Magdalena Ritter	79	11	28
A.	"	19,	Christian Krug	63	10	9
A.	"	21,	Mary A. Knauß	54	11	28

				Jahr	Monat	Tag
M.	März	28,	Sarah Miller	72	11	24
M.	"	29,	Salome Heinly	69	10	8
R.	April	2,	Elisabeth Knauß	70	10	13
R.	"	24,	William F. Miller	19	4	24
A.	"	25,	Daniel Klees	61		26
M.	Mai	1,	Peter Breinig	79	2	12
A.	"	6,	Susanne Ruhe	73		14
H.	"	13,	Sarah C. Dech	19	10	11
A.	Juli	27,	Ruben M. Gernet	48	3	10
R.	"	29,	Angelina Correl	25	9	4
A.	"	31,	John Eckert	75		22
S.	Aug.	8,	Ruben C. Marsteller	43	7	13
M.	"	11,	Maria Kuns	61	2	
Blaue K."		15,	Alice V. Blank	15	5	13
S.	"	16,	Heinrich Weiß	59	10	17
Salz.	"	25,	Friedrich Klein	80	7	1
A.	Okt.	8,	Mary Kunz	69	11	8
H.	"	8,	Joseph Illick	69	9	29
H.	"	9,	Sarah Rohn	62	2	23
A.	Nov.	9,	Adam Kunz	77	8	1
Howers-town	"	22,	Salome Biery	73	6	3
A.	Dez.	8,	Sarah Anna Schlauch	53	4	16
S.	"	20,	Reuben Trumbauer	41	5	12

1876.

				Jahr	Monat	Tag
R.	Jan.	24,	Elisabeth Hellmar	73	6	1
Salz.	Febr.	2,	Elisabeth Merkel	82	3	8
M.	"	11,	Mary Ann Heth	18	10	9
A.	"	15,	Charles Gangwer	51		
H.	"	28,	Maria Heineg	53	9	10
M.	März	15,	James B. Trexler	25	9	5
Salz.	April	3,	Henry W. Schloßer	41	1	6
H.	"	4,	Susanna Schärer	74	2	10
Salz.	"	23,	Joseph Schloßer	74	11	3
S.	Mai	1,	Sessina Clewell	23	9	26

				Jahr	Monat	Tag
Salz.	Mai	2,	Maria M. Keßler	65	2	3
H.	"	19,	Paul Fatzinger	47	9	17
S.	"	20,	Maria Doetterer	85	11	22
H.	Juni	4,	John Kibb	83	3	7
A.	"	17,	Aaron Mosser	42		16
H.	Juli	9,	Elisabeth Schneider	72	6	25
A.	"	11,	Anna M. Hersch	70	8	10
Salz.	Sept.	4,	Eva Elisabeth Meßer	61	9	13
Salz.	"	4,	Lovina Rudolph	34	4	27
A.	"	16,	Pheon Jarret	67	7	7
R.	"	23,	Charles Zöllner	73	9	12
H.	Nov.	18,	Elisabeth Huber	34	10	16
A.	"	20,	Karl L. Gallmeier	76		23
A.	"	26,	Julianna Gallmeier	69	9	21
A.	"	27,	Sarah Wolf	58	2	15
H.	Dez.	11,	Sarah E. Hechman	41	7	25
R.	"	30,	Alfred L. Schnabel	19	11	15

1877.

A.	Jan.	8,	Maria A. Kleckner	65	3	
S.	"	8,	Katharina Reinhart	74	7	8
A.	"	19,	Daniel Fußelman	72		
S.	"	30,	Friedrich Hüttinger	73	9	19
H.	Febr.	25,	Fayetta Schurz	40	1	21
H.	"	25,	Christina Daniel	69	9	29
R.	"	26,	Charles P. Moyer	33	5	8
R.	März	2,	Sarah A. R. Mill	31	11	2
A.	"	8,	Peter Wyckoff	69		19
A.	"	11,	Tilghman Kleckner	47	2	11
A.	"	12,	Robert Jost	54	2	10
R.	"	12,	Maria Bauer	60		26
S.	"	19,	Christian Gernet	71	7	19
A.	"	26,	Annie Bush	75	1	22
R.	April	11,	Jakob Stump	68	1	23
M.	"	20,	Ruben Schankweiler	64	5	13
S.	Mai	30,	Matilda Green	43	4	22

				Jahr	Monat	Tag
S.	Juni	11,	Adam Ueberroth	75	7	26
A.	"	19,	Annie E. Preston	68	1	26
Kreiters-
ville	Juli	4,	Susanna Daniel	66	8	2
	"	16,	Barbara Siemens (Armenhaus)	83	7	
	"	19,	Heinrich Fink (Armenhaus) . . .	75	5	28
Salz.	Aug.	14,	Michael Ritter .	82	11	
Salz.	"	25,	Elisabeth Schlosser	72	4	20
A.	Nov.	7,	Margaretha Saylor	75		10
A.	"	9,	Martha Roth	25	7	11
M.	"	25,	Willy Haidt	43	11	17
S.	Dez.	12,	Jakob Harwi	82	8	29
M.	"	17,	Charles Moyer	16	2	22
M.	"	29,	Katharina E. Moyer	51	10	10

1878.

S.	Jan.	9,	Johann Rieger	56	5	25
S.	"	23,	Abigail Ihrig	67	9	14
H.	"	25,	John A. Fatzinger	15	9	5
M.	Febr.	2,	Georg Dankel	89		9
A.	März	27,	Sarah Koch	64	4	20
S.	"	28,	Georg Gernet	74	9	9
H.	April	4,	Clinton Muschlitz	19	4	29
M.	"	11,	Rebekka Schmidt	78	10	18
M.	"	12,	William H. Schmeier	31	7	27
S.	"	21,	Katharina Diehl	75	2	9
S.	"	24,	Elisabeth Seibert	64	4	4
A.	Mai	1,	Mary Hutter	86	8	19
S.	Juni	2,	Friedrich Kuns	77		27
S.	"	11,	Susanna F. Marsteller	35	8	6
M.	"	13,	Stephan Fegely	48	4	20
M.	"	16,	Emma Kath. Weiler	26	2	2
S.	"	26,	Jonas S. Lerch	34	10	9
R.	Juli	21,	Susanna C. Roth	18	8	20
Salz.	Aug.	1,	Elisabeth Schmidt	61	9	15
H.	"	2,	Joseph Lichtenwalner	76	1	29

				Jahr	Monat	Tag
S.	Aug.	6,	Jakob Merkel	61	3	29
S.	"	25,	Susanna Neuhart	75	4	4
R.	Sept.	1,	Maria Nagel	81		
H.	"	16,	Karoline Kibb	68	6	14
S.	"	20,	Susanna Weber	76	7	25
A.	Okt.	1,	Elisabeth Eberhard	81	4	3
Salz.	"	7,	Sarah A. Diehl	41	6	22
M.	Nov.	2,	Benjamin Schmeier	85		8
A.	"	13,	Salomon Kramer	75	3	28
S.	Dez.	18,	Heinrich D. Cope	65	2	12
R.	"	30,	Susanna Andreas	39	5	19
S.	"	31,	Libia Lerch	68	8	14

1879.

				Jahr	Monat	Tag
S.	Jan.	5,	Heinrich Rickenberg	79	6	
R.	"	14,	Emmeline Nagel	29		24
S.	"	21,	Samuel Cope	72		
S.	"	21,	Asmus Mack	18	8	22
S.	"	24,	Emmina Ambrunn	24	2	6
S.	"	25,	Georg Henn	74	7	26
S.	"	29,	Salome Geissinger	76	10	11
S.	Febr.	19,	Abraham Blank	73	6	6
S.	"	25,	Edward Ruhf	60	6	11
M.	März	27,	Nancy Cope	70	5	25
M.	Mai	1,	Karolina Schmeier	40	1	18
S.	Juni	1,	Henriette Yaeger	41	1	7
R.	"	6,	Dorothea Haner	81	11	27
H.	"	8,	Susanna Hoch	59		16
S.	"	30,	Charles Gangwer	56	1	5
R.	Juli	16,	Libia Fatzinger	74		
M.	"	29,	Franklin Heth	19	1	16
A.	Aug.	2,	Salomon Ihrig	52	2	12
A.	"	7,	Eliza Tice	56	1	
H.	"	21,	Anna Reidenouer	65		1
H.	"	31,	Jakob Wolf	75	2	7
S.	Sept.	24,	Hiram Thomas Reichard	17	10	24

				Jahr	Monat	Tag
A.	Sept.	26,	Rebekka Lucas	70	5	15
H.	"	29,	Jakob Miller	77	9	27
A.	Okt.	7,	Charles Scholl	68	4	25
M.	"	16,	Sarah A. E. Marsteller	43	9	1
A.	Nov.	4,	Sarah Cole	44	8	29
H.	"	7,	Elisabeth Hummel	75	4	17
R.	"	22,	Jane E. R. Sand	18	3	26
A.	"	23,	Daniel Runemacher	73	11	
A.	Dez.	26,	Nancy A. Kramer	78	6	21
A.	"	27,	Hannah Stem	91	3	5

1880.

H.	Jan.	2,	Emma E. Huber	19		18
Salz.	"	5,	Hannah Schmidt	74	2	20
R.	"	20,	Lilly A. Nagel		1	20
H.	"	24,	Charles A. Boger		1	3
S.	"	24,	Georg Dolle	6	9	
M.	Feb.	4,	Jefferson Heydt	17	9	8
R.	"	12,	Clinton C. A. Heckman	3	6	23
R.	"	16,	Louisa Kraber	53	11	29
M.	"	22,	James R. Tregler	6	1	5
R.	"	23,	Jesse Acker	72	9	22
H.	März	5,	Susanna Heckman	67	4	4
M.	"	9,	Harry A. Tregler	2	11	20
H.	"	23,	Adam Fatzinger	89	3	6
H.	April	12,	Julianna Huber	72	10	26
S.	"	19,	Thomas J. Ziegenfuß	6	5	3
R.	"	30,	John W. Dannecker	1	11	7
R.	Mai	18,	Carl F. Dannecker	5	9	18
Salz.	"	22,	Abbesina M. Moritz	4	3	20
R.	Juli	17,	Alfred T. Hoehle	4		27
R.	"	20,	Emmelina Claber	42	4	27
M.	"	27,	Lorah Herrman	82		
A.	Aug.	1,	Jennie Laubach		10	5
M.	"	9,	Howard S. Clewell	2		14
S.	"	18,	Salomon Ueberroth	76	4	14

				Jahr	Monat	Tag
R.	Aug.	27,	John Eberhard	75	7	21
M.	"	28,	Howard D. Smoyer	2	8	17
S.	Sept.	10,	Heinrich Wittman	28	1	29
S.	"	21,	Maria Cope	75	7	4
R.	Okt.	21,	Charles Kratzer	76	8	23
M.	Nov.	7,	Peter Klein	76	6	16
S.	"	13,	Sylvester Weber	24	5	19
S.	"	18,	Conrad Leible	55	6	13
S.	"	24,	Franklin J. Treichler	6	8	21
Salz.	Dez.	12,	Jesaias Ueberroth	68	6	10
S.	"	14,	Laura J. Ehrig	1	11	12
M.	"	23,	Jbella C. Friederich	3	8	17

1881.

				Jahr	Monat	Tag
S.	Jan.	12,	Mary Herman	21		
M.	"	14,	Käthe L. Friederich	1	2	24
R.	"	28,	Della M. Moyer	3	11	25
H.	"	29,	Adamissa Laub	2	10	20
H.	Feb.	14,	William Laub	60	6	20
H.	"	25,	Maria Anna Huber	78	3	16
M.	März	9,	Angelina S. Emig	8	2	22
M.	"	13,	Katharina E. Bickel	8	5	3
Salz.	"	21,	William H. F. Merz	23	6	25
M.	"	26,	Charles C. Emig	3	3	14
Salz.	"	27,	Emma L. Jhrig			13
H.	"	29,	Salomon Steinmetz	71	4	24
H.	"	29,	Eduard G. Ritter		8	29
H.	"	30,	Anna C. Nunemacher	6	4	25
M.	April	3,	Jonathan Breinig	79	2	3
S.	"	4,	Elias Eschbach	55	7	16
S.	"	13,	Martin Ruhf	76	1	7
H.	"	29,	Maria Fatzinger	85	2	7
H.	Mai	14,	Mary J. Nunemacher	11	4	13
M.	"	25,	Nathan Schankweiler	64	2	20
A.	"	31,	Erwin W. H. Hertzel		4	15
M.	Juni	8,	Quinton T. Schmeier	1	5	8

				Jahr	Monat	Tag
A.	Juni	29,	Thomas Ihrig	57	2	5
R.	Juli	8,	Monroe J. Tice	24	2	15
S.	"	8,	William H. Stern	9	6	16
H.	"	9,	Sarah Nunemacher	26	7	18
M.	"	9,	Elisabeth L. Preneinger		8	
M.	Aug.	5,	Sarah Fritz	64	3	28
S.	"	7,	August H. Keenan	27		10
S.	"	8,	Peter Haritz	88	3	28
H.	"	14,	Heinrich J. Knoll	35	7	14
M.	"	17,	Stephan Schmeier	69	4	5
R.	"	31,	Anna M. Ritter	78	10	2
M.	Sept.	1,	Thomas Schmoyer	67	2	17
S.	"	7,	Oliver W. Hornung	1	10	15
H.	"	19,	Annie M. Fatzinger	16	9	13
H.	"	20,	Henry F. Minnich	48	11	12
S.	Okt.	11,	Eva G. Kuhn		2	6
S.	"	13,	Lidia Ruhf	63	9	20
A.	"	20,	George Hauer	73	11	25
	"	24,	D. Charles F. Dickenschied	89		26
S.	"	29,	Tilghman Groß	48	1	15
Salz.	"	29,	Michael Stuber	68	2	5
Salz.	Nov.	5,	Katharina Kinkaid	79		14
S.	"	13,	Friederich Augustus Miller	48		8
S.	"	17,	Katharina Riegel	80	7	20
S.	"	26,	Charles Diehl	71	3	26
S.	Dez.	7,	William H. Siegfried	3	7	26

1882.

				Jahr	Monat	Tag
S.	Jan.	2,	Charles Senger	78	8	17
M.	"	7,	William Heydt	56	8	22
H.	"	20,	Philip Huber	80	11	7
M.	Febr.	17,	Johann Schmeier	56	3	19
A.	"	20,	Edmund D. Leisenring	65	6	7
A.	"	27,	Salomon Gorr	70	5	2
M.	März	2,	Harvy A. Miller	17	10	
S.	"	3,	Salomon Kunstman	69	11	19

				Jahr	Monat	Tag
M.	März	7,	David Miller	39	8	17
A.	"	12,	Alfred J. M. Laubach		8	25
Salz.	"	16,	Susanna Deily	76	8	17
S.	"	18,	Mathilda Steinmiller	43	3	4
A.	"	19,	Eliza Saeger	73	4	1
M.	"	26,	Henry Knappenberger	54	9	13
Salz.	"	28,	Joseph Funk	74		
R.	April	2,	Adam Miller	60	3	16
S.	"	5,	Esther Clauser	36	6	9
M.	"	10,	Elisabeth E. Schmeier		6	7
A.	"	12,	Daniel König	70		
S.	"	18,	Samuel Schneider	73	7	11
H.	"	27,	James Reh	66	11	17
M.	"	29,	Morris C. Warmkessel	5	6	9
R.	Mai	7,	Oliver C. Moyer	1	3	26
S.	"	7,	Emma L. Dietzel	8	7	21
M.	"	17,	Georg W. B. Schmoyer	8	1	12
R.	"	19,	Sarah Beitler	38	2	8
S.	"	24,	Mathilda Mauser	35	10	27
S.	Juni	1,	Anna Katharina Ihrig	88	8	10
H.	"	3,	George Lazarus	82	7	2
M.	"	11,	James A. Miller	21	8	28
S.	Juli	15,	David Gernet	71	11	7
S.	"	17,	Harven M. Ritter		3	3
M.	Aug.	6,	Heinrich W. Gaumer	52	4	3
S.	"	8,	Immanuel A. G. Blank	2	10	
S.	"	23,	Sarah Marsteller	81	8	
S.	"	26,	Clewellyn Clauser		11	6
A.	Sept.	2,	Katharina Walz	81	6	
H.	"	6,	Philippina Schneider	79	9	22
H.	"	8,	Edwin C. Schiffert	38	9	18
M.	"	15,	Katharina Albrecht	58	6	18
M.	"	27,	Charles E. Knopp	1	11	9
A.	"	29,	Samuel Nunemacher	75	2	10
R.	Okt.	19,	Peter Miller	47	6	8
H.	Nov.	3,	Anna Maria Farmmer	57	4	7
S.	"	9,	David Race	77	3	9

75

				Jahr	Monat	Tag
H.	Nov.	19,	H. E. Boyer..........		2	8
S.	Dez.	1,	Heinrich Jaeger........	83	11	17
Salz.	"	8,	Rebekka Miller........	78	9	8
M.	"	10,	Emma Baer..........	29	1	11
S.	"	11,	Albert James.........	10	4	14
S.	"	12,	Katharina Brang.......	45	8	20
H.	"	15,	Mary Margareth Wolf.....	35	4	17
R.	"	23,	Nikolaus Sterner.......	85	11	22
H.	"	29,	Maria Zoellner.........	66	5	24

1883.

S.	Jan.	4,	John J. Keßler........	29	5	19
A.	"	31,	Elisabeth Muse...	89		
Salz.	Febr.	4,	Lovina Schneider......	60	10	5
H.	"	21,	Philemon Schneider......	78		16
M.	"	25,	Dorothea Schankweiler....	2	10	19
S.	März	2,	James Cornelius Grimpe...	26	2	18
S.	"	4,	Clara Alice van Billiard...	1	4	17
H.	"	8,	Abba A. Nunemacher.....	16		24
M.	"	11,	Charles J. Bauer......		9	11
M.	"	29,	Katharina Schmidt......	81	4	19
A.	April	4,	H. J. G. Weil........		8	18
R.	"	11,	Charles Ritter........	77	2	29
H.	Mai	2,	Magdalena Colver......	74	5	3
R.	Juni	3,	John Kaiser.........	57	8	10
M.	"	16,	Minnie G. Schmeier.....	6	11	17
Salz.	Juli	2,	William Frey........	14	10	25
"	"	19,	Daniel Moritz.........	83	6	18
H.	"	27,	Joseph Gräber........	67	5	1
H.	Aug.	10,	Susanna Moyer.......	84	5	12
M.	"	11,	Wimmie A. Lohrman.....		5	20
S.	"	26,	Jacob Rohr.........		9	26
R.	Sept.	1,	Georg Winfield Wisser....	1	11	8
M.	"	1,	Agnes E. Zacharias.....	27	1	
M.	"	7,	John Grebel.........	84	8	10
H.	"	8,	Ida Edith Hoch.......			11

				Jahr	Monat	Tag
S.	Sept.	13,	Salomon Hartman	82	2	29
H.	"	15,	Samuel Jacob Buß		10	8
Beth.	"	15,	Maria Geißinger	77		
R.	"	22,	John Fahlstich	39	6	18
R.	Okt.	11,	Lovina Ott	63	10	10
R.	Nov.	27,	Thomas Ritter	75	6	18
H.	"	29,	Ellen Mary Buß	14	5	25
M.	"	27,	Katharina Breinig	75	1	11

1884.

				Jahr	Monat	Tag
M.	Jan.	1,	Eliza Jane Bittenbender	16	7	5
S.	"	11,	Katharina Reinhart	56	7	1
R.	Feb.	1,	Mary Hickens	15	2	8
H.	"	4,	Elisabeth Lesker	86		4
S.	"	5,	John Peter Morgan	14	7	21
H.	"	6,	Elisabeth Buß	88	1	17
S.	"	11,	Joseph Gernet	68	8	16
A.	"	24,	Georg Probst	84	6	11
M.	"	28,	Burssa C. Gaumer	5	11	16
H.	März	8,	Nathan Schneider	55	1	17
S.	"	22,	Maria Hertline		5	24
S.	"	24,	Karolina Bauß	35	5	
S.	April	17,	Amelia R. Lambert	22	4	7
A.	"	25,	Ellen M. Wint	5	8	7
M.	Mai	1,	Daniel Schankweiler	70	1	17
M.	"	4,	Elmer E. Lichtenwallner	19	6	3
S.	"	19,	Dianna Mohr	52	1	19
M.	Juni	22,	Jonathan Knappenberger	43	4	5
R.	Juli	25,	Annie M. C. Auer	1	2	13
M.	Aug.	9,	Katharina A. Abel-Trexler	50	3	27
H.	"	11,	Karoline M. Buß	42	10	27
R.	"	21,	Hetty A. Derr		8	5
S.	Sept.	11,	Maria Fatzinger	55	6	9
S.	"	21,	Jakob März	83	3	
M.	"	22,	Thomas Schuler	84	6	
R.	Nov.	9,	Ruben Flores	62	9	1

				Jahr	Monat	Tag
S.	Dez.	13,	Valentin Hornung	84	7	8
R.	"	22,	Mabel O. Deily	1	5	5
M.	"	31,	Minnie Jane Schankweiler	14	5	28

1885.

				Jahr	Monat	Tag
M.	Jan.	9,	Jakob Breinig	8	5	17
S.	"	12,	William Diehl	80		
H.	Feb.	17,	Daniel Schneider	84	8	
R.	März	31,	Leonhart Meeser	64	3	25
S.	"	26,	Adolph Wiese	8	6	25
H.	April	13,	Amelia E. Reichard	23	7	
R.	"	30,	Robert L. Worman		11	27
R.	Mai	27,	Abelina Wendel	37		
M.	Juni	10,	Rosa Schmoyer	41	4	1

MEMOIRS
OF
REV. JOSHUA YEAGER.

CHAPTER I.

Rev. Yeager's Parentage.

Of the grandparents on his father's side, Father Yeager knew but little, except that they came from Germany, and that there was in his father's family a book, which he had frequently seen, in which a beautiful prayer had been written by his grandfather. This, in connection with what he learned from his parents, evinced that Grandfather Yeager with his household had served God, and trained his family in the fear and admonition of the Lord.

Rev. Johann Conrad Yeager, the father of Rev. Joshua Yeager, and his mother, Barbara, whose maiden name was Schmidt, were both born in York County, Pa., near the town of York.

Father Johann Conrad Yeager was a cigar-maker, and kept a small tobacco store in the town of York. He had already three children when he concluded to devote himself to the office of the Christian ministry. The circumstance which led him thereto was the following: One day, as Mr. Yeager was sitting at his bench, engaged in making cigars, his pastor, Rev. Dr. Gœhring, who served the Lutheran congregation at York, and on whose ministry Mr. Yeager had been a faithful attendant, came to his store to buy some cigars. Dr. Gœhring had had his mind on Mr. Yeager for quite a while, believing him to be destined for the ministry. This thought was not a stranger, it is believed, to Mr. Yeager himself, though he never gave vent to it, from the fact that he little thought it possible that, situated as he was, such a design could be consummated. Dr. Gœhring on this occasion approached Mr. Yeager, and, looking over his shoulders as he was engaged in rolling cigars, said: "Johann, I want you to come to my house; you have gifts for something better than cigar-making. You should become a minister of the gospel." Mr. Yeager had enjoyed the privilege of attending school in his youth, and by faithful study had gained such knowledge as the schools of his day afforded. With this limited preparatory education he came to Dr. Gœhring, and entered on a course of study for the ministry. Among the branches undertaken by him was the very difficult study of Greek, in which language he afterwards always studied the texts of his sermons. After one year's study under Dr. Gœhring, while he at the same time also continued his little business, by which means he gained a livelihood for his family, he went, by recommendation of Dr. Gœhring, to Philadelphia. Here, as was the custom in those days, candidates for the ministry pursued their studies under the city pastors, receiving such instruction and attention as these men could give them in connection with their pastoral labors. Mr. Yeager became the student of Drs. Schmidt, Schæffer and Helmuth. The instruction, whatever there was of it, was thorough and practical. Mr. Yeager, being a very faithful student, at the expiration of one year had made such progress that his preceptors presented him to the Synod for examination. He was found prepared to enter the ministry of the Lutheran Church, and was licensed by the Synod of Pennsylvania.

After his reception into the Synod he was called to serve three small congregations in New Jersey, a short distance beyond Easton, the old so-called "Straw Church" in Greenwich township, Warren Co., constituting one of his congregations. While he was pastor here, he at one time came to Easton to purchase a few articles at the store of Mr. Herschter. Mr. H. had knowledge of Mr. Yeager and had heard many favorable reports of his work. Mr. Yeager was in straitened circumstances and poorly clad. Mr. Herschter viewed his seedy clothes and then questioned him in relation to his wants. "I see many things in your store," Mr. Yeager said, "that I ought to have, and of which my family stands in need, but I have no money to purchase them, and so I must be content without them." "Go," said Mr. Herschter to his clerk, "cut off a suit of clothes for Mr. Yeager, fit him a hat, cut off a dress for his wife, weigh twenty pounds of sugar, some coffee and other articles needed in the family." "Take them along," said Mr. H., "and have a suit made up first of all for yourself, so that you may have a presentable appearance when you go away from home." "Yes," said Mr. Y., "but I have no money to pay for these articles." "No matter about that now," said Mr. H.; "you can come in a year or two, when you have earned some money, and make payment." The hearts of Mr. Y. and of his wife and children were made glad by such kindness shown them in their extremity by this Christian friend. A year or two rolled by. Mr. Yeager's labors were crowned with success. He was doing a good work in his parish. But still the state of his exchequer was not flush. He, however, had not forgotten his benefactor, and came again to the store one day to pay part of his indebtedness. "How are you getting along now, Mr. Y.?" said Mr. H. "Right well," replied Mr. Y.; "and I have come to pay part of my bill, though I am still too poor to pay the entire amount." "Give him a receipt," said Mr. H., "for the whole. I hear so many good things of you that I am amply repaid, and I will cancel your entire bill." That Mr. Yeager was made happy beyond measure by this unexpected kindness, needs scarcely be stated. He went home rejoicing.

Mr. Yeager's second charge was Williams township, Northampton Co., and Saucon (Friedensville), Lehigh Co. The Saucon congregation was organized by him. He preached temporarily in Mr. Morey's barn during the time that the church edifice was being built. This was in 1793. Dryland, Schoener's and Allentown were subsequently added to the charge. During all this time he lived in Williams township. He now moved to Hanover, having bought a farm there of 230 acres. There his son Joshua, the subject of this narrative, was born, he having been the youngest of a family of nine sons and two daughters. Rev. J. Conrad Yeager labored in this charge with great success to the end of his life, which occurred in 1832.

CHAPTER II.

Rev. Joshua Yeager's Youth.

Rev. Joshua Yeager was born September 23d, 1802. He was baptized by his father in infancy and, after careful and conscientious instruction in the principles of the Christian religion, was confirmed and received by him into communion of the Evangelical Lutheran Church. In the house of Father Yeager regular instruction was given by the head of the family to all its members, on week-day evenings, in reading, writing and arithmetic. The opportunities for a very liberal education, of course, were necessarily limited, when compared with the school privileges of the present time. But what was lacking in a secular education was abundantly supplemented by the religious instruction imparted under the paternal roof. In those days religious instruction was regarded as "Hauptsache," a part of our education, which now, alas! is not only made secondary, but in many families almost totally neglected. The pious fathers of that elder day practiced the divine injunction, "Seek ye first the kingdom of God," in instructing in, and impressing on the hearts and minds of the young, the great plan of salvation. To delegate so important and vital a matter to the one hour's instruction a week in the Sunday-school, where such instruction is ofttimes very imperfectly given, and to the secular week-day school, where no religious teaching is tolerated, would have been justly looked upon with holy horror and righteous indignation by the men of God of a hundred years ago, who realized the solemn responsibility of their office as priests at the family altar. Reading of the Scriptures and writing out what was remembered, to the extent of a sheet a day, constituted part of his home instruction in the family of Father Yeager. His son Joshua had, it is true, received this thorough instruction, yet his education was quite limited in the sense that the word "liberal education" is, at present, understood.

After he had attained the age that he could make himself useful on the farm, his daily employment consisted in manual labor, which, on a farm of 236 acres, left but little time for study or recreation.

While following the plow one Summer day, his father came out and accompanied him to the farther end of the field. Joshua could hardly reconcile this unusual occurrence. But, when the end of the furrow was reached, his father said to him: "Wait a little while. I have something to tell you. I want you, with God's help, to become a minister." This unexpected suggestion really frightened Mr. Yeager. "Come to my room to-morrow morning," continued Father Y. "Leave your plow, there are others to attend to it. I wish to give you a three months' trial to ascertain whether you have talent for the ministry; if you have, you shall continue your studies—if not, I will then tell you so." Father Yeager handed his son a Latin grammar, saying: "This is a comparatively easy study, but it will furnish you a knowledge of the system of grammar in general, which is so necessary for the study of all languages. Study this two hours, and then ask me all the questions you can, about what you understand and all that you do not understand. After that come down and go into the garden, and take such exercise and do such work as you may wish. In the evening you will again take two hours of study, and thus continue on." In this way Mr. Yeager studied. His father was a drill-master and disciplinarian, and knew how to create and maintain an interest on the part of his student. Especially, however, did he observe and keep a close surveillance on the conduct of his son. He impressed him with the importance and responsibility of the work, and constantly urged upon him to observe such a conduct as is becoming a candidate for the Christian ministry, and which may meet with the approval of God and man. This education, so often neglected on the part of those to whom young men who have the ministry in view are intrusted, but which is so essential to the formation of the character of the true minister of Jesus Christ, exerted a most powerful and an abiding influence on the mind of young Yeager. To this may be attributed, perhaps as much as to anything else, that devotion, earnestness and zeal which characterized Rev. Joshua Yeager's ministry through the long period of well nigh three score years among a people whom he served so long and loved so well.

At the expiration of three months, Mr. Y. received the cheerfully given encouragement from his father to continue his studies; for he had given evidence, in his application and the progress made, that the father was not mistaken in selecting this his youngest son as the proper subject for his mantle to fall on, a few years hence. The brothers attended to the farm, and Joshua pursued his studies with diligence for four years. These four years spent by the side of his father, under his drills and watchful care, the text-books of ancient and modern languages, dogmatics, Church history, homiletics, exegetics, hermeneutics carefully mastered and recited under the father's searching system of questioning, the practical catechetics and pastoral theology by his father's side, in his large field of labor, were worth as much, probably, as twice four years in the theological seminary. The instruction given was always by the catechetical method, and the questions asked were not only such as might be answered from the text-books studied; they embraced an extensive field of research, and required the study not only of one text-book on the subject, but possibly half a dozen. The system of Father Yeager's questioning was that which is so highly commended by all advanced educators, namely, the drawing-out process, or, in other words, the questioning which awakens thought and investigation, the method that does not answer the question for the student, but simply gives him a clew and assists him in unraveling the mystery himself. Thus did Mr. Yeager often retire with questions and problems unsolved, which occupied his thoughts through the silent hours of the night, while during the daytime he was constantly engaged in close thought and meditation on the subject whose study he was pursuing.

CHAPTER III.

Rev. Yeager's Ministry.

At the meeting of the Evangelical Lutheran Ministerium of Pennsylvania, held in the week of Trinity Sunday, 1827, Mr. Yeager was examined with two other candidates for licensure. Rev. Dr. F. W. Geissenhainer, of New York City, was the chairman of the Examining Committee. The examination was very thorough. Mr. Yeager well remembers how he was examined on Oriental customs, and when requested to translate the account of the Transfiguration in Math. xvii into German from the Greek, Dr. Geissenhainer seemed well satisfied with the translation till the Greek verb προσκυνεῖν was reached, when he was excited and almost angered at Mr. Yeager's rendering, as he translated it: "they bowed as if they seemed to worship." Dr. Geissenhainer thundered out, "What! not seemed so, it *was* so," and remarked, "it can be seen with whom he studied." The three candidates made a very satisfactory examination and were admitted to the Synod as licentiates.

At the Synodical meeting of the following year, which was held at Reading, Mr. Yeager's preparations were reported "*very good.*" On this occasion he also preached before the Synod on the last evening of the session, Tuesday evening, July 3d, 1828, on the text: 1. Tim. iv, 12–16.

From 1827 to 1831 he was the assistant of his father in his four congregations, Friedensville, Allentown, Schoenersville and Hecktown. In 1831 his father gave him the Friedensville and Allentown congregation and retained for himself the other two. Upon his father's decease, in 1832, he was also elected pastor of the other congregations.

Joshua Yeager's large field of labor extended over an immense territory, and at least a dozen congregations have sprung, in part or entirely, from his original pastorate, such as Apple's Church, Hellertown, South Bethlehem, Bethlehem, West Bethlehem, Salisbury, Altona, Rittersville, Catasauqua, Howertown, Bath, St. Paul's, St. Michael's, St. John's and St. Peter's, Allentown, etc.

He remained the pastor of the Allentown Church (St. Paul's), till 1853, twenty-two years. This congregation enjoyed unprecedented prosperity during Father Yeager's pastorate. He preached regularly every two weeks and held also week-day evening services. About the time of his withdrawal from the congregation, Rev. Dr. B. M. Schmucker, who followed Dr. Yeager in a very few months to the better world, was called as assistant pastor by the English speaking portion of the congregation.

The Friedensville Church was served longest of all by him as regular pastor, from May 22d, 1831, to Trinity Sunday, 1885, fifty-four years. Adding to this the period during which he served the congregation as assistant of his father, his service extended over fifty-eight years.

Of the Schoenersville Church he was pastor a year less. He was elected pastor of this church in December, 1832, and continued till Trinity Sunday, 1885, over fifty-three years. In connection with his father his ministration extended over the same length of time.

The Lehigh Church, in Lower Macungie, Lehigh County, he served from August 21st, 1842, to Trinity Sunday, 1885, forty-three years.

The Rittersville Church was built in 1842, the congregation having been organized by Father Yeager out of Schoenersville. Here he preached his last regular sermon on Ascension Day, 1885.

Besides these four congregations, he also served Jerusalem Church, in Salisbury, from 1843 to 1883, Macungie from 1856 to 1867, and Hecktown, Northampton County, from 1832 to 1842.

The following is a synopsis of his official acts:

Entered the ministry in 1827.

Children baptized,	6,859
Confirmed,	3,875
Communed,	50,000
Buried,	2,763
Married,	2,000

CHAPTER IV.

Characteristics of his Life.

The life of Father Yeager, whose history extends over more than four score years, was characterized by constant activity and great laboriousness. Accustomed in his early years to hard manual labor, he was not easily discouraged when in his ministry difficulties had to be encountered. Endowed with a strong constitution, which was well preserved by the observance of hygienic laws, even to old age, he endured exposure and performed physical and mental work almost without a parallel in the history of God's ministers. His tall, erect, manly form attracted attention wherever he went. Strangers stopped, as they passed him on the street, to admire his splendid physique. He never missed an appointment by sickness, nor from any other cause. He was an almost complete stranger to the ordinary ailments of humanity.

His preparations for the pulpit were always carefully and conscientiously made, and, hence, his audiences always listened to him with close attention. As a rule, which he had obtained from his father, he selected his text and began his preparations for Sunday on the Monday preceding. Hence, he was never found unprepared, and always had something interesting for his hearers. His discourses were brief and pointed, prepared with special reference to the conviction and conversion of sinners.

As he was noted for his neatness in dress and the careful arrangement of his toilet, even in its minutest detail, so his sermons were prepared with scrupulous exactness; his skeletons, which he always had before him when in the pulpit, evinced a systematic arrangement such as is seldom found in the discourses of the most finished pulpit orator. His sermons were characterized by special earnestness and deep emotion. This was not studied, but heartfelt. Father Yeager in tears, in the pulpit and before his catechetical classes, was not an unusual sight. These were no tears of sympathy at funerals, but the outpourings of his soul for the love of souls.

This is the more remarkable when we remember that Father Yeager entered the ministry in a day when the pulpit was particularly noted for its coldness, when head religion, and not heart religion, held sway in many of our churches in America and Germany. He could aver with all his heart: "I believe that Jesus Christ, true God, begotten of the Father from eternity, and also true man born of the Virgin Mary, is *my* Lord." In Him he believed and Him he preached, of Him he spoke to the sick and dying, and to Him he pointed the sinner seeking salvation. He firmly believed and preached the inspired word in his ministry of almost three score years, and thousands of souls were given him as the seal of such a ministry.

On one occasion, those who were not so favorably disposed towards him laid hold of an inadvertent expression with the design to injure him. In one of his sermons he exclaimed, in the fervor of his soul, closing the Bible: "Do you believe all that is contained in this book? I don't believe it." The apparent ambiguity of the expression was seized upon and Father Yeager decried as a rationalist. But this, as all such efforts necessarily must, reverted to the injury not of Father Yeager, but of those who had watched the opportunity to injure him. It gave him an opportunity to preach an explanatory sermon and to state in emphatic language, such as he was capable of employing, that he had said: "Do you believe all that is contained in the Bible? I do not believe that you do, or else your actions would be vastly different." The sermon had a telling effect, and made an impression which is not forgotten to this day.

On another occasion, while pastor of St. Paul's, at Allentown, he had to encounter an element of freethinkers, which had developed there and made attacks not only on his pulpit teaching, but even upon his character. It happened, while he was conducting his services one Sunday, that two snakes were observed by those in the gallery, gamboling and playing on the sounding board of the pulpit, disappearing in a very short time. This occasion, while foreboding terror to the superstitious, was seized on by the "New Light" party and published, not only in he county papers, but even in *Day's Historical Col-*

lections of Pennsylvania, 1843, and thus scattered broadcast, designedly to his detriment. The adverse sentiment which they tried to create, however, like the serpent on the sounding board, recoiled upon his enemies, when, upon examination, it was found that the snakes had made their way through a cracked wall, and were not of the old serpent of Paradise, and that that serpent was to be looked for rather in the angels of light, who, in disguise, were promulgating the false doctrines which Father Yeager was so strenuously and successfully combating.

Many similar incidents could be related here, which occurred in a life of such length and prominence, but they would all combine to illustrate how this man of God, by his intrepidity, sustained by sovereign grace, in which he was so firm a believer, and which he proclaimed so many, many years, was fitted for the special work of his day and generation. A circumstance may yet be mentioned in this connection which illustrates in Father Yeager's life that we, as co-workers with Christ, having a steady purpose and a high resolve, may make our life and labors a success.

He, though he always enjoyed good health, owing, by the help of God, to his temperate manner of living and the care of his body, had, nevertheless, in his youth contracted, by severe study, spells of indigestion, from which he suffered occasionally in early life. Applying to half a dozen physicians without being relieved, he at last came to a distinguished doctor, and applied to him for medicine. The reply was: "I will give you none. But every evening, when you have finished your studies, take a wood-saw and saw hickory wood into stove-lengths for half an hour—take a similar dose in the morning." This advice was followed, and the relief came. Father Yeager ever afterwards recommended this medicine. The moral is that much of the indisposition from and aversion to hard work, in the student's and minister's life of to-day, could be cured thus, instead of reverting to questionable diversions, by which mind, body and soul are enervated and unfitted for the arduous task of life.

But the strong man, the giant frame, the acute intellect, had to succumb at last. Joshua Yeager had looked forward from the day that he laid down the active ministry, Trinity Sunday, 1885, for the time of his departure. He had wished to die in the harness, but it pleased the Lord to give him a brief rest before his course on earth was finished. Like St. John, he was permitted yet, for several years, to appear in the midst of his people, whom he had served so long and loved so well, saying unto them: "Little children, love one another," and lifting his hands in benediction over them. On Decoration Day, 1888, as he was seated at his parlor window, where he loved to look out on the busy scenes of life, he was stricken with apoplexy and became helpless, though his intellect remained active and did not entirely forsake him till quite near his end. On the 1st of August, however, it pleased Almighty

God, in His wise and gracious providence, to call this aged servant to his rest, he having attained the age of 85 years, 10 months and 8 days. On the following Thursday funeral services were held at the late residence of the deceased, conducted by Rev. Dr. S. A. Repass, of St. John's English Evangelical Lutheran Church of Allentown, and in St. Michael's Lutheran Church, where Rev. B. W. Schmauk, a former pastor and special friend, and Rev. Dr. G. F. Spieker, the present pastor, delivered addresses, a very large concourse of people having assembled. Rev. Dr. A. R. Horne, his successor in the charge which he had served, read a biographical sketch of the deceased, and also performed the burial service on Fairview Cemetery, all of which was done in accordance with his desire expressed years before.

A son, Robert J. Yeager, of Allentown, and a daughter, Mrs. J. B. Reeme, of Chicago, survive. His wife, who was Maria, a daughter of Jacob and Maria Grimm, of Friedensville, died 11 years earlier than he. His daughter Amanda, first wife of J. B. Reeme, his son, Dr. Theodore C. Yeager and an unmarried daughter, Sarah W., also preceded him to the eternal world. Six grandchildren also survive, namely, Minnie W. and Norton, children of Dr. Theodore C. Yeager; Albert and Andrew, sons of Robert J. Yeager; and Effie B. and Annetta, daughters of J. B. Reeme, Esq.

Well done, good and faithful servant; enter thou into thy reward, while we remember those who have spoken unto us the Word of Life.

MARRIAGES.

(The years run from Trinity Sunday to Trinity Sunday. Thus, 1829-30 denotes married between Trinity Sunday, 1829, and Trinity Sunday, 1830, etc. The German orthography is followed in most instances.)

1827-29.

Benjamin Kitt to Juliana Geiger.
Johann Koch to Salome Fuestelman.
Benjamin Busch to Maria Stenger.
Carl Mohr to Dorothea Gleiss.
Samuel Quier to Henrietta Jarret.
Andreas Freund to Sarah Wolf (widow).
Thomas Bachman to Catharina Nelig.
Abraham Dietz to Maria Biers.
Peter Huber to Maria Wormann.

1829-30.

Abraham Rohr to Maria Seem.
Jacob Albrecht to Catharina Rohr.
Thomas Herrman to Rebecca Ritter.
Johann Illick to Maria Jung.
Jacob Reichert to Elisabeth Stein (widow).
David Mootz to Magdalena Fellman.
Thomas Meyer (widower) to Elisabeth Wolf.
Johann Volk to Catharina Moll.
Christian Klewell to Diana Klotz.
Georg Haberacker to Sarah Roth.

Carl Kolver to Maria Kammerer.
States B. M. Yants to Elisabeth Haas.
Georg Minch to Hanna Rommel.
Philip Flexer to Elisabeth Gangwer.
Dr. John Romig to Mathilda Martin.
Jacob Kämmerer to Maria Gackenbach.
Carl Kocher to Sarah Spinner.

1830-31.

Joseph Schaefer to Caroline Harlacher.
Peter Schaefer to Sarah Miller.
Carl Ueberroth to Elisa Kneip.
Carl Albrecht to Hetty Neuhart.
Samuel Gingkinger to Elisabeth Jarret.
Christian Schueler to Elisabeth Lorenz.
Franklin Butz to Catharina Larosch.
Johannes Heist to Maria Linn.
Francis Gross to Sarah A. Schiffert.
Michael Schaudt to Anna Borz.
Johann Bader to Hanna Brecht.
Jacob Stehr to Catharina Weber.
Martin Koenig to Hanna Buchecker.
Carl Kratzer to Anna Eberhardt.
David Moritz to Anna Waldmann.
Adam Mensch to Maria Weiler.
Daniel Schumacher to Catharina Scheurer.
Jacob Schneider to Catharina William.
Nathan Miller to Elisabeth Butz.
Abraham Lerch to Elisabeth Froehn.
George Barl to Elisabeth Dillgart.

Heinrich Marsteller to Maria Laug.
Heinrich Rausch to Elisabeth Matz.
Philip Haffa to Esther Green.

1831–32.

Thomas Knappenberger to Salome Gruber.
Carl Gross to Lydia Engelman.
Daniel Deyle to Susanna Fetzer.
Heinrich Ziegenfuss to Sarah Masteller.
Heinrich Reinbold to Maria Neidlinger.
Jacob Kelchner to Hanna Yundt.
Francis Seagreaves to Glerosia Butz.
Philip Sellers to Elisabeth Worman.
Abraham Harlacher to Maria Meyer.
Salomon Heller to Susanna Illick.
Jacob Ecker to Catharina Derr.
Salomon Miller to Nancy Reinschmidt.
Johannes Walden to Elisabeth Siegfried.
Heinrich Seip to Sarah Miller.
Carl Jacoby to Sarah Martin.
Abraham Ludwig to Anna Gangwer.
Carl Beitler to Maria Lehr.
Johannes Mark to Anna Neuhardt.
Daniel Selor to Elisabeth Scheuerman.
Johannes Vogel to Maria Gangwer.
Adam Kunz to Carolina Stem.
Peter Landes to Christina Nunenmacher.
Samuel Schneider to Esther Mory.
Samuel Schneider to Maria Dreisbach.
Daniel Kindig to Elisabeth Musselman.

Francis Trexler to Catharina Hiltebeitel.
Salomon Gangwer to Elisabeth Egner.
Heinrich Vogelman to Hanna Wind.
Georg Schatter to Elisabeth Klein.
Joseph Hoffert to Sarah Marsteller.
Heinrich Bieber to Rebecca Straub.

1832–33.

Lorenz Jaeger to Elisabeth Minch.
Paul Steidinger to Hanna Hauser.
Peter Mill to Susanna Eschbach.
Abraham Bliem to Catharina Juston.
Edward Haff to Elisabeth Kunfert.
Abraham Steinberger to Rebecca Trissler.
Peter Hey to Elisabeth Frankenfield.
Joseph Landes to Rebecca Schmidt.
Isaac Strauss to Judith Schneider.
Salomon Wieder to Elisabeth Ritter (widow).
Isaac L. Thomas to Elisabeth Cope.
Johann Weil to Rebecca Quier.
James Fatzinger to Judith Siegfried.
Wilhelm Saeger to Hanna Gangwer.
Johannes Schweitzer to Hanna Dewalt.
William H. Albrecht to Maria Schaefer.
Jacob Meyer to Margaretha Woodering.
Joh. Peifer to Elisabeth Yost.
Isaac Stehr to Lydia Yost.
Peter Bader to Anna Hoffert.
Johann Bachman to Anna Fritz.
Jacob Leibensperger to Florinda Klein.

Thomas Moser to Hanna Siegfried.
August Ruhe to Debora Gangwer.
Elias Zellner to Catharina Siegel.

1833-34.

Abraham Van Horn to Elisabeth Arnolt.
Heinrich Beitler to Elisabeth Scheuerer.
Johannes Wertz to Elisabeth Burger.
Samuel Stoehr to Susanna Bernt.
Heinrich Ueberroth to Juliana Seip.
Jesse Ueberroth to Louisa Quier.
Florentin Hoehler to Sarah Osenbach.
Samuel Straub to Maria Miller.
Jacob Hoch to Eva Kolb.
Joseph Nagel to Salome Biege.
Edward Schneider to Hanna Kunfert.
Abraham Worman to Hetty Kaemmerer.
Johann Kraemer to Sarah Brinker.
Christian Agster to Maria Siegendahl.
Heinrich Knauer to Maria Kloeckner.
Georg Miller to Anna Rickert.
Jacob A. Ludwig to Esther Brinker.
Joseph Frey to Maria Fenner.
Wilhelm Derr to Hanna Schmidt.
Michael Ritter to Elouisa Miller.
Elias Arnt to Clorista Daniel.
Benjamin Harper to Catharina Keim.
Lorenz Mester to Sarah Reichenbach.
Jesse Keck to Judith Ueberroth.
Jacob Stoehr to Maria Engelman.

Jacob Remmel to Elisabeth Dickson.
Jacob Baer to Hanna Vogel.
Joseph Gangewer to Anna Julina Cope.
Wilhelm Miller to Catharina Brobst.
Reuben Bieber to Priscilla Bier.
Johann Herman to Christina Burger.
Georg Sprau to Maria Peterson.
Jeremias Schmidt to Henrietta Horn.
Jacob Lautenschlaeger to Maria Ritter.
Lewis Schweitzer to Juliana Steinberger.
Jesse Ochs to Sarah Christ.
J. Best (widower) to Elisabeth Beistel (widow).
Wilhelm H. Blumer to Susanna Biery.
Carl Scholl to Henrietta Kneip.
George Luckenbach to Maria Strieby.
Johann Knauss to Themy Schell.
Thomas Fatzinger to Maria Jung.
Manasses Neuhart to Louisa Muss.
Valentin Schmidt to Carolina Buntstein.

1834–35.

Friederich Metz to Elisabeth Hoffmann.
Jacob Ritter to Anna Klein.
Daniel Koenig to Eliza Ann Koenig.
Nathan Lautenschlaeger to Rebecca Horn.
George Dieterich to Regina Geister.
Immanuel Trexler to Carolina Huber.
Jesse Quier to Lydia Schmidt.
Joseph Engler to Lucy Ann Selor.
Elias Hauskunst to Elisabeth Lazarus.

Reuben Paul to Lavinia Haupt.
Abraham Wohlbach to Anna Hepler.
Wilhelm Rohn to Sarah Weber.
Adam Epp to Maria Schmidt.
Conrad Linder to Christianna Friederika Kengel.
Wilhelm Mill to Maria A. Knappenberger.
David Campbel to Elisabeth Koenig.
Joh. Fatzinger to Carolina Kremser.
Peter Minich to Elisabeth Falstich.
Jacob Kram to Susanna Busch.
Daniel Zoellner to Maria Deily.
Joh. Gernet to Catharina Mory.
Samuel Herrmann to Abigail Miller.
Salomon Heil to Susanna Ritter.
Friedrich Wagner to Lucinda Weber.
Carl Meyer to Maria Waldmann.
Gideon Barkert to Isabella Gehn.
Jonathan Meyer to Elisabeth Reichert.
Samuel Boeder to Elisabeth Reichert.
Georg Martin to Elisabeth Rumfeld.
Georg Dickson to Lucy Ann Hunsberger.
Daniel Schaefer to Susanna Schneider.
Georg Schmoll to Anna Spinner.
Friederich Musskop to Elisabeth Andrie.
Abraham Kocher to Elisabeth Schiffert.
Abraham Quier to Carolina Giffert.
Peter Leschter to Maria Ellwig.

1835-36.
Michael Ziegenfuss to Mathilda Fretz.

Nicolaus Hauk to Catharina Bauer.
Robert E. Wright to Maria H. Hütter.
David Stuber to Lydia Hauer.
David Thorn to Juliana Ritz.
Johannes Seip to Maria Ueberroth.
Johannes Boos to Susanna Frey.
Edward Schnerr to Anna Wagner.
Peter Bernd to Maria M. Kommes.
Abraham Yellis to Elisabeth Trumbauer.
Joh. Moll to Maria Edelmann.
Michael Poh to Lydia Resch.
Heinrich Stichler to Dianna Reinschmidt.
Carl Hoffert to Maria Stumpf.
Simon Frey to Elisabeth Meyer.
Arthur Ritter to Elisabeth Vogel.
Edward D. Fatzinger to Maria B. Nonnemacher.
Joh. Leibensperger to Anna Schaeffer.
David Moll to Elizabeth Weber.
James Stoehr to Anna Yohe.
Elias Eister to Helena Drescher.
Mendes Albrecht to Maria A. Weber.
Samuel Heckmann to Anna Neff.
Reuben Fink to Juliana Grim.
Heinrich Eschbach to Lydia Bobb.
Georg Rohrbach to Sarah Paul.
Michael Schaefer to Anna Arnold.
Samuel Glace to Isabella Schwarz.
Heinrich Blum to Margaretha Kiefer.
Rudolf Oberly to Sarah Ueberroth.
Joh. Steinberger to Juliana Ueberroth.

Joh. Daniel Eisenbraun to Margaretha Troxel.
Jacob Kiefer to Maria Meyer.
Joh. Troxel to Sarah Seip.
Wilhelm Scheweler to Maria Diehl.
Valentin Schlemmer to Margaretha Siegendahl.
Levi Simon to Susanna Schneider.
Peter Schmidt to Maria Karn.
Wilhelm Mill to Elisabeth Getter.
Heinrich Jaeger to Henrietta Walbert.
Carl Edelman to Lisetta Ludwig.
Peter Schmidt to Josephina Quier.
Joseph Jones to Elisabeth Keck.
John C. Cole to Lissetta Newhard.
Wilhelm Daniel to Susanna Schneider.

1836–37.

Reuben Schmidt to Anna Mack.
Anthony Siegfried to Lucinda Kleckner.
Jonas B. Kammerer to Lavinia Kaufmann.
Isaac Seiler to Sarah Schneider.
Jacob Nagle to Margaretha Albrecht.
Jacob Bast to Maria Anna Colver.
Isaac Moser to Maria Kaufman.
Samuel Weber to Sittne George.
Carl Weikel to Anna Schneider.
Joh. Wuster to Christina Haizmiener.
Christian Eppert to Maria Schmidt.
Thomas Greg to Hetty Meyer.
Adam Hauck to Lucinda Juengling.
Lorenz Riede to Friederika Sprankel.

Samuel Gumpert to Eliza Kraemer.
Thomas Schneider to Lydia Kichlein.
Amos Ettinger to Susanna Lautenschlaeger.
Georg Deily to Elisabeth Keiper.
Daniel Roth to Maria A. Seip.
Carl Diehl to Juliana Reinhart.
Jacob Stumpf to Rebecca Osenbach.
Joseph Gross to Anna Hoffert.
Carl Deily to Sarah Bell.
Friederich Frankenfield to Maria Boyer.
Nikolaus Remmel to Charlotte Heuer.
Adam Sold to Elizabeth Zuber.
Wilhelm Michael to Marian Lehr.
David Bauman to Susanna Lenz.
Robert Daniel to Lissetta Schneider.
Augustus Gaumer to Carolina Sterner.
Valentin Schaefer to Wilhelmina Ringhäuser.
Jacob Funk to Elisa Caly.
Carl Gebel to Sarah Nagel.

1837–38.

Jacob Friedrich Mahler to Anna Cath. Liffler.
Joseph Berkenstock to Elisabeth Kleckner.
Georg Ziegenfuss to Anna Mathilda Getter.
Abraham Heckmann to Lovina Knauss.
Carl Hinkel to Maria Hauer.
Augustus Gross to Sarah Mester.
Owen Saeger to Elisabeth Ruhe.
Heinrich Bacher to Hannah Hiltenbeitel.
Abraham Diemer to Catharina Odenwelter.

Joh. Georg Geister to Judith D. Lang.
Abraham Lawell to Judith Hall.
Johann Frankenfield to Sarah A. Rothrock.
David Erdmann to Anna Egner.
Paul Lautenberger to Julia Anna Hoffert.
Carl Nagel to Carolina Frey.
Joh. W. Mast to Sarah Fink.
Georg Beck to Rebecca Bechtel.
Jacob Lindikuhl to Cath. Guth.
Daniel Ritter to Lovina Schweitzer.
Robert S. Brown to Carolina M. Grim.
Reuben Schorz to Maria Dewalt.
Carl Beck to Elisabeth Frankenfield.
William Mattern to Elisabeth Eckert.
Nathan Moll to Rosanna Lie.
Edward Knauss to Elowina Ueberroth.
Friedrich Walter to Hetty Rumfeld.
Peter Guth to Carolina Juengling.
Joh. Egge to Elisabeth Seip.
Samuel Landes to Sarah Meier.
Peter Lehr to Elisabeth Zacharias.
James Bauer to Maria Rum.
Joseph Meyer to Maria Musskopf.
Andreas Hummel to Eliza Schneider.
Stephan Ritter to Lydia Transue.
Joel Miller to Lydia Strieby.

1838–39.

Reuben Philips to Susanna Schiffert.
Martin Ruhf to Lydia Rumfeld.

Georg Ritter to Elenora Knauss.
James Ray to Elisabeth Ritter.
Penmus Egge to Lydia Addison.
Wilhelm Knauss to Hannah Waldmann.
Jonathan Rumfeld to Catharina Zeller.
Carl Blank to Trustilla Frey.
Abraham Troxel to Sarah Lehr.
Reuben Schmidt to Elizabeth Brinker.
Carl Knappenberger to Lucy Ann Seip.
Christian Fischer to Maria Keiter.
Samuel Funk to Elisabeth Boger.
Joh. Huber to Elisabeth Fatzinger.
Joseph Dech to Elisabeth Ritter.
Joh. Diefenderfer to Rebecca Schwarz.
Joh. Martin Ritter to Rebecca Marcks.
Daniel Lazarus to Louisa Meyer.
Jacob Mohr to Susanna Schelly.
Heinrich Hoch to Susanna Rohn.
Israel Trexler to Catharina Osmann.
Daniel Koenig to Hanna Reiss.
Christian Koenig to Catharina Frick.
Joseph Stuber to Rebecca Clewell.
Alexander Grote to Sabina Wagner.
Martin Nunemacher to Maria Alshaus.
Jonathan Trexler to Clarissa Martin.
Wilhelm Kuhnsman to Lydia Jung.

1839–40.

Joh. Stuber to Sarah Licht.
Philip Zoellner to Catharina Gross.

Joseph Kichlein to Elizabeth Fatzinger.
Abraham Huber to Hannah Vogel.
Friederich Gutfleck to Sophie Spannuth.
Reuben Ritter to Maria Marcks.
David Ueberroth to Maria Siegfried.
Michael Blatt to Magdalena Lehr.
Christian Souer to Catharina Reinhart.
Peter Moll to Rebecca Hunsberger.
Simon Schneider to Abigail Levan.
Jacob Wiegner to Rebecca Gaukler.
Carl Schmidt to Cath. Wenner.
Alexander Moritz to Hannah Weber.
Joh. Ritter to Maria A. Wind.
Carl Wagner to Henrietta Seip.
Reuben Kleckner to Amanda L. Jacoby.
David Stephen to Juliana Jaeger.
Peter Mohr to Wilhelmina Miller.
Peter Specht to Elisabeth Resch.
Joseph Neuman to Christina Reichenbach.
Elias Ellinger to Elisabeth Herbst.
Joseph Harres to Polly Rensheimer.
Nathan Friederich to Lovina Kiechel.
Joseph Meyer to Nelly Heinrich.
Ephraim Tomson to Rebecca Keller.
Johann Schimpf to Maria Kleckner.

1840-41.

Michael Zoellner to Maria A. Schwarz.
Franz A. Hoepstein to Sophia M. E. Seelen.
Carl Edelmann to Sarah Weser.

Daniel Frey to Elisabeth Colver.
Samuel Zoellner to Sarah Gruber.
Carl Deschler to Hannah Sterner.
Carl Funk to Cath. Lorasch.
Jacob Ehret to Carolina Herbig.
Daniel Spriegel to Philippina Neuhardt.
Gideon Friederich to Hannah Leibensperger.
Martin Mager to Elisabeth Knechel.
Michael Stuber to Maria Schneider.
Jesse Kidd to Sarah Hoch.
Joh. H. Yost to Salome Mory.
Aaron Yost to Cath. Kocher.
Friederich Eilenberger to Lovina Emmery.
Heinrich Funk to Elisabeth Nunemacher.
Daniel Ritter to Eliza A. Dewald.
Margen Appel to Sarah Yost.
Georg Helfrich to Hetty Grof.
Andreas Walter to Hetty Schneider.
Jonas Burger to Lovina Ehret.
Carl Frankenfield to Sarah Laury.
Joh. Menninger to Susanna Xander.
Joh. Linn to Catharina Ohlenwein.
Adam Schneider to Sarah Remmel.
Peter Nunemacher to Rebecca Haupt.
Thomas Neuhart to Lydia Fetzer.
Solomon Dech to Mathilda M. Dreisbach.
Carl Nitterauer to Maria Eschbach.
Georg Estert to Elisabeth Hunsberger.
Carl Ueberroth to Maria Derr.
Carl Romig to Louisa Schwander.

1841-42.

James Prestent to Maria A. Telor.
Gideon Ritter to Theresa Ziegler.
Wilhelm Edelman to Deborah Grim.
Henry L. Vandyke to Rebecca Kleckner.
Daniel Fogelmann to Maria Keiper.
Wilhelm Zoellner to Susanna Deily.
Michael Giffert to Elisabeth Weber.
Edward Clewell to Fyetta Wesener.
Reuben Faust to Eliza Hohle.
Aaron Wind to Leah Walder.
Josias Vogel to Juliana Balliet.
Carl Wenner to Judith Gaumer.
William Sterner to Leanna Huber.
Daniel Siegfried to Henrietta Kleckner.
Thomas Jacoby to Christina Anna Brisel.
Jonas Herpel to Mathilda Hottenstein.
George Schmidt to Catharina Eschbach.
Edmund Reichert to Maria A. Reiter.
Joseph Saeger to Maria Quier.
Joseph Masteller to Maria Mohr.
Solomon Blank to Susanna Stein.
Daniel Ritter to Maria A. Fretz.
Joseph Nunemacher to Matilda Ginkinger.
Michael Zoellner to Cath. Metzger.
Jesse Weber to Maria Ann Appel.
Aaron Bast to Catharina Frey.
Heinrich Nunemacher to Carolina Fetzer.
Samuel Joerg to Maria Musselman.
Solomon Waldmann to Mary Ann Ihrig.

William Laub to Catharina Schweitzer.
Heinrich Buerger to Christina Beck.
Thomas Ginkinger to Elisabeth Miller.
Daniel Fatzinger to Angelina Bickert.

1842–43.

Reuben Peterson to Selinda Schneider.
Isaac Raub to Maria Kumfer.
Georg W. Heckman to Catharina Seip.
Johann Nunemacher to Lucy Ann Knauss.
William Transu to Ellen Raub.
Joh. L. Hanky to Maria Jung.
Carl Hinkel to Elisabeth Gerhardt.
Joseph Correl to Cath. Lautenschlaeger.
Simon Ritter to Belinda Breinig.
William Eschenbach to Henrietta Steinberger.
Carl Heinz to Maria Schurz.
Gabriel Tempfon to Maria Huth.
Samuel Krauss to Catharina Anna Gerhardt.
Solomon Bader to Catharina Schitz.
David Neuhart to Catharina Weil.
Jacob Ihrig to Carolina Kaucher.
Samuel Transue to Rebecca Reiss.
Abraham Rohn to Sarah Eigner.
James Neitlinger to Sarah Hunsberger.
Alexander W. Loder to Maria Jaeger.
Thomas Bachmann to Ebesina Beisel.
William Meyer to Sarah Fatzinger.
Adam Meyer to Rebecca Kiechel.
Carl E. Christ to Salome Wind.

David Gernet to Rebecca Deily.
Adam Y. Hauk to Hannah Muth.
Joseph Deily to Sarah Keiper.
Reuben Engelman to Sarah A. Stoehr.
Nathan Schäfer to Sophia Jung.
William Baer to Eliza Gold.
Daniel Dieterich to Sarah Geister.
Heinrich Wolf to Elisabeth Koch.
Peter Engler to Maria Lang.
Isaac Griesemer to Gertrude Wolf.
Carl Deily to Sibylla Deily.
Jacob Fatzinger to Susanna Mack.
Jeremias Fischer to Maria Heckman.
David Schitz to Maria Merkel.
Franklin Person to Maria Clewell.
Carl Vogel to Rebecca Lechleiter.
Thomas Walter to Mathilda Weber.
Philip Maus to Sarah Ott.
Aaron Tomson to Hetty Vogel.
Reuben Steckel to Mathilda Kleppinger.
Daniel Klein to Elisabeth Klemmer.
Franklin Jung to Hannah Goebel.

1843–44.

David Reichard to Anna Keiper.
Andreas Keim to Elisabeth Braun.
Abraham Reis to Elisabeth Wind.
Georg Wenner to Sarah A. Unangst.
Josiah Bast to Anna Kindig.
George Engler to Mathilda Wottering.

Carl Osenbach to Henrietta Reichard.
Heinrich Weinsheimer to Rebecca Saeger.
David Rau to Sarah Yundt.
Carl Gross to Sarah A. Reimer.
Thaddeus Gilbert to Sarah Trexler.
Jesse Rumfeld to Maria Bachman.
Wilhelm Reimer to Sophia Rothrock.
William Ihrig to Hanna Funk.
Heinrich Schweikefer to Louisa Hoehle.
Joh. Braun to Sarah A. Keiper.
Carl L. Gingkinger to Elisabeth Ruth.
David Wendling to Sarah Ruth.
Joh. Beitelman to Mathilda Mellon.
Joh. Schmeyer to Maria Lichtenwalter.
Martin Jung to Maria Frankenfield.
Salomon Boehm to Juliana Merkel.
Thomas Dony to Lovina Keiper.
Owen Bortz to Hanna Wenner.
Andreas S. Clewell to Rebecca Michel.
Carl Neuhard to Maria Meyer.
Josiah Nagel to Sarah Frey.
Michael Stuber to Juliana Lein (widow).
Joh. Hoffert to Judith Wenner.
Carl Klein to Maria Staehler.
William Schwan to Lovina Bernt.
Aaron Walter to Catharina A. Jordan.
George Scherer to Carolina Luckenbach.
Samuel Schmeier to Elisabeth Jaeger.
Jacob Ueberroth to Elisabeth Ihrig.
Michael Frankenfield to Lucy Ann Rau.

Amandes Hoffert to Anna M. Raub.
Samuel Colver to Maria Deily.

1844–45.

Peter Rufe to Amalia Kluge.
Jesse Fusselman to Catharina Reichard.
James Schmeier to Lovina Steffy.
Solomon Ziegler to Maria Schaefer.
Stephan Bier to Maria Dankel.
Robert Halfpenny to Theresa Gangwer.
Carl Gangwer to Susanna Schaefer.
Carl Rieb to Sarah Simon.
James Foegely to Maria Bernhardt.
Carl Klein to Carolina Ludwig.
Thomas Staehler to Sophia Erly.
Nathan Nagel to Catharina Rufe.
Valentine Hiller to Maria Steinmarkt.
Peter Wenner to Elemina Trexler.
Heinrich Miller to Lydia Ritter.
Nathan Ritter to Hannah Schanz.
Jacob Rob to Lovina Adam.
Rudolph Schmidt to Sarah Ochs.
Jesse Reichard to Lissetta S. Diefendörfer.
Samuel Keiper to Sibylla Zoellner.
Christoph Seibold to Friederika A. Prinz.
Philip Sander to Susanna Funk.
Joseph Reichard to Florentina Frankenfield.
Carl Wendling to Maria Schmeier.
Heinrich Person to Rebecca Keck.
Christian L. Kidd to Maria Schmetzer.

Elias Kaemmerer to Hetty Butz.
Raham Schuler to Elisabeth Ritter.
Peter Xander to Eva Reinhardt.
William Nagel to Rebecca Kreiling.
Edward Dewald to Helena Breinig.
Thomas Schoener to Sarah Jung.
Thomas Weber to Lovina Laubach.
Aaron Mohr to Judith Wind.
Samuel S. Sheimer to Henrietta Jung.
Carl R. Heller to Eva Elisabeth Burt.
Daniel Heckman to Eliza A. Lawall.
Heinrich Frey to Isabella Wottering.
Jacob Ackerman to Carolina Zoellner.

1845-46.

Dr. David O. Mosser to Susanna Breinig.
Jacob Schleifer to Maria Christmann.
Stephan Ritter to Elisabeth Fusselman.
Carl Ihrig to Sibylla Kaemmerer.
Milton Wind to Maria Keinert.
Daniel Ritter to Maria Schaefer.
Carl Fatzinger to Belinda Lichtenwalter.
William Rieb to Fyetta Yoder.
Levi Ritter to Hetty Wesco.
Allen S. Barron to Amanda Steckel.
Carl Weber to Hanna Landes.
David H. Linn to Elisabeth Steinmetz.
Jacob Nuss to Lucy Ann Schaefer.
Manasses Moser to Catharina Hop.
Daniel Quier to Anna M. Horning.

Georg Long to Catharina Rischel.
Nathan Keinert to Lydia Dohny.
Carl Reichard to Maria Owen.
Georg Blank to Martha A. Stoehr.
Jacob Kron to Hannah Schneider.
Joseph Flory to Harrietta Schleiter.
Georg Biers to Hannah Koenig.
Tobias Sterner to Sarah A. Kunsman.
Franklin Hersch to Emma Jaeger.
Stephan Fenstermacher to Lucy Ann Buchman.
William Balliet to Louisa Giess.
Peter Diehmer to Antinetta Wolf.
Peter Reichard to Leah Deily.
Jacob Stuber to Sarah A. Jung.
William Ritter to Sarah A. Neumeier.
Hiram Brobst to Eliza Eckert.
Carl Hauer to Catharina Bast.
Heinrich Jung to Catharina Wolf.

1846–47.

Georg Breinig to Catharina Schmidt.
William Dachrodt to Henrietta Ackermann.
Joh. Trexler to Harrietta Miller.
Reuben L. Miller to Eva Odenwelder.
Samuel Henn to Hanna Hunt.
Jonas Borz to Helena Wetzel.
Peter Mohr to Harrietta Ueberroth.
Heinrich Frey to Susanna Wesener.
James Busch to Maria Trexler.
Edward H. Hitzman to Maria A. Steinberger.

Heinrich Jacoby to Rebecca Ackerman.
William H. Diefenderfer to Mathilda Haak.
Aaron Ihrig to Elisabeth Arnold.
James L. Pflueger to Elisabeth Keim.
Aaron Liem to Lovina Heckman.
Heinrich Fatzinger to Henrietta Strauss.
Thomas Friederich to Catharina M. Biery.
Joh. Gutheil to Maria Schneider.
Joh. Beitler to Catharina Hicker.
Joseph Clase to Carolina Stuber.
James Jung to Christina Kneller.
Heinrich Kichlein to Sarah Osmun.
Simon Friederich to Lydia Roth.
Louis L. Schelden to Mathilda Butz.
James Schneider to Sarah Diefenderfer.
Heinrich Hess to Carolina Schmidt.
Heinrich Fatzinger to Maria Singer.
Reuben Hausman to Maria Anna Geisser.
Reuben Bock to Harrietta Cole.
Benjamin D. Hagenbuch to Lydia Walter.
Carl Deily to Catharina Aurelia Lein.
Nathan Gehman to Lovina Erdman.
Jacob Saeger to Clara Feil.
Peter Remmel to Sarah A. Dickson.
James W. Willson to Mathilda Keck.
Tobias Schmidt to Catharina Kercher.
Carl Mueller to Mohela Schaefer.

1847-48.
Johann Kratzer to Henrietta Breder.

Georg Boyer to Anna Jul. Albrecht.
Levi Frankenfield to Eliza Roth.
Johann Hunter to Amanda L. Hoffert.
Reuben Osmun to Sarah A. Moebes.
Aaron Schmeier to Lovina Breinig.
Conrad Herman to Lydia Leibengut.
William Walp to Maria A. Mohr.
Carl Eschbach to Catharina Graef.
William Schmidt to Catharina Moll.
William Heckman to Ansanette Nagel.
Joh. Engler to Sarah Heller.
William Stellwagen to Rebecca Peterson.
Abraham Hunsberger to Maria Bachert.
August Jung to Anna Detterer.
Johann Wolf to Mariette Lawall.
Levi Derr to Catharina Kindig.
William Bachmann to Louisa Yohe.
George Berger to Carolina Derr.
Allen Kraemer to Lovina Horn.
Carl Sterner to Sarah Trapp.
David Fatzinger to Rebecca Mosser.
Stephan Anthony to Nancy A. Mumy.
Joseph Yeakel to Josephina Niess.
Robert Yost to Clarissa Geisinger.
Daniel Roth to Sarah Happer.
Jacob Gaumer to Anna C. Mattern.
Georg A. Klein to Lydia Beissel.
Georg Fischer to Miss Stumm.

1848-49.

Simon Sterner to Caroline Ackerman.
Jacob Scherer to Helena Strassberger.
Tilghman Baumer to Maria Muth.
Absalom Sterner to Wilhelmina Lazarus.
David Nelly to Mary Jane Krafert.
Thomas Jaeger to Ursilla Burk.
Peter Wittman to Louisa Mory.
Reuben Samos to Alpia Meyer.
William Bast to Maria Reiss.
Nathan Siegfried to Sarah Hanse.
David Keim to Elleminda Catharina Lerch.
Heinrich Romig to Carolina Mohr.
Gustav Reinhold Lauschner to Christ. Pfennig.
Joh. H. Humphrey to Fanny Braun.
Philip Woodring to Maria Saylor.
Richard Rimer to Eliza Ann Schmidt.
Martin Ritter to Rebecca Yost.
William Keller to Sarah A. Hoffert.
Peter Kleckner to Carolina Knerr.
Michael Huehler to Maria Knerr.
Daniel Friederich to Sarah A. Eisenhardt.
Carl Gangwer to Margaretha Harned.
Samuel Stein to Aurelia Paul.
William Neuhard to Carolina Hartman.
Carl Walz to Catharina Bender.
Eli Eschbach to Lucy Ann Gangawere.
Peter Bauer to Cecilia Marsteller.
Johann Walz to Christianna Keim.
David Schaefer to Mathilda Schmidt.

Carl Kaemmerer to Sadie Erdmann.
Solomon Laross to Maria Nagel.
Philip Neuhard to Carolina Breder.
Solomon Seibert to Mary Ann Rau.
James S. Eschbach to Emilie Sterner.
Jacob Kolb to Catharina Fyetta Gaukler.
Georg Ruhf to Elisabeth Kingate.
Samuel Steidinger to Eliza Dennes.
Eli Hoffert to Louisa Lautenberger.
William Nagel to Mary Wetzel.
Thomas Anthony to Elisabeth Jung.
Joshua Benner to Mary M. Scott.
Johann Nagel to Anna Hermann.
Carl Hoehle to Abigail Acker.

1849–50.

Joseph Musselman to Susanna Cole.
James Schneider to Mary E. Lazarus.
David Jung to Maria Pflueger.
Edwin Siegfried to Lucy Ann Groman.
Jacob Fried. Haller to Maria Magd. Gallmeier.
Thomas R. Davis to Catharina Fusselman.
Aaron Marsteller to Leah Lazarus.
Joseph Clewell to Catharina Rau.
Thomas B. Schlemer to Mathilda E. Cope.
Heinrich A. F. Degning to Louisa Koller.
Joel Roth to Catharina Schaefer.
Eli Osmun to Emilie Schneider.
Joh. Burger to Olinda Lerch.
Carl Keiser to Clara Schuler.

Aaron Fuchs to Sarah Halteman.
Francis Schelling to Sarah Schleiter.
Carl Volk to Rosalinda Schmeier.
Georg Huettroth to Fanny Weiss.
James Keck to Mary A. Stettler.
Thomas Hertzel to Mamie Breinig.
Johann Hanft to Helena Schmidt.
William Weidner to Eliza Blank.
Heinrich J. Meyer to Fyetta Ritter.
Carl Rau to Maria Neuhardt.
Benjamin F. Trexler to Dianna Walter.
Franklin Schmidt to Carolina Volk.
Israel J. Harres to Sarah A. Bader.
Stephan Schachtely to Florentina Kern.
Reuben Lichtenwallner to Tousilla Breder.
Adam Luckenbach to Louisa Frey.
Enos Ackerman to Catharina Keim.
Carl Barba to Elisabeth Mann.
Edward Jacob Kuhns to Rosanna Lerch.
Elias Trumbauer to Angelina Mill.
Joh. H. Jost to Mary Ahlum.
Stephan Ackerman to Catharina Detterer.
Abraham Hunsberger to Elisabeth Kuhns.
Daniel Jaeger to Leah Backenstoss.
Johann Siegfried to Catharina Ruhf.
Reuben Roth to Maria Levan.
Thomas Wilson to Hanna Biehn.
Edward Hellman to Emelina Scholl.
Reuben Bergstresser to Maria Walter.
Christian Schmidt to Catharina Veitinger.

William Neuhardt to Maria Weil.
Lewis Weaver to Susanna Licht.
Georg Fink to Eliza Fried.
Joh. K. Dech to Catharina Kläuss.
Jacob Weber to Carolina Ihrig.
Heinr. Franklin Marsteller to Elovina Schmeier.
William Stump to Henrietta Stadtler.
Lewis Ritter to Mary Henn.
Daniel H. Yost to Elisabeth Deschler.
Daniel Kuhns to Sarah Scheib.
Ephraim Jung to Mary A. Koenig.
Harrison Jung to Isabella Seip.
Johann Edvens to Catharina Dreisbach.

1850-51.

Joseph Jung to Harriette Dewalt.
Jacob Fuchs to Cadora Edelman.
William Roth to Maria Scheurer.
Robert Vogel to Susanna Unangst.
Peter W. Fitzky to Clara Ros. Beringer.
Nikolaus Boyer to Franziska Rethly.
Joseph Lenhart to Eliza Happer.
Heinrich Keppler to Lydia Moll.
Jacob Kuhns to Anna L. Beck.
Heinrich Gittinger to Rebecca Clewell.
Isaac Gangwer to Mathilda Geissinger.
Edwin Schnabel to Isabella Nagel.
Joshua Hense to Mathilda Stem.
Heinrich J. Beck to Adelina Biery.
Benjamin Weitzel to Catharina Halteman.

Thomas Jaeger to Sabina Balliet.
Nathan Weber to Maria Hoh.
Christoph Voelker to Eliza Reiss.
Peter Reinschmidt to Elisabeth Woodring.
Johann M. Ritter to Mathilda Moritz.
Solomon T. Keck to Mathilda Hartman.
Jacob Merkel to Elisabeth Harres.
William Ritter to Elisabeth Kremser.
James Weil to Maria Lobach.
Jesse Wieser to Susanna Ihrig.
Caspar Hinkel to Anna M. Schmeier.
William Reinhardt to Catharina Knecht.
Reuben Flores to Carolina Keim.
Daniel Ihrig to Arabella Hauer.
Heinrich Eberhardt to Henrietta Hoffert.
Johann Jones to Hanna Mory.
Johann Reichard to Magdalena Schmidt.
Heinrich Seip to Mathilda Fried.
David Sendel to Susanna E. Sterner.
Heinrich Kremser to Mathilda Ritter.
Johann Erdman to Anna M. Roth.
Benjamin Kleckner to Maria Ochs.
William Scheimer to Hanna Schanz.
Jacob Weber to Hetty Trexler.
William Stein to Hetty Hartman.
Andrew S. Keck to Maria E. B. Gangewer.
Mandes Nagel to Mathilda Scholl.
Joh. Gottlieb Spies to Maria Walz.
Carl Umbescheiden to Maria Breiner.
Daniel A. Scholl to Anna M. Schneider.

Heinrich Koenig to Ann M. M. Jung.
David Rosenberger to Maria A. Schwartley.
Joh. N. Hiestand to Carolina Reger.
Friederich Kanz to Anna Eliza Marsteller.
Carl Stuber to Catharina Reichard.
Stephan Berlin to Juliana Peter.
Charles Keck to Ellenor Koenig.
Michael Kehrer to Eliza Weber.
Richard Deily to Eliza Albrecht.
Thomas Baum to Christianna Major.
Thomas Reichard to Rebecca Beitler.
James W. Rau to Maria A. Stuber.
Carl Kuntz to Lovina Ihrig.
Georg Wm. Willenbuecher to Eva Elisab. Fink.
William Brunner to Henrietta Bachmann.
Johann Kuhns to Sabina Buss.
Edward Gangwer to Eliza Ann Bergstresser.
Nathan Deibert to Lovina Landes.
John Stibgen to Mathilda West.
Edward Ruhf to Elisabeth Jung.
George Landes to Isabella Neuhard.
Heinrich A. Scholl to Adeline Meyer.
William Fatzinger to Eliza Wenninger.
Thomas Rosenberger to Rebecca Dillinger.
Levi Bilgart to Catharina Linn.
Solomon H. Ludwig to Maria Kaemmerer.
Edward Schanz to Carolina Lenz.
Martin Meisner to Catharina Trexler.
Levan Hoffert to Sarah Neuhardt.

1852.

Feb. 1, Abraham Gangawer to Susanna Schwenk.
" 2, Heinrich Koenig to Friederika Daeufer.
" 22, Abr. G. Klemmer to Anna E. Dimming.
" 24, Owen Leopold to Maria Daniel.
March 7, Daniel L. Bogh to Elizabeth Jung.
" 30, Tilghman Gangawer to Louisa Siegfried.
May 16, Charles L. Hollman to Maria Kroman.
" 21, Franklin Weiss to Catharina Keiter.
" 23, Nathaniel Hillegas to Elamina Acker.
July 11, Gideon Roth to Mathilda Ludwig.
" 25, Edward Reichard to Catharina Geissinger.
Aug. 1, George F. Gibson to Louisa S. Keiter.
Sept. 2, Henry Fischel to Ann Maria Hart.
" 4, Samuel Daniel to Eliza Deily.
" 26, Joseph Meyer to Lydia Ann Reichard.
Oct. 3, Jonas Hagey to Cecilia Wohlbach.
" 10, Richard Ambrun to Elizabeth Nauman.
" 17, Simon Wolf to Carolina Heilman.
" 21, David Miller to Maria Wolf.
" 31, Johann Scherer to Helena Wimmer.
Nov. 4, Edmund Yost to Maria Amanda Schwarz.
" 21, Edwin Troxel to Carolina Ihrig.
" 25, Heinrich Sellers to Mary Ann Yost.
Dec. 15, Lewis Boyer to Susanna Walter.
" 19, Joseph H. Mies to Mary Ann Beonds.
" 26, Robert Kingate to Catharina M. Wendel.
" 28, Johann M. Hock to Margaretha Mebus.
" 30, Heinrich Ritz to Keziah Ross.

1853.

Jan. 2, Andreas Bruder to Dianna Schneider.
" 9, Franklin Reichard to Leah Schwenk.
" 27, Charles Lick to Carolina Guth.
" 27, Philip Andres to Maria Resh.
" 30, Paul Reichard to Lucy Ann Bruder.
" 31, Levi Oberholtzer to Christina Andres.
Feb. 1, Peter Reichard to Lovina Brong.
" 20, William D. Long to Maria Keim.
" 20, Heinrich Wolf to Isabella Fegely.
" 22, Joh. A. Dech to Henrietta Eigner.
" 24, Stephan Kichel to Anna J. Leibensperger.
" 27, Thomas Diehm to Maria Sterner.
March 5, Peter Yelles to Theresa Miller.
" 12, Allen Balliet to Sarah Hoffman.
" 17, Isaac Huber to Catharina Fatzinger.
" 20, Heinrich Muss to Mathilda Wagner.
" 27, Samuel H. Ginkinger to Mary A. Rinker.
April 25, Martin Wagner to Catharine Schuelzer.
" 28, Charles Becker to Carolina Yeager.
May 15, Joseph Koch to Mathilda Keiper.
" 21, William Engler to Henrietta Stettler.
June 14, Jos. Spengler to Elizab. Schoenenberger.
" 19, Francis J. Freimann to Clarissa Weiandt.
" 26, Edwin Roth to Susanna Dennsardt.
" 26, Tilghman Ueberroth to Carolina Klein.
July 10, John Trapp to Catharina Nunnemacher.
" 10, Johann Leidig to Susanna Weil.
" 10, James Kramer to Christianna Free.
" 24, Carl W. Hoffert to Mathilda Sell.

July 26, Joh. Raitline to Sarah Quier.
" 26, Jonas Mest to Hetty D. Fatzinger.
Aug. 21, Jonas Schmidt to Maria Miller.
" 28, Lewis Weher to Mathilda Kratzer.
" 28, Peter Odenheimer to Melinda Schwander.
Sept. 18, Eli Kratzer to Carolina Reinard.
Oct. 2, Jonathan Sterner to Carolina Marsteller.
" 2, Joseph Schlosser to Juliana Weber.
" 2, Joh. J. Jarret to Phoebe Fenstermacher.
" 4, Heinrich T. Roeder to Eliza Schleiter.
" 4, Herman Jaeger to Margaretha Wetzel.
" 16, Friederich Gangawer to Dianna Frey.
" 30, Edward Scheimer to Ann Cath. Kraemer.
Nov. 6, Leonhard Moeser to Rebecca Frey.
" 6, Nathan Weiler to Marietta Ziegler.
" 6, Heinrich Merkel to Elizabeth Koch.
" 17, Rev. S. K. Brobst to Maria E. Ritter.
" 27, Nikolaus Ewald to Eva W. Wagner.
Dec. 15, Joseph Biery to Eliza Gaumer.
" 17, Georg Heller to Christina Cecilia Henig.
" 25, Solomon Ihrig to Dianna Fatzinger.
" 25, James H. Mill to Anna M. Romig.
" 25, William Van Houpton to Mary Landis.
" 27, Charles Rob. Clewell to Sarah A. Roth.

1854.

Jan. 1, Stephan Ruhf to Sarah Riker.
" 1, Joh. Georg Deininger to Rebecca Stein.
" 1, George T. Reichard to Emilie P. Ritter.
" 10, James H. Schmeier to Rebecca Schneider.

Jan.   15, Johann H. Ruth to Sarah E. Schmeier.
"   19, William F. Stuber to Lovina S. Yingling.
"   25, Johann Duth to Emilie Rhein.
"   29, Abraham Steinberger to Amanda Rickert.
Feb.   2, Christian F. Stelzer to Carolina C. Deily.
March 5, Carl Detweiler to Mary Ann Reinschmidt.
"   19, Bernhardt Zentner to Maria Hornung.
April 2, Jon. B. Kaemmerer to Carolina Knerr.
"   9, Josiah G. Youngken to Maria H. Minnich.
"   19, Dukin Grimshaw to Eliza Quinn.
May   14, Heinrich Mayer to Mary Cressman.
"   25, William B. Gebhardt to Mary Ann Cope.
"   29, Valentin J. Staut to Elizabeth S. Yoder.
June   1, Georg Klein to Rebecca Schaefer.
"   4, William Gungkel to Henrietta Brinker.
"   6, Robert J. Yeager to Mathilda Deily.
"   11, Enos Weierbach to Sarah A. Heller.
"   18, James R. Rodny to Ellen W. Bader.
Aug.   13, Benjamin Wetzel to Elizabeth Schneider.
"   13, William H. Jordan to Henrietta Reichard.
"   13, Wm. Ziegenfuss to Eliza H. Nunemacher.
Sept. 3, Reuben Knauss to Melinda Schlosser.
"   5, Dennis H. Dreisbach to Mary J. Benner.
"   12, Samuel Kressler to Juliana Huth.
"   12, Heinrich Kraemer to Carolina Roth.
"   17, Moses Schneider to Maria Laubach.
Oct.   5, Israel E. Harres to Fyette E. Bader.
"   15, Jonas F. Hellmer to Elisabeth Retz.
"   19, Carl T. Jaeger to Leah Gaugawer.
"   26, Dan. M. Lichtenwallner to S. C. Scheffler.

Oct. 31, Charles Graffin to Mary Schneider.
Nov. 14, Tilghman Ochs to Susanna Long.
" 19, Moses Kaemerer to Elovina D. Long.
Dec. 12, Solomon Klotz to Hetty Ann Dieterich.
" 17, Geo. H. Monnstier to Christina Hoffman.
" 24, Heinrich Rau to Sibylla Linn.
" 26, Michael Kehrer to Anna M. Braun.

1855.

Jan. 9, Heinrich Reichard to Mathilda Nace.
" 14, Edward L. Dech to Violetta Cath. Sterner.
" 16, James Diehl to Rebecca Johnson.
" 22, Ferdin'd H. J. Fischer to Sarah L. Fried.
Feb. 1, Joh. F. K. Rensheimer to Harriette Mory.
" 11, Edwin Miller to Fyette Fatzinger.
" 11, Christian Hoerner to Anna Zellner.
" 20, Heinrich W. Ihrig to Anna R. Kiehn.
" 25, Jonas Emmerich to Hetty Bauer.
March 6, James Fehler to Susanna Schweitzer.
" 8, Tilghman Kuhns to Eliza Silfies.
" 11, Levi Butz to Emeline Schmeier.
" 20, Tilghman Weil to Hannah Nunemacher.
" 25, Carl F. L. Weber to Catharina H. Ihrig.
" 25, James A. Trexler to Margaretha Sattler.
April 3, Solomon Schiffert to Anna M. Seibert.
" 8, Johann Ihrig to Maria A. Kincade.
" 8, Tilghman Seip to Catharina Long.
May 3, Napoleon Gauff to Cath. E. Kaemmerer.
" 12, Tilghman Moll to Emeline Hauer.
" 15, Tilghman Schmeier to M. C. Christman.

May   20, Wm. H. Hateman to S. E. Nunemacher.
June 26, Daniel Eberhardt to Polly Sterner.
July   15, Heinrich K. Reis to Faganna Lick.
"   29, Friederich Miller to Clarissa Diehl.
"   20, August Bohlen to Lydia Albrecht.
"   31, Israel Schuler to Maria Acker.
Sept. 16, Tilghman Horn to Carolina Faveur.
"   16, Franklin Beck to Mary Weiler.
"   17, Carl Behms to Maria Erz.
"   25, Harrison Beitler to Ann Elisa Harrison.
Oct.   2, Georg Weldy to Christina Neiman.
"   7, Owen Roth to Fyetta Minnich.
"   7, William Wolf to Carolina Scheeren.
"   14, Reuben Benner to Clarissa Keiper.
"   19, James McAllister to Maria Sellers.
"   21, Benj. F. Knauss to Sarah A. Steininger.
Nov. 3, David H. Wheeler to Dianna L. Quier.
"   13, Georg Huth to Lovina Hoch.
"   20, David Miller to Susanna Keck.
Dec. 2, James Kimmett to Emelinda Keiper.
"   4, Jacob Miller to Carolina R. Schneider.
"   8, Allen O. Frankenfield to Ellen Hoffert.
"   9, Daniel Bachman to Clarissa Neuhardt.
"   18, Christian F. Bogh to Hannah Meyer.
"   20, Tilgh. Kingcate to Fyetta Leipensperger.
"   25, Thomas Schiffert to Sarah Schuler.
"   25, Wm. H. Wieder to Louisa Kammerer.
"   30, Philip S. Diehl to Leah Hoover.

1856.

Jan. 22, Erin Semmel to Mary Hisky.
" 29, Benneville Faegely to Elisabeth Haman.
Feb. 19, Jacob Gangawer to Susanna Dreisbach.
" 24, Franklin Ihrig to Sarah Benner.
March 4, David Gilbert to Abigail Walbert.
" 27, Ferdinand W. Wind to Susanna E. Kidd.
" 30, Georg Dewald to Sarah Weil.
April 1, Peter Hornung to Maria Huber.
" 29, Stephan Brickel to Gottlieben Beringer.
May 11, James Weil to Dianna Beitler.
" 27, Fred. H. Hanschuh to Hannah L. Fried.
June 1, Samuel Ruhf to Amanda Harlacher.
" 17, Abraham Frankenfield to Math. Stocker.
July 4, William Heller to Susanna Jung.
" 6, Reuben Raub to Sarah Savitz.
Aug. 12, Friederich Wolf to Mary Ihrig.
" 26, Levi Freeman to Elovina Sterner.
Sept. 14, Hugh Huber to Carolina R. Boyer.
" 21, Johann Kammerer to Hannah Guth.
" 30, Edm. F. Tice to Pauline S. Eberhardt.
Oct. 2, Paul Fatzinger to Susanna E. Meyer.
" 7, Reuben Merkel to Lovina C. Weil.
" 9, Benjamin Wendling to Elisabeth Wagner.
" 12, Jesse Layton to Maria Gaumer.
" 12, William Helfrich to Cath. A. Heilman.
Nov. 13, William Mohr to Elisabeth Mebus.
" 16, Francis Kaemmerer to Am. Reinhardt.
" 18, John H. Laubach to Sarah A. Blank.
" 18, Carl H. H. Fischer to Elisabeth High.

Nov. 25, Daniel Boger to Lydia Mohr.
" 25, Solomon Schneider to Julianna Ritter.
Dec. 7, Heinrich Muss to Marsina.Guth.
" 7, Heinrich Schaerer to Sarah McGinnes.
" 13, Friederich Hellwig to Sarah Reichard.
" 28, William H. Hoehle to Polly Acker.

1857.

Jan. 4, Alfred Nagel to Maria Schneider.
" 18, G. J. Wanner to Elisabeth Muschlitz.
" 27, Adam Woolever to Eliza Ann Saylor.
Feb. 8, Jonathan Miller to Rebecca Scholl.
" 15, Aaron Geist to Eliza Long.
" 15, James Butz to Eliza Kaemmerer.
" 17, William H. Miller to Lovina Gorr.
" 17, Wayne Bitting to Carolina Diehl.
" 22, Alexander H. Mertz to Amanda Bitting.
" 22, John Schreck to Mary Mertz.
March 8, Charles S. Laciar to Mary Scholl.
" 15, Heinrich Roth to Hannah Scherer.
" 24, Heinrich Held to Sarah A. Knedler.
" 29, Samuel Ehret to Elisabeth Weidner.
April 12, Addison R. Wind to Catharina Kern.
" 12, William H. Clewell to Elemina L. Mohr.
" 19, Amos Grand to Anna M. John.
" 28, Levi Weber to Rosina Brither.
May 24, Tilghman Herzel to Elemina Menges.
" 31, Obadiah Ueberroth to Annaline Herbst.
June 21, Jeremias Ritter to Lucy Ann Weber.
July 12, Joseph Melsheimer to Bertha Brodbeck.

July 12,. Tilghman Fatzinger to Sophia Schneider.
Aug. 1, Alfred Wuchter to Sabine Cope.
" 6, Horatio Wesner to Eliza Klauss.
" 28, Joh. Jacob Long to Anna M. Nunemacher.
Sept. 13, John Johnson to Clarissa Benner.
Oct. 1, Peter S. Schmeier to Sus. Diefenderfer.
" 10, Manasses Schmidt to Polly Sterner.
" 11, Joh. Hartzel to Sarah Heinrich.
" 13, Jacob Lawall to Ann Catharine Buss.
" 27, Lewis Schaller to Louisa Nunemacher.
Nov. 12, Solomon Ueberroth to Sarah Ann Jost.
" 15, Charles Keinert to Susanna Ihrig.
" 22, Jonas Emrich to Sarah Giess.
Dec. 8, William D. Rohn to Carolina M. Meyer.
" 13, Georg H. Roth to Susanna L. Siegfried.
" 25, John Lenz to Catharina Fatzinger.
" 26, Thomas Nace to Elisabeth Bachman.
" 27, Heinrich Fried to Sarah Eliza Kleckner.

1858.

Jan. 3, Franklin Dimmig to Henrietta Meyer.
" 10, Charles H. Klein to Mathilda Miller.
" 17, Heinrich A. Halteman to Sus. M. Ihrig.
" 19, Johann Eckert to Eliza Reichard.
" 24, Joseph Diehl to Mary Ann Weber.
Feb. 4, Georg Gauf to Anna M. Giess.
" 6, Josiah Rieger to Dianna Merkel.
" 7, Friederich Klein to Sophia Lossig.
" 16, William Ortt to Maria Cope.
" 21, Edmund J. Reinhard to Sarah Beitler.

Feb. 21, Oliver Nagel to Elenora Werkheiser.
March 13, Leonhard Werkheiser to Nancy S. Hauer.
" 16, Jacob F. Diehl to Catharine N. Ritter.
" 21, Christian Hohl to Sarah Fogelman.
April 4, Richard Mellon to Elisabeth Weber.
" 25, Daniel Deily to Nancy Sterner.
May 20, Abraham Boyer to Elisabeth Appel.
" 23, Edwin Quier to Mathilda Harmany.
" 23, David Renner to Tilara Reinhart.
" 23, William Cook to Lucinda Gaumer.
" 30, Heinrich Bilgart to Lydia Huber.
June 1, Charles Brodhead to Camilla Shimer.
" 15, Charles Merkel to Hetty Oswald.
July 1, Reuben Trexler to Isabella Heller.
" 3, David Schneider to Susanna Miller.
Aug. 8, Heinrich Friholfer to Eliza Hiltenbeitel.
" 15, Andreas Wirth to Aurelia Ritter.
" 24, Asher D. Scheimer to Maria Riegel.
Sept. 11, Johann Ruhf to Catharina A. Wampold.
" 16, Dr. Sam. R. Rittenhouse to A. M. Schaefer.
" 30, William H. Kuhns to Maria Musselman.
Oct. 14, Tilghman Kraemer to Catharina Long.
" 17, William Hornung to Elisabeth Emmerig.
" 19, Francis C. Deily to Sarah A. Dech.
" 19, Samuel Roth to Hannah G. Siegfried.
" 26, Johann N. Hoffman to Babette Koblenzer.
Nov. 14, Edwin Ritter to Rebecca Dickson.
" 21, Tilghman Kidd to Eliza A. Bickert.
" 22, Franklin Braeder to Mary Ann Kleckner.
" 22, David Schneider to Sarah A. Gamber.

Nov. 29, Theodore Gundlach to Mary A. Harwi.
Dec. 5, Cyrus Wasser to Susanna Berkenstock.
" 12, Ephraim Huber to Maria E. Schuler.
" 25, Samuel Mohr to Agnes Rau.
" 26, Joseph Wolf to Frenia Frankenfield.

1859.

Jan. 9, William H. Kraemer to Sarah Strauss.
" 16, Josiah E. Schweitzer to Camilla W. Illick.
Feb. 6, Johann Sterner to Rufine Schadt.
" 20, Ephraim Moll to Helena Sauerwein.
March 1, William H. Weil to Martha Anna Giess.
" 20, Anthony Fix to Maria L. Weikel.
April 2, Alfred Yale to Susanna Schumacher.
" 24, Jarvis Roth to Sarah Carl.
" 24, Joh. R. Reichard to Mary A. Deily.
May 8, Paul Gollmer to Isabella Kraemer.
" 15, H. T. Fogelman to Elis. Bartholomäus.
" 22, John Hoh to Mary Ann Friederich.
June 12, Josiah Fahlstich to Matilda Rinker.
July 4, Solomon Rickert to Eliza A. Kratzer.
Aug. 7, Samuel Gross to Elette Kumfer.
" 7, Charles P. Lehr to Eliza Paul.
" 14, David Leibensperger to Cath. Schlosser.
" 17, Enos Eckert to Fyetta Xander.
" 18, Jonas Koch to Sarah Platz.
" 20, Thomas Engler to Susanna Peter.
" 21, Johann Marsteller to Sarah Heinly.
" 25, Joseph H. Lerch to Maria A. Berkenstock.
Sept. 11, Henry S. Miller to Lovina Fenstermacher.

Sept. 29, Charles H. Blank to Sarah Eigner.
Oct. 2, Adam Miller to Emeline Klauss.
" 9, Franz Schmidt to Bertha Gessner.
" 10, George W. Kinsey to Sarah L. Detweiler.
Nov. 1, Heinrich Schmidt to Amanda Wiand.
" 5, Benj. Zimmerman to Hetty Scheuerer.
" 6, Peter Ruth to Rebecca Schanz.
Dec. 1, J. Ruhf (widower) to Polly Reiss (widow).
" 10, Daniel S. Gifft to Madina Kanz.
" 11, Tilghman Jacoby to Emeline Stattler.
" 15, William Rebbert to Rebecca Fetzer.
" 26, Philip Hauer to Anna Eckert.
" 31, Jas. T. Seagreaves to Sarah Jane Schmidt.

1860.

Jan. 11, Manasses Klein to Sarah A. Kohl.
" 22, Tilghman Ihrig to Elisabeth Funk.
" 31, Isaac Gangawer to Maria A. Detweiler.
Feb. 28, Dr. Peter B. Breinig to Isabella Appel.
March 3, Adam Hauer to Amanda Schmidt.
" 6, David W. Scholl to Anna M. Hartman.
" 6, Rev. Beal M. Schmucker to Christ. Pretz.
" 25, Thomas Ed. Kidd to Eliza M. Wagner.
" 31, Zacharias Singer to Anna M. Schmidt.
April 8, Tilghman Fatzinger to Mary Clader.
" 8, Georg F. Poh to Polly Ann Balliet.
" 29, Edwin Hoffert to Sabina Derr.
May 15, Dr. Aug. A. Freyman to Mary C. Doerle.
" 19, Geo. Diefenderfer to Marietta Fatzinger.
" 27, William Frey to Mathilda Sterner.

May 27, James Fahnel to Lovina Harmony.
June 10, Abraham R. Trexler to Sarah Walp.
" 10, Georg Spaeth to Rebecca Kuhns.
" 16, Joseph Keller to Polly Braun.
July 5, Lake Erie Huber to Anna M. Heller.
Sept. 16, Edwin Fogelman to Mary Lerch.
" 22, William Eckert to Lovina Eckert.
" 29, William F. Ruth to Elisabeth C. Dorney.
Oct. 2, William E. Illick to Mary Kunkel.
Nov. 10, Demas Schuler to Anna M. Lauer.
" 18, Jacob K. Staengle to Lydia Giltner.
Dec. 2, Francis Texter to Mathilda Nunemacher.
" 25, Johann Harwi to Maria Gangwer.
" 25, Heinrich Schlosser to Elisabeth Fahlstich.

1861.

Jan. 10, Charles Zellner to Maria Reb. Freiman.
" 22, William Halman to Selnia Krauss.
Feb. 2, Charles Breinig to Eliza Ruth.
" 23, Harrison Knappenberger to H. Weidner.
March 12, Francis Kraemer to Carolina Landis.
May 19, Jacob Hartman to Sabina Uhler.
" 26, Heinrich Fahlstich to Rebecca Trexler.
June 9, David Reichard to Susanna Weiss.
" 13, Rev. Wm. J. Mennig to Sarah A. Weber.
July 21, Manoah Warmkessel to Sarah Merkel.
" 22, Heinrich W. Ihrig to Emilie Missemer.
Aug. 11, Heinrich E. Ubrich to Mary Ann Schell.
" 18, Samuel Kincaid to Amanda Siegfried.
" 18, Joseph Wimmer to Eliza Bader.

Sept. 7, David Ihrig to Elisabeth Ernst.
" 21, Martin Frankenfield to Sarah A. Steuben.
" 25, Charles Ettinger to Rebecca Romig.
" 29, Joh. G. Blank to Emma L. Kaemmerer.
Oct. 29, Samuel Hoh to Fyetta Wint.
" 27, Charles Hainse to Priscilla Fink.
Dec. 8, Jacob Hopper to Mary A. E. Hauser.
" 10, Joseph Bachmann to Mathilda C. Jost.
" 17, John Groman to Sarah Fretz.

1862.

Jan. 12, Richard Lafaver to Ann Jane Schneider.
" 15, Heinrich Fried to Susanna Abbott.
Feb. 1, Samuel Kidd to Louisa Diehm.
" 4, David Hartman to Rebecca Schwenker.
" 22, Dr. Henry S. Clemens to E. M. Hartman.
March 25, Daniel J. Rhoads to Sarah Romig.
April 1, Peter M. Landes to Susanna W. Yeager.
" 5, Charles B. Schmeier to Rosa M. Albrecht.
June 8, David W. Scholl to Matilda Geissinger.
" 29, Johann W. Reichard to Elizabeth McHose.
July 31, David Ueberroth to Cornelia Stuber.
Aug. 3, Johann J. Rothe to Louisa Stiegler.
Sept. 11, Johann F. Pflueger to Anna M. J. Frey.
Oct. 5, Heinrich Miller to Carolina Leibensperger.
" 11, Isaac Gerhard to Lucy Ann Schoener.
Nov. 23, Johann Rinker to Sarah Schwander.
Dec. 26, Heinrich Bortz to Sarah Baer.
" 28, Jacob Gernet to Mary Jane Funk.

1863.

Jan.	17, Franklin Wint to Ansonetta Stueben.
"	24, Herman Buss to Emmeline Weber.
"	25, William Schankweiler to Sarah Sicher.
Feb.	7, John Beitler to Sarah Cahoon.
March	14, Theo. Merkofer to Susanna Schaefer.
April	9, Heinrich F. Sterner to Abigail Schneck.
"	21, Herman Burckhardt to Fyetta Mertz.
May	3, Heinrich Mill to Sarah Messer.
"	16, Benj. Ely (widower) to Eliz. Bauer (widow).
"	23, Jonas F. Gorr to Sarah C. Gaumer.
June	9, Thomas Reichert to Rebecca Doll.
"	14, Dr. Amos J. Harres to Amanda Schleiffer.
"	16, Charles H. Weber to Barbara Ann Stofflet.
July	5, William Linn to Susanna German.
"	26, Levi J. Beitler to Sarah A Zellner.
Aug.	4, Edwin Cope to Maria Braeder.
"	23, Abraham Ruhf to Eliza Romig.
Sept.	13, Cyrus Lapp to Rebecca Dech.
"	13, James Huber to Elizabeth Heckman.
"	13, Reuben H. Illick to Dianna Meyer.
"	29, Martin L. Yost to Amanda Gabel.
"	29, John J. Yost to Mary Reichard.
Oct.	3, Isaac Erb to Catharina Dierolf.
"	6, Jonathan J. Paul to Sarah Weiser.
"	25, Christ. Scheid to Veronika Leibensperger.
Nov.	12, L. S. Lichtenwallner to C. Leibensperger.
"	19, William Burger to Louisa Stecher.
"	21, William Laury to Elizabeth Illick.
Dec.	10, Jacob Reichard to Sarah A. Ott.

Dec. 13, James Beitler to Sarah A. Schneider.
" 24, Asher M. Schortz to Fyetta Colver.
" 30, Edwin W. Fried to Ellen Siegfried.

1864.

Jan. 16, John Ettinger to Abigail Betz.
" 31, Emmanuel Schaefer to Maria Leopold.
Feb. 1, Charles Heist to Anna M. Marbach.
" 7, Jacob S. Kidd to Christianna Neutlinger.
" 15, Heinrich Hoevel to Eliza Keck.
" 20, Gustav Hoffman to Anna Radtman.
" 28, Milton Ruhf to Catharina Schmidt.
March 27, William Gaumer to Eliza Ettinger.
" 27, James Friederich to Maria Knerr.
April 16, Samuel Missimer to Anna Dreigler.
" 17, Asher Bush to Amanda Leibensperger.
May 7, Wilson Reiss to Mary Ann Romig.
June 4, William Henry to Elizabeth Mosser.
July 16, Heinrich Frey to Catharina Hartzel.
Aug. 13, Milton Eckert to Mary Nagel.
" 16, Edwin Moritz to Amanda Yost.
Oct. 8, Jonas Schmeier to Elvine Schmeier.
" 9, Heinrich H. Hinkel to Amanda Abel.
" 13, William Eckert to Elizabeth Bachman.
Nov. 19, Tilgh. Lichtenwallner to Clarissa Dewalt.
" 29, David Gernet to Catharina Stump.
Dec. 11, Martin R. Frey to Elizabeth Steinbach.
" 18, Francis H. Jaeger to Rebecca Breinig.
" 21, John Moll to Elvina Berger.
" 28, William Raub to Ellen Berkenstock.
" 31, Levi Sterner to Sarah Cath. Kunsman.

1865.

Jan. 1, David Kratzer to Clarissa J. Stump.
" 29, Amandus Heinrich to Eliza Herz.
" 29, Franklin Ritter to Fyanna Dickson.
Feb. 11, Charles Albrecht to Rebecca Fegely.
" 12, Oliver C. Zellner to Mary Ann Spengler.
" 26, Thomas Albrecht to Rebecca Reis.
April 2, Sigmund F. Gnann to Elmira Schmidt.
" 6, J. Matthew Hummel to Elizabeth Mohr.
" 9, Edward Yost to Sarah Allam.
" 23, Friederich Ehlers to Emmalinda Ihrig.
" 29, John W. Hecker to Anna E. Scherer.
" 30, C. L. Lautenschlaeger to E. Hunsicker.
May 1, Heinrich J. Moyer to Eliza M. Minnich.
" 6, Julius Landrock to Susanna Nagel.
" 7, Charles W. Roth to Catharina Koch.
" 22, Herman Schiffer to Catharina Schneider.
June 4, Stephen Remely to Ellenora Albrecht.
" 24, Johann Braun to Catharina Henn.
" 25, Edwin H. Bickel to Sarah A. Scholl.
July 1, Owen R. Wilt to Annie Linn.
" 2, Edwin Schmidt to Christina Fahlstich.
" 23, Daniel J. Kraemer to Judith Peter.
Aug. 24, Thomas F. Laubach to Sarah A. Borz.
" 26, Amandus Roth to Sophia Hauer.
Sept. 10, Heinrich G. Reinhart to Lovina Koch.
" 16, Alfred S. Leiser to Malissina Nagel.
" 17, Harrison Mill to Sarah A. Stump.
" 28, Elias R. Benner to Belinda J. Lapp.
" 28, Jacob Yoder to Barbara Newkommer

Oct. 3, Walter Kunz to Emma Deibert.
" 5, Milton Lautenschlaeger to Sus. Spinner.
" 22, Allen A. Christman to Mary A. Fahlstich.
Nov. 11, Friederich Trager to Sarah Allem.
" 12, Maybury S. Weidner to Sarah Acker.
Dec. 2, Jonas Lauer to Lydia Amanda Schmeier.
" 13, William H. Decker to Sue Annie Mohr.
" 24, John S. Trumbower to Ellen C. Ritter.

1866.

Jan. 18, Harrison Boyer to Matilda R. Nagel.
" 21, Benneville Christman to Maria Hill.
" 23, Peter Kern to Sarah E. Buss.
Feb. 4, Heinrich Emmerich to Fyetta Trapp.
" 11, Georg A. Xander to Ellenfriede Hauer.
" 15, Johann Graeber to Maria Spiess.
" 18, Edwin Flexer to Amilia Schmidt.
" 20, Alfred E. Roth to Mary Ann Heiny.
March 11, Johann Koch to Christianna Zappenfeld.
" 13, Jacob Wittman to Anna G. Berdhold.
" 17, Wm. H. Kraemer to Matilda J. Denhart.
" 18, Salomon H. Nagel to Susanna Yeager.
" 25, Jacob Siess to Ann Woods.
" 27, Jacob Sell to Catharina A. Beck.
" 31, Jas. P. Schmeier to Mary A. Lichtenwallner.
April 7, Samuel Yehl to Rebecca Gloss.
June 7, William D. Rohn to Henrietta Dech.
" 9, William F. Keck to Catharina Neuhardt.
" 9, Johann Knopf to Elmira Werner.
" 17, William Stuber to Hannah Ernst.

June 18, George Adams to Annie Ritter.
" 30, Heinrich Stein to Susanna Mosser.
July 24, Edwin F. Deily to Matilda Solliday.
" 29, Charles F. Ihrig to Faganna Kramm.
" 29, Charles Yoachim to Mary Frey.
Aug. 11, William H. Strawn to Marsiann Lacy.
" 26, John Neumeyer to Mary Jane Fritz.
" 26, Peter Lester to Sarah E. Nagel.
Sept. 15, Friederich Wilt to Anna M. Lang.
Oct. 7, William J. Illick to Mary Miller.
" 11, Johann Scholle to Catharina Mensch.
" 20, Samuel Dutt to Catharina Smith.
Nov. 4, Franklin D. Fried to Amanda Eliz. Derr.
" 18, John Fahlstich to Eliza Schlosser.
" 18, Allen W. Trexler to Mary E. Ahner.
" 18, John Kingcaid to Isabella Kunkel.
" 18, Solomon Reinschmidt to Mary Schmidt.
" 24, William Wint to Hannah Geissinger.

1867.

Jan. 1, Charles H. Miller to Eliza N. Remmel.
Feb. 10, Friedrich Aug. Miller to Sophia Hillegas.
" 12, Daniel J. Reinhart to Clarissa Kraemer.
March 2, John Williams to Carolina Gilbert.
" 14, John Metzger to Matilda Blank.
" 17, Christian Mauser to Matilda Frey.
" 19, Aaron Laub to Lucinda Weber.
April 11, Math. Ziegenfuss to Mary A. Frankenfield.
" 26, Jonas Weber to Floryanne Hausmann.
May 4, Horatio Shankweiler to Cecilia Bloch.

May 9, Morgan Mory to Malinda Wint.
" 12, James Moritz to Amanda Sterner.
June 1, Calvin A. Brown to Mary J. Huber.
" 8, Edward F. Huber to Annie E. Moyer.
July 27, Christian Rath to Odelia Meyer.
" 30, William Jacob Volz to Anna Bloss.
Aug. 24, Charles Savitz to Rebecca Osmun.
" 31, Alfred Ritter to Catharina Erdman.
Sept. 2, Johann Schmidt to Elisabeth Weiss.
" 22, James Kraeder to Sarah A. Schwinker.
" 29, Lewis Keiper to Susanna Barret.
Oct. 26, Berned Velker to Lydia Keeler.
Nov. 3, Benj. J. Schmeier to Matilda S. Moyer.
" 12, Elias A. Schmeier to Mary E. Albrecht.
" 16, Andrew J. Osmun to Ellen J. Brong.
" 17, Edmund O. Reichard to Adelina Moritz.
" 23, Sol. H. Schmeier to Clara S. Schmeier.
" 23, Francis S. Hartman to Ellen R. Andreas.
Dec. 8, Geo. J. Reichard to Sus. R. Muthhard.
" 19, Jacob Ihrig to Carolina Keppler.
" 24, Edwin Schneider to Aravesta Yost.
" 24, Frank Hausman to Mary Giess.
" 24, Peter Foy to Sarah A. Owens.
" 26, Rudolph Solt to Anna M. Schoeneberger.
" 26, Jeremias Schaefer to Ellen J. Kidd.

1868.

Jan. 5, James Sterner to Senia Fatzinger.
" 26, Carl L. Stahl to Ellen Fahlstich.
Feb. 4, Reuben H. Daniel to Mary A. Schortz.

Feb. 15, Joseph Stern to Lovina Kunsman.
" 20, Geo. Raudenbush to Am. Knappenberger.
April 4, Washington Wetzel to Cath. Fegely.
" 9, Sol. H. Gross to Amanda Ihrig.
" 11, William H. Hoch to Sarah Fischer.
" 19, Joshua Nagel to Emma Leipensperger.
May 12, Charles A. Saul to Martha Fatzinger.
" 16, Charles B. Klein to Sarah Lichtenwallner.
" 23, George Bechtel to Caroline Gery.
" 31, Charles Moyer to Ansanetta Jacoby.
" 31, Thomas Leiser to Ellen Trexler.
June 6, Levi Hiestand to Catharina Schmeier.
" 6, William W. Hartman to Anna M. Frey.
" 6, Frank S. Lichtenwallner to Mary A. Butz.
Aug. 8, Geo. W. White to Annie S. Seagreaves.
" 20, F. G. A. Schade to Helena S. Berg.
Sept. 3, Mifflin N. Keck to Matilda P. Edelman.
" 6, William Giess to Mary Ann Bruder.
" 13, John Houk to Matilda Wilt.
Oct. 1, Henry J. Romig to Mary M. Warmkessel.
" 3, Paul Branger to Catharina Langenstrauss.
" 4, William Leishner to Mary E. Durron.
" 5, Daniel M. Kindig to Leanna Kramm.
" 11, Alfred Moritz to Lucinda Hoch.
" 18, Franz Wieser to Mary Ann Lerch.
" 27, Jackson Trumbauer to Susan S. Weber.
Dec. 1, Josiah J. Laubach to Leanna Schneck.
" 25, Robert M. Jacoby to Mary J. Stachler.

1869.

Jan. 10, John Q. A. Schneider to Amelia Fink.
" 23, Henry Keeler to Mary Jane Reinbold.
Feb. 1, William H. Roth to Elamina Trexler.
" 2, Winfield S. Troxel to Sevilla Stahlnecker.
" 13, John J. Hamman to Am'da S. Neumoyer.
" 27, Wm. H. Wagenast to Sus. C. Schmeier.
" 27, Peter Angstat to Sarah Lenhart.
March 16, Frank Hisky to Sarah A. Halteman.
April 18, Franklin C. Becker to Marg. B. Schaefer.
" 22, Peter Conrad to Mary Eckert.
May 1, Friedrich Schweier to Ellen Mebes.
" 9, James Leiser to Mary Schmidt.
" 16, David Reinhart to Ursilla Seibert.
" 17, Daniel Scheetz to Matilda C. Seip.
" 20, Owen F. Fatzinger to Savilla S. Wint.
" 30, George P. Breinig to Josephine Henn.
June 6, William A. Hinkel to Catharine J. Nagel.
" 6, John Everett to Elmira Gnann.
" 19, Benjamin Schmidt to Martha Fegely.
" 26, H. B. Knappenberger to Martha A. Butz.
" 27, Henry T. Ginkinger to Catharine Clees.
July 4, Theodore Siegfried to Clara Reinschmidt.
Aug. 8, Joseph Torrence to Elvina Jacoby.
" 19, Conrad Daniel to Mary Schneider.
" 21, Martin Leisenring to Mary Miller.
Sept. 4, Edwin Butz to Faganna Miller.
" 28, Frank M. Diehm to Emma R. Klotz.
" 28, John A. Schaefer to Hannah E. Reiss.
" 30, Edward H. Buchecker to Clara Groman.

Oct. 10, William Bauer to Eliza Romig.
" 16, Samuel Schmeier to Leah Yeager.
Dec. 2, David Friederich to Sarah Moyer.
" 11, James Brang to Mary Buss.
" 25, Oliver J. Pflueger to Hetty M. Youndt.
25, Charles H. Trexler to Elisabeth Hall.
25, Franklin Hock to Clemina Lodge.

1870.

Jan. 25, Abraham Blank, Jr., to Mary J. Knauss.
Feb. 6, Edward F. Osenbach to Dianna M. Roth.
" 10, Oliver Rinker to Sarah Bailey.
March 18, William Shadler to Theresa Staufer.
" 26, William Leopold to Sarah Jacoby.
28, Georg Ott to Lavina Roth.
" 29, Conrad F. Stahl to Catharina C. Krapf.
April 6, Joh. Bundeman to Hannah T. Reifinger.
" 16, Franklin Ihrig to Mary Miller.
" 30, William H. Mohr to Mary A. Rufe.
May 8, Charles A. Huber to Abyssinia Schneider.
" 8, Allen A. Balliet to Mary A. Balliet.
" 10, Jacob Miller, Jr., to Elizabeth M. Kuntz.
" 20, Levi J. Ruhf to Catharina A. Kaiser.
" 21, William Rumfeld to Amanda Kessler.
" 26, Robert W. Ihrig to Ellen A. Sterner.
June 19, Oliver W. Merkel to Emma M. Gangwer.
July 3, William H. Jacob to Rebecca Bilgart.
" 3, Tilghman G. S. Osenbach to Alice Henn.
" 3, Daniel Minnich to Montana Meyer.
Sept. 11, Abraham Frey to Annie Kleckner.

Sep. 26, Mattheus Maier to Mary Lukleder.
Oct. 1, Milton N. Dotterer to Susan Rumfeld.
" 16, Alfr. C. Osenbach to Matilda A. Albrecht.
" 16, Sam. S. Stump to Amanda L. Eberhard.
" 16, Chas. A. Nunemacher to Ellen Reinhard.
" 20, Jacob S. Ettinger to Sarah J. Frutchey.
Nov. 2, John Schrunk to Alavesta Keiper.
" 12, Georg W. Neitz to Emma J. Schmeier.
Dec. 6, F. W. Martin to Emma C. Schaefer.
" 20, Owen Kurtz to Theresa M. Cressman.
" 24, Allison W. Ritter to Eliza A. Kaemmerer.
" 24, Wm. Weinsheimer to Anna M. Kuder.
" 25, James A. Trexler to Ellen J. Trumbauer.

1871.

Jan. 22, Clinton A. Reinhard to A. E. Schneider.
" 29, Hiram J. Roth to Martha J. Schankweiler.
Feb. 11, John H. Holzerman to Sarah E. Cope.
" 19, Alfred Nagel to Emma Roller.
March 4, Reuben M. Schaeffer to M. A. Trumbauer.
" 9, Johann N. Schmidt to Wilhelmine Scheeff.
" 11, Henry A. Schmeier to Elamina C. Butz.
April 20, J. F. Reichard to Annie Lawall.
May 20, John Frank to Alavesta Wack.
" 20, Theophilus Pflueger to Annie E. Weber.
" 28, Jackson T. Stuber to Annie Herrman.
June 10, Heinrich Hartlein to Sarah Gernet.
" 11, Heinrich Berger to Eliza Ehret.
" 11, Isaac B. Keller to Annie Klauss.
July 2, Robert J. Eschbach to Matilda Henn.

July 4, David Friederich to Mary Oswald.
" 15, Irwin Ruhf to Mathilda Weis.
" 22, John Beck to Catharina Brinker.
" 22, Edward Diehl to Fyetta Koch.
" 30, James Kemmerer to Mary Bür.
Aug. 5, William Mack to Sarah Weierbach.
" 20, William Brong to Mary Newhard.
Sept. 16, Gottfried Holl to Barbara Grossman.
" 28, Josiah F. Fatzinger to Amanda Riehl.
Oct. 29, Lewis Wasser to Carry Roeder.
Nov. 5, Solomon Reinbold to Judith Deily.
" 13, Wilson T. Ginkinger to A. M. Schneider.
" 25, Jacob Leibensperger to Sarah E. Knauss.
Dec. 9, Charles H. Staehr to Emma J. Moyer.
" 16, Allen Nunemacher to Sarah Weber.
" 22, John L. Stiles to Emma F. Staehr.
" 23, Milton A. Saeger to Elizabeth Seil.
" 30, William S. Reeser to Cath. S. Peterson.
" 30, Charles D. Hanke to Sarah Gery.
" 30, Mahlon Gery to Mary Fillman.

1872.

Feb. 4, Christoph Herzog and his wife Margaretha (golden wedding).
" 17, Jeremiah S. Quier to Eliza A. Kleppinger.
" 18, Irwin L. Hess to Emma C. Miller.
" 18, Henry H. Wetherhold to Mary J. Remel.
" 22, Theodore E. Trexler to Sarah A. Hopper.
March 10, Jacob Reis to Helena S. Deily.
" 10, Stephan Gangewer to Lizzie Musselman.

March 31, Benjamin F. Benecoff to Ellen Brinker.
" 31, Rudolf Kern to Carolina Schneider.
April 13, James Heiselmoyer to Matilda Fink.
" 21, Hiram C. Deily to Louisa Derr.
" 21, Abrah. Hottenstein to Paulina Holzwart.
May 5, Thomas Hoehle to Augusta Flores.
" 18, James Schaub to Elmira Rickert.
" 18, Daniel Gaukler to Leonora Hunsberger.
" 18, George Moyer to Rebecca Barnar.
" 18, James Schmidt to Sarah Schaeffer.
" 26, Alfred Diehl to Susan Kern.
June 9, Thomas Schweikeffer to Martha Wilson.
" 15, Alfred Dankel to Eliza Ann Strunk.
" 17, Edwin Mebus to Sarah A. Mebus.
" 30, Walter J. Leschter to Emma E. Shapel.
July 20, Jeremiah C. Fritz to Hannah M. Gernet.
" 27, George Reinbold to Mary L. Funk.
" 28, August W. Long to Mary Leibensperger.
Aug. 18, Heinrich Hoepner to Juliana Springer.
" 18, Edwin G. Schneider to Emma C. Kratzer.
" 24, Peter Siegfried to Sarah Reichard.
" 27, Milton M. Kindig to Clara R. Brader.
Sept. 24, George W. Johnson to Amanda Long.
Oct. 6, James Bliem to Emma E. Ohl.
" 26, Samuel Smith to Amanda Young.
" 31, Alfred S. Lerch to Sarah A. Gangwer.
Nov. 10, Tilghman Remmel to Eliza A. Ramaly.
" 30, William A. Sieger to Amelia Fischer.
Dec. 12, Dr. Charles F. Pflueger to Cecilia Walbert.
" 28, Asher K. Schmidt to Camilla A. J. Ritter.

1873.

Jan. 1, Matthew Schmidt to Catharina Benner.
"   21, James W. Schmeier to Mary A. Kocher.
Feb. 22, William S. Burger to Mary A. Heberling.
March 6, Richard Nagel to Sarah Music.
"   18, Henry Michel to Eliza J. Deily.
"   24, Richard W. Saeger to Amanda Miller.
April 3, Daniel Keinert to Rebecca Paul.
"   5, William Bast to Annie Keiter.
"   30, William H. Wood to Mary A. Losh.
May   4, Lake Erie Huber to Mary A. E. Schmeier.
"   31, James D. Klauss to Aquilla M. Sieger.
June 2, August Keller to Lovina Daubert.
"   3, Frank Seip to Amanda Kunkel.
"   11, Solomon Ihrig to Susanna Boger.
"   28, Albert Yeager to Louisa Mosser.
"   29, Frank Warmkessel to Mary L. Kern.
July 5, Alfred Tice to Kate McGinley.
"   12, Marcus Gernet to Sarah A. Klinker.
"   20, Wm. H. H. Schmidt to Martha N. S. Mack.
"   20, John H. Leiby to Annie E. Ehrig.
"   27, John S. Knerr to Dianna Fischer.
Aug. 5, Sylvester M. Hauer to Henriette Schafer.
Sept. 20, Enos Ritter to Maria Friederich.
"   25, Theodore E. Schmidt to Ansenetta Lohr.
Oct. 2, William Reed to Emelinda Kressler.
"   18, Christian Schlegel to Margaretha Seebalt.
"   19, Johann J. Meyer to Tusanella Eckert.
"   25, Charles Funk to Dianna Veater.
Nov. 11, Charles F. Horn to Elisabeth Howard.

Nov.   13, Alfred L. Young to Sarah C. Raub.
Dec.   4, Jonas L. Lerch to Mathilda Keiper.
"   25, Charles I. Nunemacher to Sarah Dickson.
"   25, John Donnecker to Mary J. Mertz.

1874.

Jan.   24, Franz Erling to Mary Arnold.
"   31, Joseph H. Eckmeder to Helena Dickson.
Feb.   3, William Moyer to Mary A. Beitler.
"   14, George Moyer to Lydia Schmidt.
"   14, Josiah J. Hummel to Emma Brunner.
"   14, James B. Stoudt to Elisabeth Stricker.
"   17, Charles Ritter to Elisabeth Kichlein.
"   28, Conrad Guenthart to Ellen Nagel.
March 17, Wm. H. Gangwer to Car. S. Reichenbach.
"   29, Joh. Weil to Mary Hillegas.
"   30, Henry Ritter to Sarah Sensenbach.
April 16, Immanuel U. Trexler to Marg. Boehm.
May   5, Albert C. Belden to Hannah E. Mosser.
"   23, Jonathan T. Romig to Judith E. Levan.
June   6, William Leobold to Amanda Beere.
"   18, David S. Ludwig to Emma Haines.
"   27, Paul E. Schantz to Esther L. Searles.
July   12, Daniel Schaefer to Elamina Weber.
Aug.   2, Daniel D. Moyer to Lily F. Bratch.
"   22, Carl Fridsche to Anna Schneider.
"   7, Adaman G. Smith to Louisa J. Keck.
Sept. 6, Charles Fatzinger to Annie Layden.
"   12, George W. Helms to Annie M. Rupp.
Oct.   17, A. S. Miller to Maria Neumeyer.

Oct. 25, Charles L. Trexler to Emma M. Fried.
" 29, Henry C. Missimer to Ellen M. Seitz.
Nov. 17, Newton Rinker to Emma R. Berkenstock.
" 22, Wm. H. Schortz to E. S. Lichtenwallner.
" 28, William J. Beitler to Hetty F. Walp.
" 28, Thomas Boyer to Caroline Strasser.
Dec. 3, William Reinbold to Melinda Bernt.
" 25, Joh. A. Schneider to Elemanda Reitz.
" 26, Wilson F. Ritter to Eliza Bartholomew.

1875.

Jan. 3, Allen Stuber to Lovina Ihrig.
" 6, Gott. M. Scherer to Franzisca Schlecker.
" 16, John H. Holzeman to Sarah J. Linn.
Feb. 9, James H. Breinig to Isadora E. Yost.
March 9, Henry S. Sendel to Louisa C. Becker.
" 13, Amandes A. Albrecht to Chrissura Rauch.
" 29, Joseph H. Eastman to Mary E. Bauder.
April 10, George F. Deily to Sarah E. Miller.
" 25, Charles Cook to Emma M. Reichard.
" 29, Levi Herzog to Ellen A. Neuhart.
May 9, Joseph B. Rohr to Emmeline Jacoby.
" 16, Wilson R. Deily to Mary L. Strohm.
" 20, Wilson F. Bahl to Sarah Wint.
" 20, Samuel A. Dech to Mary J. Fatzinger.
July 4, Samuel M. Mebus to Sarah L. Frey.
Aug. 19, Frank S. Harlacher to Emma S. Deily.
Sept. 6, Lewis Levan to Mary Trexler.
" 18, Frank Miller to Ellwina Preisser.
Oct. 10, Leander J. Laub to Luella W. Trexler.

Oct. 23, Christian W. Oehler to Catharina Vogel.
" 23, Peter Malburg to Sarah M. Schmidt.
" 30, John Wesley Lormor to Kate Grenwalt.
Dec. 9, Alfred J. Clader to L. L. Lichtenwallner.

1876.

Jan. 15, Henry P. Nagle to Eliza Kidd.
" 22, Benjamin Wolf to Eliza Roeder.
Feb. 6, Reuben Peterson to Susan Heckman.
" 17, Jere. Fenstermacher to Sunia E. C. Ritter.
March 2, Oliver Laub to Sunia Jacoby.
" 28, Calvin H. Miller to Mary A. Simon.
April 1, John J. Reinert to Kate McCandress.
" 23, John S. Young to Amanda Strassberger.
May 6, Calvin Schober to Ella Vogel.
" 13, Edwin T. Carl to Mary E. Goebel.
June 15, O. J. Schmoyer to Susan Lichtenwallner.
" 25, John Roller to Elisabeth Mellon.
July 8, Reuben R. Weidner to Alice E. Clewell.
" 22, Jacob Brick to Elamina Quier.
" 23, Samuel Hinkel to Emma J. Layden.
" 27, Benjamin A. Schmeier to Cecilia Gaumer.
" 29, Milt. Nunnemacher to Mary Berkenstock.
Aug. 2, Jas. M. Trumbauer to Alice E. Seiberling.
" 13, Eugene Stahlnecker to Mary A. C. Mohn.
" 20, George Schlosser to Emma Cope.
Sept. 16, Manasses Dietz to Martha Hillegas.
Oct. 8, Thomas Minich to Camilla Osenbach.
" 19, Cyrillus Larose to Agnes L. Schmeier.
Nov. 4, Charles Werner to Sarah A. Christ.

Nov. 5, Charles Acker to Clara Diefenderfer.
" 12, John G. Kessler to Marietta Eschbach.
" 13, Lewis Gerzner to Maria Mohr.

1877.

Jan. 4, Reuben Schortz to Carolina Santee.
" 13, John G. Mayer to Catharina Schmidt.
" 20, Morris M. Wendel to Adelina Mosser.
" 28, Benj. F. Reichart to Annie E. Schmidt.
" 28, Lewis S. Stein to Maria M. S. Mill.
Feb. 15, Nathaniel J. Kidd to Mary Weaver.
" 24, George W. Troxel to Carrie Newkom.
March 1, John Schmidt to Elizabeth Schlosser.
" 10, Wm. E. Willenbuecher to A. M. J. Esser.
April 22, Samuel N. Fox to Elmira F. Long.
May 6, Peter T. Weaver to Maria M. Amey.
" 20, Henry Deiver to Ida Clifton.
" 20, Joseph M. Wind to Ida E. Good.
" 24, Alvin M. Schmoyer to Cassie S. Gaumer.
June 14, Alfred Ritter to Mary A. Hill.
July 31, Joseph Goldschmidt to Belinda E. Moyer.
Sept. 13, Carl M. Mosser to Carolina S. Ihrig.
Nov. 18, Charles Zentner to Elizabeth Minnich.
" 24, Allen L. Rumfeld to Martha I. Engleman.
Dec. 1, Robert A. Rau to Emma Barner.
" 21, Allen Reichard to Camilla Brader.
" 22, Lycurgus A. Weierbach to Aman. M. Nace.
" 22, Campbell W. Jones to Sibylla Hausman.
" 25, Peter W. Alles to Mary M. A. Lantzer.

1878.

Jan. 1, Thomas C. Breinig to Car. Leipensperger.
" 20, Frank Brinker to Catharina Eisenhart.
Feb. 9, Edwin T. Fatzinger to Mary Hittinger.
" 16, Jonathan D. Wieser to A. M. Donnecker.
" 26, Wm. H. F. Eberhard to Ida Jane Osewald.
March 2, Levi J. Riegel to Emmelina Weber.
" 9, Albert Trapp to Emma Rohr.
" 17, Charles A. Muschlitz to Bertha Miller.
" 19, Asher M. Schortz to Emma L. Reinhard.
April 4, Joseph Daylor to Elmira A. Kidd.
" 7, Solomon Herzel to Angelina Kahler.
" 21, Israel Rudolph to Mary Hottenstein.
June 17, Emanuel M. Ruch to Mary J. Muschlitz.
" 23, Samuel G. Torrence to Sarah Jacoby.
Aug. 11, Frank Steinmetz to Agnes Kidd.
" 15, Frank Hardner to Agnes Diehl.
" 15, Daniel Leibensperger to Matilda Frick.
" 17, Rich. D. Leisenring to E. J. Marsteller.
Sept. 12, Alexander B. Ellsworth to Mary Wetzel.
" 25, Jerome Christman to Mary Deily.
Oct. 10, Oscar Newhard to Louisa Grant.
" 19, Wm. H. Reinbold to S. A. Nunemacher.
Nov. 16, Milton C. Ritter to Ida E. Walter.
Dec. 7, Jacob A. Koch to Lizzie S. Walbert.
" 21, Frank L. Burger to Emma C. Marsteller.
" 21, George A. Kleppinger to Sarah A. Rockel.
" 27, Wm. R. Yeager to Henrietta W. Yeager.

1879.

Jan. 29, Henry E. Dell to Kate Peters.
March 23, Albert F. Mosser to Jane Sarah Schelten.
April 5, Erwin H. Weidner to Ellen C. Yeager.
" 10, George Springer to Hettie Fischel.
" 26, Levere J. Gangwer to Flora E. Kilpatrick.
May 25, Franklin L. Hartman to Mary L. Harwi.
" 26, George A. Kreitz to Emma R. Wachter.
" 29, Franklin R. Sharer to Lydia Bilgart.
June 8, William F. Tice to Martha L. Lilly.
" 16, Owen R. Oberly to Ellen Dieter.
" 21, Charles Biers to Isabella Geyer.
July 5, Austin B. Weiler to Laura Bittenbender.
Aug. 23, Wm. H. Zentner to Alavesta S. Miller.
" 30, S. Harry Bachman to Ellen Hodes.
Sept. 2, Erwin Knapp to Lucy Borger.
" 6, William Hoffert to Emma Schwenk.
" 18, Allen F. Stromminger to Mary A. Gernet.
" 28, Wm. T. Osenbach to Clementine M. Clader.
" 30, Uriah Lynn to Amanda Delp.
Oct. 11, Anaman J. Gangwer to Jane Kilpatrick.
" 16, Calvin Vogenitz to Sophia Siegel.
" 18, William K. Schneider to Mary D. Merkel.
" 30, Christian Nicholas to Sarah M. Grimm.
Nov. 29, George Bechtel to Lillie Frankenfield.
Dec. 2, Peter A. Kuntz to Miss Ambrunn.
" 5, R. C. Schmoyer to Kate A. Lichtenwallner.
" 13, William J. Ritter to Sarah C. Young.
" 25, Peter Hansson to Alice Frank.
" 25, Samuel D. Deily to Alice O. Nagel.
" 28, Franklin J. Wehr to Mary A. J. Reichart.

1880.

Jan. 17, Jacob Bergstresser to Josephina Hoffman.
" 17, Edwin Lichtenwallner to E. M. C. Knauss.
" 29, Daniel D. Trexler to Annie M. Fell.
Feb. 21, James Moyer to Kate Steckert.
" 23, Emanuel Keinert to Annie Schwarz.
" 28, William H. Ehrich to Rosa A. B. Gardner.
March 25, Allen S. Geissinger to A. T. Kauffman.
" 29, Erasmus Miller to Louisa Gilbert.
" 30, Harrison Berner to Leanna Biers.
April 8, Alfred H. Worman to Laura J. Kratzer.
" 17, Simon Ditt to Hannah Herrman.
May 15, Oscar Brader to Eliza Ruhf.
July 17, Franklin S. Derr to Emma Kratzer.
" 22, Lewis F. Wenner to Tuvillia S. Eisenhard.
" 31, William H. Swartz to Martha E. Burkit.
Aug. 15, Adam W. Sandt to Clara M. Statler.
" 21, Morris Clewell to Alice Bensinger.
" 22, Alexander S. Deily to Lydia M. Smith.
Sept. 4, Theodore O. Moyer to Fyanna M. Ritter.
" 25, Edwin A. Laibla to Emma L. Merkels.
" 25, Richard Schlegel to Catharina Yeager.
" 25, Alfred Kramer to Annie Frankenfield.
Oct. 16, Thomas O. Reichard to Amelia E. Wehr.
Nov. 28, Henry J. Knoll to Amanda J. Wint.
Dec. 11, Erwin D. Miller to Eliza Neumoyer.
" 23, Leopold Herrman to Augusta Friedrich.

1881.

Jan. 9, G. D. B. Schmeier to Susan Warmkessel.

Jan. 13, Milton Rader to Maria Miller.
"   18, B. F. Albright to Emma C. Diefenderfer.
"   31, Robert Moll to Mary Traub.
April 23, Wm. R. Yeager to Margaret A. Weaver.
"   29, Joseph Breisch to Tuvillia Reinert.
May   3, Friederich Bene to Louisa Stuber.
"   12, Eli Frankenfield to Emma Osenbach.
"   21, John Adams to Catharina Keck.
June   5, Milton T. Reichard to Emma M. Zerfass.
"   18, George W. Weil to Melinda Shugar.
"   30, Oliver C. Ritter to Ellen N. Roller.
"   30, Gustave A. Meyer to Alice L. Golmer.
July 16, Jacob D. Harwi to Mary A. Berger.
Aug. 20, Charles C. Bauer to Catharine E. Wetzel.
Sept. 3, James F. Jacoby to Lizzie F. Bachman.
"   3, William H. Blacker to Clara E. Ehret.
"   9, Harrison F. Long to Angelina N. Fox.
"   29, Milton H. Kramer to Annie M. Schmidt.
Oct. 29, Lewis H. Schlosser to Louisa Klotz.
"   30, William H. Wiser to Sarah A. Haman.
Nov. 24, Oscar F. Weber to Emma S. Yeager.
"   26, Charles D. Trexler to Anna M. Schmeier.
Dec. 17, Lewis F. Holzerman to Matilda Brinker.
"   26, John F. Roller to Alice Fogel.
"   26, Peter Biegley to Amanda Reichart.

1882.

Jan. 14, Ambrose Gehman to Alavesta L. Butz.
Feb.   6, Reuben Deshler to Mary A. Zellner.
April 9, Charles Reichard to Emma Wolf.

161

May   2, George A. Sauer to Clorilla Eck.
"   16, James Sacks to Bella J. Stephens.
"   20, Amandus Seipel to Emma Nace.
"   20, Martin Zellner to Emma Koehler.
"   27, Morris C. Rœder to Sarah E. Sterner.
"   27, Richard C. Gackenbach to Alice Wagner.
"   28, John W. Deily to Alavesta S. A. Weil.
June 24, John Fisher to Annie C. Dewald.
July 29, Howard B. Breisch to Emma M. Martz.
Aug. 18, Heinrich J. Huck to Sarah J. Yeager.
Sep. 17, Marcellus F. Boyer to Sarah A. Frey.
"   24, Charles A. Auer to Sarah A. E. Berger.
Oct. 21, Tilghman F. Kidd to Elenora S. Faust.
"   29, Orange D. Nagel to Jane C. Sterner.
"   31, Henry Roback to Mary Ehret.
Nov. 25, Oliver A. Wagner to Sarah Fink.
"   25, Alfred Cope to Araminda Lambert.
"   25, Joseph Lagleder to Amanda King.
"   26, Charles Siegfried to Amelia Nagel.
"   26, Preston Biegley to Laura E. Wieser.
Dec.   3, William Hecker to Emma Klein.
"   16, Alfred P. Wenner to Mary M. Gaumer.
"   16, Charles A. Frey to Sarah P. Muschlitz.

1883.

Jan. 27, Preston A. Lambert to Ida F. Markel.
March 8, Theodore W. Clewell to Fidena Butz.
May   8, Daniel S Hummel to Ida Ritter.
June 26, Alfred Harwi to Emma E. Brug.
July   8, Alfred W. Moyer to Lilly A. Clader.

July 21, Alfred F. Fahlstich to Catharine Schmidt.
Sept. 1, George Rudolph to Clara Cope.
" 18, Wm. H. Foltz to Mary J. Harwi.
Oct. 13, Cyrus L. Hoch to Annie E. Rinker.
" 13, George Neumoyer to Olympia Eckert.
" 17, Llewellyn E. Mosser to Flora R. Lentz.
Nov. 10, William H. Deily to Alice M. Reinhard.
" 18, Walter R. Scheierer to Philippa Ruhe.
Dec. 24, Benj. F. Kemmerer to Jane I. West.
" 29, Amandus Schmidt to Jane A. Mohr.
" 29, Milton Ritter to Emily E. Dotterer.

1884.

Jan. 26, George A. Ueberroth to Lillie H. Weiss.
" 26, Edwin A. Benner to Mary A. Vogel.
March 8, Allen W. Buss to Annie E. Werner.
" 30, James Leisser to Mary S. M. Deily.
May 9, Frank H. Helfrich to Clara C. Schweitzer.
June 2, Wm. C. Dershuck to Lizzie A. Reinhard.
" 17, William Best to Lena Hetfelfinger.
" 25, George Mock to Laura Rudolph.
" 30, James S. Schneider to Susan Dries.
July 26, Augustus Wagner to Agnes Erney.
Aug. 2, Oliver E. Buss to Mary A. Kiechel.
" 2, Milton Fluck to Lena Wagner.
" 9, Andrew F. Stephan to Eliza E. Repp.
" 21, Eugene W. Schlauch to Alice S. Balliet.
" 24, William Acker to Cora Knoll.
Oct. 2, David Baer to Jane M. Fegely.
" 2, Jesse Moyer to Susanna Rottman.

Dec. 6, John J. Albright to Emma S. Koons.
" 23, W. G. Everrett to Mary E. Reph.
" 25, Frank J. J. Miller to Louisa S. Fegely.
" 27, William F. Texter to Maggie A. Bickert.

1885.

Jan. 18, Obadiah Trexler to Claraine Ruhe.
Feb. 1, Joh. H. Ueberroth to Emma Schlosser.
" 1, Benj. H. Neumoyer to Emma Knechel.
March 22, James Lilly to Valeria Hendricks.
July 18, Quintus H. Cope to Alice A. Flexer.
" 25, Alfred S. Leuer to Miss Lapp.
Aug. 3, Uranus Kidd to Emma Danner.
" 22, T. H. J. Derrhamer to Lovina Hillegas.
" 29, Preston Dickson to Emma Reichard.
Sept. 24, P. D. Folk to Effie Ritter.
Dec. 10, F. K. Wolle to Emma M. Torrence.

1886.

Jan. 31, Howard Wuchter to Julia Berger.

CONFIRMATIONS.

Names of Persons Confirmed by Rev. J. Yeager in the Schoenersville Church.

MARCH 29, 1835.

Males.

1 George Bachman,
2 Thomas Frederick,
3 Francis Huber,
4 Conrad Huber,
5 Henry Illick,
6 Nathan Keim,
7 Reuben Schortz,
8 Owen Ritter,
9 Gabriel Thompson,
10 Andrew Keim,
11 Reuben Patterson,
12 Peter Beil,
13 Joseph Bast,
14 Edward Deiley,
15 Solomon Dech,
16 Charles Young,
17 Joseph Smith,
18 Joseph Stuber,
19 Samuel Young,
20 Samuel Keim,
21 William Stuber,
22 Jacob Dech,
23 Robert Daniel,
24 Felix Fenner,
25 Peter Nolf,
26 Samuel Daniel,
27 Samuel Colver,
28 Charles Osenbach,
29 Henry Fatzinger,
30 Samuel Keiper,
31 Charles Quier,
32 William Vesner,
33 Joseph Daniel,
34 George Stuber,
35 Samuel Ritter,
36 James Ray,
37 Henry Snyder.

Females.

1 Mary Ann Lapp,
2 Matilda Bachman,
3 Judith Deiley,
4 Rebecca Huber,
5 Maria Yeager,
6 Elizabeth Fatzinger,
7 Cath. Fry,
8 Juliana Knauss,
9 Juliana Fatzinger,
10 Maria Young,
11 Christiana Florey,
12 Annie Keim.

SCHOENERSVILLE CHURCH AND SCHOOL HOUSE.

13 Sydney George,
14 Maria Edelman,
15 Elemina Miller,
16 Annie E. Stuber,
17 Cath. Roth,
18 Maria Bast,
19 Maria Trone,
20 Susanna Shiffert,
21 Sarah Engler,
22 Maria Stuber,
23 Lydia R. Reaser,
24 Rebecca George, wife.
25 Cath. Fry, wife.

APRIL 23, 1837.

Males.

1 Joseph Young,
2 Henry Ritter,
3 Abraham Sterner,
4 George Sterner,
5 Adam Miller,
6 Adam Daniel,
7 Samuel Roth,
8 Daniel Fogleman,
9 Joseph Moyer,
10 Wm. Moyer,
11 Chas. Mertz,
12 Samuel George,
13 August Getz,
14 Charles Daniel,
15 Peter Snyder,
16 Chas. Deiley,
17 Jos. Deiley.

Females.

1 Catharina Wolf,
2 Louisa Moyer,
3 Maria Schortz,
4 Julia Ritter,
5 Sarah Fatzinger,
6 Eliza Hohl,
7 Cecilia Hohl,
8 Elizabeth Kratzer,
9 Christ. Reaser,
10 Matilda Hower,
11 Cath. Daniel,
12 Sibylla Miller,
13 Anna C. Deiley,
14 Maria Deiley,
15 Caroline Rau,
16 Hettie Grim,
17 Elizabeth Florey,
18 Henrietta Fenner,
19 Eliz. Quier,
20 Juliana Clewell,
21 Sarah Daniel,
22 Belinda Breinig.

APRIL 23, 1839.

Males.

1 Thos. Frankenfield,
2 Wm. Yeager,
3 Wm. Ritter,
4 Wm. Ritter,

5 David Sweitzer,
6 Stephen Ritter,
7 Jos. Gradwohl,
8 Robt. Fogle,
9 Jos. Huber,
10 Martin Fogle,
11 Wm. Sweitzer,
12 Owen Frederick,
13 Jesse Reichard,
14 Geo. Engler,
15 Absalom Sterner,
16 Jacob Koehler,
17 Lewis Kidd,
18 Aaron Young,
19 Stephen Schrechterly,

20 Thos. Stuber,
21 David Keim,
22 Charles Glace,
23 David Young,
24 Reuben Florey,
25 Henry Fatzinger,
26 Thos. Glace,
27 David Reichard,
28 Jacob Miller,
29 Chas. Saylor,
30 Henry Butz,
31 Jos. Young,
32 Chas. Scherer,
33 Felix Bast.

Females.

1 Sarah Hohl,
2 Maria Stahr,
3 Eliz. Stahr,
4 Fyanna Vesner,
5 Maria Fry,
6 Eliz. Osenbach,
7 Eliz. Knauss,
8 Lucretia Hower,
9 Henrietta Miller,
10 Sibylla Zellner,
11 Cath. Engler,
12 Maria Ritter,
13 Elizabeth Keim,
14 Elizabeth Hohl,
15 Susanna Deiley,
16 Caroline Kidd,
17 Rebecca Brooch,

18 Cath. Brooch,
19 Hettie Huber,
20 Christ Rau,
21 Eliz. Reichard,
22 Helena Breinig,
23 Eliz. Harwick,
24 Caroline Harwick,
25 Hannah Young,
26 Alavesta Gross,
27 Sarah Moyer,
28 Eliz. Young,
29 Maria Glace,
30 Hannah Frederick,
31 Lavinia Zerfass,
32 Eliz. Brown,
33 Susanna Bast,
34 Maria Ritter.

April 10, 1841.
Males.

1 Thos. Deiley,
2 Jas. Snyder,

3 Isaac Miller,
4 Geo. Young,
5 Solomon Thompson,
6 Aaron Thompson,
7 Sam. Snyder,
8 Sydney Clewell,
9 Franklin Reichard,
10 David Huber,
11 Peter Quier,
12 Jacob Fatzinger,

13 Jos. Florey,
14 Dav. Moyer,
15 Andrew Kramer,
16 John Ritter,
17 Wm. Hohl,
18 Henry Sterner,
19 Ephraim Daniel,
20 Wm. Bast,
21 Simon Sterner.

Females.

1 Eliz. Leichtley,
2 Henrietta Young,
3 Pauline Getz,
4 Eliz. Young,
5 Cath. Sweitzer,
6 Lavinia Hohle,
7 Lavinia Seibert,
8 Henrietta Reichard,
9 Fyetta Zerfass,
10 Matilda Ritter,

11 Caroline Stuber,
12 Eliz. Newhard,
13 Melinda Snyder,
14 Christina Snyder,
15 Hannah George,
16 Abigail Breinig,
17 Cath. Scherer,
18 Anna Doney,
19 Belinda Shimer,
20 Clara Kiechel.

APRIL 16, 1843.

Males.

1 Peter Glace,
2 Owen Ott,
3 Joseph Kidd,
4 Wm. Hoffert,
5 John Newhard,
6 Reuben Lichtenwalner,
7 Wm. Reichard,
8 Wm. Fatzinger,
9 Lewis Young,
10 Geo. Hoch,
11 Peter Beiche,
12 Geo. Beiche,

13 Josiah Nagle,
14 Owen Clewell,
15 Chas. Sterner,
16 Peter Daniel,
17 Geo. Daniel,
18 Reuben Harrier,
19 Wm. Ritter,
20 Jas. A. Sweitzer,
21 Lewis Ritter,
22 Daniel Peifer,
23 John Fry.

Females.

1 Eliza A. Saylor,
2 Caroline Yeager,
3 Cath. Daniel,
4 Amelia Hohle,
5 Maria A. Snyder,
6 Naomi Breinig,
7 Susanna Vesner,
8 Maria Young,
9 Sophia Snyder,
10 Lydia Weaver,
11 Bella Kidd,
12 Maria Fatzinger,
13 Dianna Fatzinger,
14 Anna M. Minnich,
15 Matilda Quier,
16 Cath. Keim,
17 Sarah A. Fox,
18 Selinda Young,
19 Maria Frankenfield,
20 Elizabeth Frankenfield,
21 Sarah A. Reichard,
22 Paulina Frederick,
23 Cath. Newhard,
24 Caroline Kidd,
25 Eliz. Deiley,
26 Juliana Bergenstock,
27 Eliz. Sterner,
28 Eliz. Kurtz.

APRIL 13, 1845.
Males.

1 Richard Snyder,
2 Lake E. Huber,
3 David O. Saylor,
4 Matthew Winner,
5 Ferdinand Wind,
6 Herman Miller,
7 Nath. Snyder,
8 Simon Breinig,
9 Wm. Wetzler,
10 Paul Kiechel,
11 Jacob Keim,
12 Geo. Dixon,
13 Abram Hertz,
14 Sol. Deiley,
15 Ambrose Snyder.

Females.

1 Caroline Snyder,
2 Lizzie Getz,
3 Clara Getz,
4 Eliz. Snyder,
5 Amelia Snyder,
6 Maria Huber,
7 Caroline Wolf,
8 Susan Buss,
9 Sarah Dech,
10 Juliana Kidd.

FIRST SUNDAY AFTER EASTER, 1847.
Males.

1 Wm. Newhard,
2 Peter Yeakel,
3 Chas. Ritter,
4 Thos. Daniel,

5 Jer. Breinig,
6 Chas. Daniel,
7 Henry Young,
8 Edw. Saylor,
9 Hugh Huber,
10 John Dech,

11 Samuel Roth,
12 Jacob Miller,
13 Jos. Kidd,
14 Samuel Snyder,
15 Jos. Lichtenwalner.

Females.

1 Rebecca Sweitzer,
2 Diana Snyder,
3 Sarah Young,
4 Maria Buss,
5 Juliana Mill,

6 Eliz. Shipe,
7 Fyanna Snyder,
8 Cath. Snyder,
9 Anna Becker.

OCTOBER 22, 1848.

Males.

1 Asher Shimer,
2 Paul Kratzer,
3 John Keim,
4 Tilgh. Fatzinger,
5 Geo. Reichard,
6 Daniel Lichtenwalner,
7 John Crock,

8 Chas. Stamm,
9 Amos Wolf,
10 Wm. H. Wolf,
11 Daniel H. Rohn,
12 Adam Serfass,
13 Wm. Tice.

Females.

1 Caroline Snyder,
2 Eliz. Breinig,
3 Sarah Kidd,
4 Eliza Kratzer,
5 Sus. Fatzinger,
6 Juliana Weber,
7 Louisa Lerch,
8 Sarah Sherer,
9 Sarah Huber,
10 Matilda Daniel,
11 Caroline Huber,
12 Maria Wagner,

13 Maria Lambert,
14 Henrietta Getz,
15 Rebecca Shortz,
16 Matilda Deily,
17 Henrietta Egner,
18 Maria Huber,
19 Caroline Fry,
20 Cath. Rohn,
21 Maria Newhard,
22 Sophia Kreiss,
23 Eliz. Kreiss.

November 17, 1850.

Males.

1 Chas. D. Kidd,
2 Edw. Dech,
3 John Snyder,
4 Josh. Sweitzer,
5 Henry Miller,
6 Wm. Sherer,
7 Henry Fogleman,
8 Ephraim Huber,
9 Wm. D. Rohn,
10 Henry Buss,
11 Reuben Fogleman,
12 Chas. Wind,
13 Edwin Wiener.

Females.

1 Sarah Snyder,
2 Lavinia Newhard,
3 Clara Deiley,
4 Camilla Shimer,
5 Susanna R. Yeager,
6 Elemina A. Rohn,
7 Eliz. Moll,
8 Cath. Anna Lazarus,
9 Sarah A. Fogleman,
10 Mary A. Fatzinger,
11 Sarah Snyder,
12 Sarah J. Miller,
13 Mary Hoch,
14 Sarah Kidd,
15 Caroline Sherer,
16 Maria Daniel.

November 14, 1852.

Males.

1 Wm. E. Illick,
2 Reuben Lazarus,
3 Henry Lazarus,
4 Asa Rohn,
5 E. H. Hunnel,
6 Thos. Dixon,
7 Robt. Fatzinger,
8 Francis Exter,
9 Joseph Wolf.

Females.

1 Matilda Huber,
2 Rebecca Kreiss,
3 Rebecca Dixon,
4 Lavinia Hoch,
5 Matilda Solt,
6 Leah Snyder,
7 Abbie Snyder,
8 Mary A. Reichard,
9 Susanna Hoch,
10 Eliz. C. Rohn,
11 Annie M. Zellner,
12 Susanna Kidd,
13 Mary A. Miller,
14 Anna M. E. Lazarus,
15 Lavinia S. Kratzer.

November 12, 1854.

Males.

1 James B. Snyder,
2 Martin Frankenfield,
3 Reuben Illick,
4 Martin Zellner,
5 James Lichtenwalner,
6 Reuben Daniel,
7 David Wolf,
8 Peter Weaver,
9 Conrad Daniel,
10 Samuel Kidd,
11 Edwin Rohn,
12 James Huber,
13 James Solt,
14 Mich. Reichard,
15 Enoch Snyder,
16 Wm. Rohn,
17 Horatio Yeager.

Females.

1 Eva Hoch,
2 Maria Reichard,
3 Caroline Lazarus,
4 Eliz. Yeakel,
5 Juliana Wenner,
6 Anna C. Buss,
7 Eliza Falstich,
8 Maggie Daniel,
9 Susan Snyder.

November 9, 1856.

Males.

1 Geo. Lazarus,
2 Herman Buss,
3 Frank Snyder,
4 Jacob Reichard,
5 Owen Fatzinger,
6 Edw. Fatzinger,
7 Edw. Andreas,
8 Jacob Kidd,
9 Daniel Uhler,
10 Asher A. Shortz,
11 James Kidd,
12 Edw. Fatzinger,
13 David Zellner,
14 Edwin B. Fogleman,
15 James E. Hoch.

Females.

1 Amelia Ehrig,
2 Amanda Rohn,
3 Camilla Illick,
4 E. Araminda C. Snyder,
5 Maria Zellner,
6 Maria Daniel,
7
8 Maria Schuler,
9 Eliza A. Dech,
10 Sarah E. Solt,
11 Sarah A. Uhler,
12 Matilda Lazarus.

November 7, 1858.
Males.

1 James Wolf,
2 Francis Rohn,
3 John Lynn,
4 Wm. G. Wolf,
5 Cyrus F. Lapp,
6 Levi Young,
7 Nathaniel Kidd,
8 James Wind,
9 Wm. Uhler,
10 John Daniel.

Females.

1 Amanda Fogleman,
2 Mary Heiney,
3 Sarah Buss,
4 Sarah Blotz,
5 Angelina Lichtenwalner,
6 Eliza A. Snyder,
7 Maria E. Snyder,
8 Lavinia Huber,
9 Cath. E. Hoch,
10 Henrietta Stuber.

November 4, 1860.
Males.

1 Wm. H. Crock,
2 Tilgh. M. Lichtenwalner,
3 Cyrus Keim,
4 Wm. Lazarus,
5 Geo. J. Reichard,
6 Christ. Schoeneberger,
7 Jacob Hoch,
8 Edwin Kidd,
9 Wm. H. Hoch,
10 James W. Ray.
11 David Solt,
12 Owen H. Laub,
13 Frank Snyder,
14 Tilgh. Kidd,
15 Richard Gougler.

Females.

1 Belinda Lapp,
2 Amanda Dewalt,
3 Susanna Ray,
4 Aleminta Huber,
5 Elemina Dech,
6 Louisa Dixon,
7 Rebecca Dech,
8 Sibylla Wind,
9 Mary Miller,
10 Sarah Ritter,
11 Sarah Cahoon,
12 Elizabeth Hoch,
13 Elizabeth Uhler,
14 Henrietta Reichard,
15 Eliz. Rockel,
16 Mary A. Reichard,
17 Lavinia Ritter.

November 2, 1862.

Males.

1 Ben. Jacoby,
2 David Daniel,
3 James Frankenfield,
4 Chas. Huber,
5 George Crock,
6 John Hoch,
7 Wm. Solt,
8 James Fatzinger,
9 James Keim,
10 Alfred Steinmetz,
11 Austin Dech,
12 Hiram Kratzer,
13 James Moyer,
14 Adam Wuchter.

Females.

1 Sabina Daniel,
2 Mary Roth,
3 Amanda Schuyler,
4 Eliz. Lazarus,
5 Selinda Laub,
6 Christina Weaver,
7 Eliza Dieter,
8 Caroline Zellner,
9 Eliz. Ritter,
10 Isabella Snyder,
11 Ellen Kidd,
12 Mary Nonnemacher,
13 Clarissa C. Hoch,
14 Alaminda Hoch.

November 6, 1864.

Males.

1 Oliver Pflueger,
2 George Buss,
3 Alfred Fry,
4 Samuel Crock,
5 Amos Heckman,
6 Milton Steinmetz,
7 Chas. Hoch.

Females.

1 Caroline Dixon,
2 Ciniah Fatzinger,
3 Clarissa Ritter,
4 Amanda Sterner,
5 Mary Hummel,
6 Diana Ray,
7 Sarah Heckman,
8 Susanna Steinmetz,
9 Ellen Steinmetz,
10 Ellamanda Ritter.

November 4, 1866.

Males.

1 Milton Buss,
2 Lavinia Schortz,
3 George Hoch,
4 Frank Graver,

5 Martin Crock,
6 Emanuel Ritter,
7 Frank Walter,
8 Martin Illick.

Females.

1 Lavinia Laub,
2 Esther P. Pflueger,
3 Eliza Schortz,
4 Lucinda Hoch,
5 Ella Kidd,
6 Eliz. Schlegel,
7 Caroline Fisher,
8 Elemina Fatzinger,
9 Helena Dixon,
10 Teliah Hoch,
11 Ellen J. Fry.

NOVEMBER 1, 1868.

Males.

1 George F. Deily,
2 Harrison Daniel,
3 John M. Ritter.

Females.

1 Abyssinia Snyder,
2 Mary Brunner,
3 Annie Crock,
4 Mary A. Snyder,
5 Theresa M. Cressman,
6 Montana Schrehr,
7 Rebecca Dieter,
8 Elmira Hoch,
9 Maria Sterner,
10 Ceniah Ritter,
11 Camilla Ritter,
12 Alavesta Steinmetz,
13 Lydia Smith.

OCTOBER 23, 1870.

Males.

1 James Wolf,
2 Asher Steinmetz,
3 James Schortz,
4 John Resh,
5 Benj. Graver,
6 Peter Graver,
7 Wash. Reeser.

Females.

1 Sarah Rape,
2 Ellen Daniel,
3 Trusilla Ritter,
4 Sarah Dixon,
5 Amanda J. Wind,
6 Amanda J. Daniel,
7 Emma Brunner.

December 14, 1872.

Males.

1 Samuel Dech,
2 Henry L. Lapp,
3 Wm. S. Buss,
4 Milton Schlegel,
5 Robt. C. Buss,
6 Leander Laub,
7 Wilson J. Crock,
8 Oliver Laub,
9 Cyrus Hoch,
10 Oliver Sterner,
11 Chas. Brunner,
12 Preston Ritter,
13 Cornelius Cressman,
14 George H. Winch.

Females.

1 Matilda Ritter,
2 Sarah C. Dech,
3 Cath. Geidner,
4 Anna M. Snyder,
5 Lillie C. Fry,
6 Alexander Heckman.

October 25, 1874.

Males.

1 Jacob Seifert, married,
2 George Kleppinger,
3 Wm. Daniel,
4 Richard Daniel,
5 Cyrus Heckman,
6 Wilson Ritter,
7 Addison Ritter,
8 Reuben Patterson.

Females.

1 Elenora Seifert, married,
2 Louisa Reichard, married,
3 Polly Heckman,
4 Emma Reichard.

October 26, 1876.

Males.

1 Alexander Deily,
2 Allen Cressman,
3 Jacob Walter,
4 Eugene Patterson,
5 Wm. Sleider,
6 Clayton Shimer,
7 Milton Kleppinger,
8 Alfred Daniel,
9 Preston Snyder,
10 Harvey Snyder,
11 Sylvester Reichard,
12 Wm. Magges,
13 Peter Hagenbuch.

Females.

1 Mary Woodring,
2 Annie C. Dech,
3 Emma Huber,
4 Ellen Schortz,

5 Ellen Ritter,
6 Amelia Landenguth,
7 Alice Fatzinger,
8 Alice Fleight.

NOVEMBER 10, 1878.

Males.

1 Wm. Hoch,
2 George Patterson,
3 Milton Lichtenwalner,
4 Wm. Minnich,
5 Thomas Bauer,
6 James Lichtenwalner,
7 Wm. Snyder,
8 James Beitler,

9 Thomas Stuber,
10 Wm. Fatzinger,
11 Robert Muschlitz,
12 Owen Reichard,
13 Uranus Kidd,
14 Francis Dieter,
15 George Donnecker,
16 Quilly Ritter.

Females.

1 Amanda Schortz,
2 Lilly Jane Huber,
3 Flora Illick,
4 Cuely A. Snyder,

5 Mary J. Heckman,
6 Agnes Steinmetz,
7 Maria Kratzer,
8 Sarah J. Daniel.

OCTOBER 9, 1880.

Males.

1 Robt. Snyder,
2 Oliver Cressman,

3 Artenas Snyder,
4 Chas. Fatzinger.

Females.

1 Elemanda Muschlitz,
2 Amanda Huth,
3 Emma Beitler,

8 Annie Fatzinger,
9 Carrie Miller,
10 Ansanetta Nickum.

NOVEMBER 5, 1882.

Males.

1 Owen E. Deininger,

2 Harry A. Benner,

Lehigh Church.

3 Geo. E. Deininger,
4 Aaron Steinmetz,
5 Morris Snyder,
6 Harvey Ritter,
7 Freeman Keim,
8 William Huber,
9 Preston Kidd,

10 Owen Lichtenwalner,
11 John Kidd,
12 Alfred Sterner,
13 Harvey Buss,
14 Marcus G. Heckman,
15 Oliver E. Buss.

Females.

1 Clara A. M. Huber,
2 Minnie Frankenfield,
3 Ada Frankenfield,
4 Emma Hackman,
5 Ellouisa Crock,

6 Emma Lilly,
7 Ida Lichtenwalner,
8 Juliana C. Keim,
9 Henrietta Stuber,
10 Ida E. Wolfe.

NOVEMBER 1, 1884.

Males.

1 William Wolfe,
2 Henry Crock,
3 Charles Huber,
4 Samuel Keim,
5 Harry Lichtenwalner,
6 Grant J. Snyder,

7 Oliver Muschlitz,
8 Frank Fatzinger,
9 James Muschlitz,
10 Clinton Illick,
11 Harrison Moyer.

Females.

1 Jane Lilly,
2 Ida Huber,
3 Ellen Minnich,
4 Mary Fatzinger,

5 Annie Crock,
6 Mary J. Hoch,
7 Matilda Hohl,
8 Emmelia Jacoby.

Names of Persons Confirmed at Lehigh Church.

APRIL 2, 1843.

Males.

1 Henry Yoder,
2 Reuben Fegley,

3 Peter Fegley,
4 Reuben Gernert,

5 Jonas Bortz,
6 Charles Breinig,
7 Jonas Schmoyer,
8 Henry Romig,

9 Henry Knappenberger,
10 Henry Schankweiler,
11 Jonas Knappenberger.

Females.

1 Susanna Gehry,
2 Carolina Schmoyer,
3 Elvina Schmoyer,
4 Elizabeth Newmoyer,
5 Carolina Albright,

6 Helena Schoemaker,
7 Susanna Breinig,
8 Sarah Clauss,
9 Matilda Bitting.

APRIL 26, 1845.

Males.

1 Charles Schmoyer,
2 Jonas Bear,
3 James Breinig,

4 Tilghman Schmoyer,
5 Solomon Becker.

Females.

1 Lucretia Albright,
2 Maria Schmoyer,
3 Carolina Mill,
4 Elvina Breinig,
5 Yetta Brey,
6 Annie Yeager,
7 Elizabeth Schmoyer,
8 Maria Gorr,
9 Maria Muth,

10 Harrietta Knappenberger,
11 Hannah Herbst,
12 Lovina Schmoyer,
13 Carolina Mattern,
14 Annie M. Schmoyer,
15 Rosalinda Schmoyer,
16 Christianna Newmoyer,
17 Maria Ring,
18 Elizabeth Danner.

APRIL 25, 1847.

Males.

1 Henry Weiand,
2 Nicodemus Schuler,
3 John Weaver,
4 William Romig,
5 David Frederich,

6 Daniel Trexler,
7 Jacob Frederich,
8 Tilghman Dennis,
9 Henry Mill,
10 Charles Schmoyer.

Females.

1 Maria Weiand,
2 Annie Hain,
3 Annie M. Frederich,
4 Sarah Knappenberger,
5 Isabella Fegley,
6 Elizabeth Schuman,

7 Maria Frederich,
8 Sarah Kline,
9 Clarissa Schuler,
10 Ellenora Mohr,
11 Sarah Mattern.

MARCH 20, 1849.

Males.

1 Israel Schmoyer,
2 Frank Romig,
3 John Frederich,
4 Jonas Johnston,

5 Henry Billiard,
6 Levi Clauss,
7 James Weile,
8 Henry Weile.

Females.

1 Carolina Knappenberger,
2 Ellamanda Clauss,
3 Judith Frederich,
4 Carolina Frederich,
5 Mary A. Amig,

6 Eliza Kline,
7 Emeline Schmoyer,
8 Annie M. Breinig,
9 Emeline Schmoyer,
10 Annie E. Breinig.

APRIL 18, 1851.

The records of this year are missing.

1853.

Males.

1 John Durey,
2 Frank H. Yeager,
3 William T. Breinig,
4 Conrad Amig,

5 Edwin Hinckel,
6 Stephen Frederick,
7 Tilghman Boger,
8 Jonathan Knappenberger.

Females.

1 Elizabeth Schmoyer,
2 Lydia Trexler,
3 Eliza Warmkessel,

4 Rosa Breinig,
5 Amanda Schmoyer,
6 Jane A. Breinig,

7 Emma Bauder,
8 Elizabeth Hoffner,
9 Sarah Wagner,
10 Elvina Gorr,
11 Henrietta Amig.

April 15, 1855.
Males.

1 John H. B. Jarret,
2 Henry Knappenberger,
3 Jacob Wagner,
4 Henry J. C. Trexler,
5 Manuel Warmkessel,
6 Charles H. Ettinger,
7 David Bear,
8 Harrison Knappenberger.

Females.

1 Carolina Schmoyer,
2 Amelia Schwartz,
3 Amanda Dreisbach,
4 Christiana Eisenbrown,
5 Eliza M. Wagner,
6 Eliza A. Knappenberger,
7 Matilda Shankweiler,
8 Lydia Hineley,
9 Emeline Clauss,
10 Maria A. Hamman,
11 Maria A. Romig,
12 Elizabeth A. Wagner.

April 12, 1857.
Males.

1 Sassaman Kline,
2 Charles H. Hineley,
3 James Frederich,
4 Francis Boger,
5 Lewis Dennis,
6 Levi Lichtenwalner,
7 Jerres Roth,
8 Henry Schmoyer.

Females.

1 Maria A. Lichtenwalner,
2 Lovina Schmoyer,
3 Sarah Gorr,
4 Mary A. Romig,
5 Lovina Frederich,
6 Emeline Ettinger,
7 Mary A. Breinig,
8 Maria Trexler.

May 8, 1859.
Males.

1 Jacob B. Warmkessel,
2 Benneville Frederich,
3 Jacob B. Lichtenwalner,
4 Solomon G. Schmoyer,

5 William H. Shankweiler,
6 Wm. Knappenberger,
7 Elias A. Schmoyer,
8 Edwin Frederich,
9 Frank Oberdorf,
10 Edwin P. Schmoyer.

Females.

1 Catharine M. Bickel,
2 Annie L. Shearer,
3 Carolina Johnston,
4 Ellenora Shankweiler,
5 Amanda Boger,
6 Elizabeth Hineley,
7 Carolina Clauss,
8 Matilda R. Clauss,
9 Maria A. Kline,
10 Eliza Ettinger,
11 Rebecca Billiard,
12 Helena Schmoyer,
13 Melinda Roth.

April 7, 1861.

Males.

1 Henry Romig,
2 Stephen Trexler,
3 Mifflin E. Keck,
4 Wm. M. Keck,
5 Horatio Shankweiler,
6 James P. Schmoyer,
7 Obadiah Miller,
8 Edwin Fritz.

Females.

1 Catharine Trexler,
2 Hannah Schmoyer,
3 Matilda Schmoyer,
4 Ellenora Schmoyer,
5 Deborah Keck,
6 Alavesta Kuhns,
7 Marguretta Frederich,
8 Matilda Frederich,
9 Deliah Warmkessel,
10 Catharine Schmoyer,
11 Rebecca Miller,
12 Annie Schuler,
13 Sarah Bittenbender,
14 Susanna Schmoyer,
15 Amelia Knappenberger,
16 Rosalinda Fegley.

1863.

Males.

1 Seth Lichtenwalner,
2 Wm. H. Schmoyer,
3 Hiram M. Ettinger,
4 Jonas Hander,
5 Benj. A. Schmoyer,
6 Lewis S. Schmoyer,
7 Henry Romig.

Females.

1 Maria M. Warmkessel,
2 Sarah Lichtenwalner,
3 Emma A. Kuhns,
4 Carolina Blitenloe,
5 Mary E. Fritz,
6 Susanna Boger,
7 Mary A. Boger,
8 Maria Albright,
9 Sarah A. Gilbert,
10 Margaretta Shankweiler,
11 Amanda Kline,
12 Sarah E. Gift,
13 Elvina Boger,
14 Eliza A. Dengler.

APRIL 1, 1865.
Males.

1 Oliver N. Mosser,
2 George N. Kuhns,
3 Cyrus P. Slide,
4 George A. Clauss,
5 Wm. Knappenberger,
6 James Shankweiler,
7 Henry P. Knappenberger,
8 Franklin Warmkessel,
9 Charles Heist,
10 Benj. J. Schmoyer,
11 Milton A. Schmoyer,
12 John A. Albright,
13 Jeremiah C. Fritz,
14 Jeremiah S. Kuhns.

Females.

1 Hannah A. Mosser,
2 Hannah C. Maberry,
3 Catharine Miller,
4 Jane A. Schmoyer,
5 Amelia Schmoyer,
6 Eliza T. Schmoyer,
7 Susanna C. Schmoyer,
8 Martha A. Kuhns,
9 Catharine Warmkessel,
10 Amanda J. Knappenberger.

MARCH 31, 1867.
Males.

1 George W. Schmoyer,
2 Chas. E. Lichtenwalner,
3 Thomas Bast,
4 James T. Clauss,
5 Peter Diefenderfer,
6 Elias S. Frederich,
7 Samuel J. Smith,
8 James Trexler,
9 Euallen J. Schmoyer,
10 Alfred Trexler,
11 Charles Bower,
12 Daniel Dangler,
13 Alexander Swanger,
14 Addison Miller,
15 Amaziah Miller,
16 George Knedler.

183

Females.

1 Emma J. Schmoyer,
2 Ellen J. Warmkessel,
3 Susanna Lichtenwalner,
4 Cath. Laudenslager, —
5 Helena Koch,
6 Emma M. Breinig,
7 Emma L. Schmoyer,
8 Annie J. Clauss,
9 Annie M. Snyder,
10 Martha Ann E. Shankweiler,
11 Amelia A. Shankweiler,
12 Sarah A. Shankweiler,
13 Agnes L. Schmoyer,
14 Annie Frederich,
15 Mary A. Romig,
16 Annie M. Knappenberger,
17 Mary A. Warst,
18 Susanna E. Dengler,
19 Alavesta E. Mohr,
20 Mary A. E. Bast.

MARCH 28, 1869.
Males.

1 Joshua L. Schmoyer,
2 George E. A. Bear,
3 Augustus Weaver,
4 George D. B. Schmoyer,
5 David S. Ludwig,
6 Oscar J. Schmoyer,
7 Joseph A. Warmkessel,
8 James F. A. Smith,
9 David Knappenberger,
10 Kosmus Miller,
11 Henry A. Mohr,
12 Thomas J. Shankweiler,
13 Penrose Knappenberger,
14 James W. Schmoyer.

Females.

1 Clara Bluch,
2 Elemanda E. Knappenberger,
3 Louisa S. Kuhns,
4 Louisa E. E. Boger,
5 Carolina S. Bower,
6 Emeline Miller,
7 Eliza A. Shankweiler,
8 Augusta E. Rest,
9 Melinda S. Knappenberger,
10 Catharine S. Gaummer,
11 Emma C. Marsteller,
12 Mary M. Esser.

APRIL 9, 1871.
Males.

1 Pearce Bear,
2 Henry Gaummer,
3 Alvin S. Ludwig,
4 Charles P. Hoffman,
5 George S. Albright,
6 Benj. S. Diefenderfer,
7 Alvin Schmoyer,
8 Wm. H. Trump,
9 Horace Schmoyer,
10 Wm. Rohrbach.

Females.

1 Annie R. Boger,
2 Rosa E. Schmoyer,
3 Louisa L. Lichtenwalner,
4 Louisa E. Schmoyer,
5 Paulina L. Schmoyer,
6 Alavesta Fogel,
7 Elmira Laudenslager,
8 Elmira E. Schmoyer,
9 Hannah Schmoyer,
10 Ellen Diefenderfer,
11 Catharine Snyder,
12 Christiana Gaummer,
13 Emma Bear,
14 Emma Nice,
15 Susanna E. Warmkessel,
16 Ida V. Mosser,
17 Annie L. Ritter,
18 Amanda Wenner,
19 Catharine Shankweiler.

April 20, 1873.

Males.

1 James J. Bear,
2 James A. Miller,
3 Francis Warmkessel,
4 George S. Ludwig,
5 Seranus Bloch,
6 David G. Slenker,
7 Oscar Diefenderfer,
8 Lewis F. Wenner,
9 Alfred S. Wenner,
10 Nathan D. E. Gaummer.
11 Oscar Marsteller,
12 Wm. Schmoyer,
13 Peter H. Albright,
14 Benj. Litzenberger.

Females.

1 Aquilla Warmkessel,
2 Annie L. Bittenbender,
3 Ellen V. Schmoyer,
4 Ellen J. Schmoyer,
5 Mary Haydt,
6 Louisa L. Wendling.

April 18, 1875.

Males.

1 Francis H. Gilbert,
2 H. W. Jacob,
3 John A. Jacob,
4 James O. Jacob,
5 Wm. A. Smith,
6 John A. Dierolf,
7 Irvin D. Miller,
8 Alfred J. Litzenberger,
9 Charles E. Bear,
10 Henry S. Schlenker,
11 Charles Brensinger.

Females.

1 Ellen A. Gaummer,
2 Sarah E. Bittenbender,
3 Alice M. Resh,
4 Louisa C. Miller,
5 Sarah Schmoyer,
6 Hettie E. Diefenderfer,
7 Ellen C. Warmkessel,
8 Callistina R. Klotz,
9 Charlotta M. Schlenker,
10 Paulina A. Eisenhart,
11 Sarah E. Gilbert,
12 Elizabeth L. Dengler.

APRIL 15, 1877.

Males.

1 A. Warmkessel,
2 John J. Becker,
3 Victor M. Gaummer,
4 Lewis O. Shankweiler,
5 Morris S. Fogel,
6 Oliver J. Schmoyer,
7 Franklin Haydt,
8 Charles T. Trexler,
9 Henry H. Miller,
10 Calvin H. Miller,
11 Morris F. Nice,
12 Henry P. Nice,
13 Charles M. Schmoyer,
14 Albert T. Breinig,
15 Edwin C. Schmoyer,
16 James F. Jacoby.

Females.

1 Susanna C. Romig,
2 Amanda M. Wenner,
3 Sarah M. Laudenslager,
4 Ellen N. Miller,
5 Angelina J. Maberry,
6 Ellen J. Breinig,
7 Mary S. Breinig.

APRIL 13, 1879.

Males.

1 Jonas J. Smith,
2 Wm. M. Fritz,
3 Lewis O. Gaummer,
4 Oscar Wenner,
5 Ezekiel Stuffled.

Females.

1 Priscilla Gaummer,
2 Mary A. Gaummer,
3 Annie A. Lichty,
4 Kate E. Albright,
5 Emma D. Schmoyer,
6 Maria S. Bittenbender,
7 Sallie E. Schmoyer,
8 Marie C. Breinig.

April, 1881.
Males.

1 Jacob S. Christ,
2 John J. Resh,
3 Frank J. Miller,
4 Elmer G. Ziegenfuss,
5 Morris W. Gehman,
6 Richard S. Breinig.
7 John J. Schmoyer,
8 Elmer E. Lichtenwalner.
9 George D. Gilbert,
10 James M. Miller,
11 Lucas Warmkessel,
12 Harvey A. Miller.

Females.

1 Ellen J. Gaummer,
2 Catharine M. Butz,
3 Emma E. Breinig,
4 Ida Ritter,
5 Emma S. Kuhns,
6 Eliza M. Weaver,
7 Hannah F. Becker,
8 Annie A. Lichtenwalner,
9 Louisa M. Miller,
10 Mary M. Miller,
11 Ellenora Becker,
12 Sarah E. Bailey,
13 Catharine Zeigenfuss.

November 17, 1882.
Males.

1 Frank Butz,
2 Wm. A. Trexler,
3 Wilson J. Resh,
4 Samuel S. Schmoyer,
5 Victor D. Schmoyer,
6 Irvin B. Ritter,
7 George A. Amig,
8 Oscar E. Osenwald,
9 Oscar R. Moyer,
10 Mervin P. Ettinger,
11 Oscar D. B. Bleiler,
12 Oliver Bause,
13 Lewis Stauffer,
14 Wm. H. Trexler,
15 Wm. A. Sensenderfer,
16 Harvey F. Hausman,
17 Alfred Shankweiler,
18 Irvin Knapp,
19 Thomas Knappenberger.

Females.

1 Hannah R. Gaummer,
2 Rebecca Lichty,
3 Alice C. Schmoyer,
4 Effie Ritter,
5 Clara A. Miller,
6 Alice L. Warmkessel,
7 Ellen L. Amig,
8 Emma L. Warmkessel,
9 Ida Hinkel,
10 Caroline E. Boger,
11 Jane E. Schmoyer,
12 Amelia Ellis.
13 Eliza J. Bittenbender.

1884.

Males.

1 Morris Amig,
2 Victor W. L. Wenner,
3 Franklin Trexler,
4 George Trexler,
5 Franklin H. Jacoby,
6 Harvey E. A. Smith,
7 Willis A. D. Schmoyer,
8 Charles W. Schmoyer.

Females.

1 Clara J. E. Seip,
2 Carrie L. M. Sensenderfer,
3 Rebecca C. D. Herbert,
4 Sarah C. Hertzog,
5 Laura E. Gammer,
6 Emma A. Weaver,
7 Victoria J. Bittenbender,
8 Laura C. H. Miller,
9 Ida C. Butz,
10 Alice F. Angstett,
11 Kate Haydt,
12 Ellen C. Shankweiler,
13 Irene S. F. Sensenderfer,
14 Maggie H. Raudenbush
15 Lina A. Romig,
16 Ida M. Shankweiler,
17 Nora P. Lichty,
18 Ellen V. Shankweiler,
19 Marcella E. Bickel,
20 Mary E. S. Seislove.

Confirmed in St. Paul's Church, Allentown, Pa.

October 30, 1881.

Males.

1 Martin Ritter,
2 John Ritter,
3 Gideon Ritter,
4 Reuben Ritter,
5 Charles Knappenberger,
6 Daniel Fatzinger,
7 David Barrett,
8 Charles Reichard,
9 Charles Schreier,
10 Joseph Nunemacher,
11 William Schoppert,
12 William Gangewere,
13 George Alshouse,
14 John Seip,
15 Jonas Herz,
16 Charles Hoffert,
17 Reuben Helfrich,
18 Frederick Ruhe,
19 Jacob Hauf,
20 Nathan Miller,
21 Lorenz Ibach,
22 Charles Deily.

Females.

1 Abigail Edelman,
2 Henrietta Bean,
3 Henrietta Ruhe,
4 Mary A. Seip,
5 Catharine Laudenschlager,
6 Leah Walter,
7 Mary A. Strassberger,
8 Elizabeth Gangewere,
9 Mary A. Koch,
10 Lucy Brobst,
11 Anna Koch,
12 Sarah Seip,
13 Mary Grollinger,
14 Abigail Saeger,
15 Henrietta Beitel,
16 Lucy A. Hartzel,
17 Susanna Bauer,
18 Lucinda Holl,
19 Christianna Dachtman,
20 Carolina Sterner,
21 Regina Geister,
22 Mary Saeger,
23 Sophia Litzenberger,
24 Mary Miller,
25 Lovina Trexler,
26 Mary Schmidt,
27 Mary Young,
28 Anna Kohn.

April 7, 1833.
Males.

1 Joseph F. Newhard,
2 David Stamm,
3 Peter Bernetz,
4 Peter Rommel,
5 Israel Trexler,
6 John Fatzinger,
7 Charles Deily,
8 Owen Saeger,
9 Herman E. Stein,
10 Henry Nunemacher,
11 Edward O. Reichard,
12 William H. Mertz,
13 Jacob Nagel,
14 Daniel Ritter,
15 Samuel J. Knauss,
16 Reuben E. Beidelman,
17 Henry Bachert,
18 Daniel Frey,
19 Levi Gross,
20 Henry Ritter,
21 Nathan Lautenschlager,
22 Henry Nagel,
23 Levi Hartzel.
24 Elias Schaeffer,
25 Daniel Ritter,
26 Martin Ritter,
27 Abraham Yohe,
28 Adam Hoffert,
29 Reuben Hartzel,
30 Benjamin Krauss.

Females.

1 Lisetta Newhard,
2 Elizabeth Reichard,
3 Lucinda Kleckner,
4 Mary Beidelman,

5 Mary A. Colver,
6 Sarah Long,
7 Sarah Trexler,
8 Lovina Ritter,
9 Harriette Kneipp,
10 Louisa Ueberroth,
11 Barbara Breinig,
12 Sarah Gutekunst,
13 Rebecca Worman,
14 Emmelina Johnson,
15 Mary Beitel,
16 Lavinia Rieb,
17 Lydia Walter,
18 Matilda Stein,
19 Mary Gangawere,
20 Mary Brecht,
21 Jufinia Gangwer,
22 Lustie A. Raster,
23 Elizabeth Waldman,
24 Mary Balliet,
25 Mary Nunemacher,
26 Louisa Deily.

AUGUST 4, 1834.
Males.

1 Henry Haberacker,
2 John Horn,
3 John Nunemacher,
4 Stephen Keck,
5 Elias Kerschner,
6 Aaron Bast,
7 Michael Harwick,
8 Peter Harwick,
9 Charles Frey,
10 Jacob Ritter,
11 Peter Nunemacher,
12 Charles Stahr,
13 Daniel Gilbert,
14 Daniel Glass,
15 Charles Kratzer,
16 William Seip,
17 William Gebhard.

Females.

1 Sarah Schiffert,
2 Catharine Reinhard,
3 Sarah Ritter,
4 Anna Schreer,
5 Rebecca Scherer,
6 Elizabeth Rummel,
7 Elizabeth Brinker,
8 Elizabeth Nunemacher,
9 Sarah Kramer,
10 Catharine Dahlman,
11 Catharine Keck,
12 Lydia Ibach,
13 Rebecca Schneider,
14 Mary Egge,
15 Elizabeth Kleckner.

APRIL 1, 1836.
Males.

1 Augustus F. Halbach,
2 Samuel Edelman,
3 Charles Klein,
4 Solomon Ritter,

5 Daniel Stein,
6 Charles Ritter,
7 Ephraim Leschter,
8 Joseph Seip,
9 John Rader,
10 Michael Meschter,
11 John Ginkinger,
12 Charles Sterner,
13 Joseph Krause,
14 Eli Sager,
15 Aaron Wind,
16 Jacob Ruhe,

17 David Schantz,
18 Owen Schaus,
19 Abraham Ibach,
20 Jacob Reimel,
21 William Keck,
22 Samuel Gentner,
23 Jesse Hunsberger,
24 Jacob Yost,
25 Charles Wenner,
26 Peter Wenner,
27 Abraham Keck,
28 Ephraim Horlacher.

Females.

1 Catharine Horlacher,
2 Rebecca Stahr,
3 Anna Haupt,
4 Rebecca Kleckner,
5 Catharine Weil,
6 Sarah A. Ludwig,
7 Matilda Moeller,
8 Mary Trexler,
9 Mary Yost,
10 Elizabeth Ritter,
11 Sarah Ritter,
12 Rebecca Frey,
13 Lucinda Klotz,
14 Mary Keiter,
15 Susanna Lautenschlager,
16 Rebecca Ueberroth,
17 Elizabeth Fatzinger,
18 Mary Helfrich,
19 Matilda Ritter,
20 Sarah Gangawer,

21 Sabina Saeger,
22 Sarah Miller,
23 Mary Reichart,
24 Sarah Bacher,
25 Elizabeth Bacher,
26 Mary Kratzer,
27 Sarah Reimel,
28 Mary Young,
29 Sarah Mester,
30 Sarah Kramer,
31 Sarah Nagel,
32 Alavesta Hertz,
33 Elizabeth Miller,
34 Alavesta Miller,
35 Catharine Bast,
36 Carolina Reichert,
37 Mary Schneider,
38 Elizabeth Stein,
39 Hannah Roth.

APRIL 1, 1838.
Males.

1 George Gross,   2 Charles Scholl,

3 Charles Nagel,
4 Charles Newhard,
5 Charles Geidner,
6 Edmund Balliet,
7 Charles Martin,
8 Aaron Keiter,
9 Thomas Hallbach,
10 Charles Drumhardt,
11 Amos Bacher,
12 George Brong,
13 Joshua M. Lowry,
14 Ephraim Wimmer,
15 Charles Reinhard,
16 Daniel Roth,
17 Charles Keck,
18 Franklin Gebhard,
19 William Nagel,
20 Charles Keiter,
21 Solomon Koch,
22 Nathan Nagel,
23 Aaron Yohe,
24 William Egge,
25 John Trexler,
26 Henry Frey,
27 Franklin Kramer,
28 George Gangwer,
29 William Seip,
30 Samuel Young,
31 Jonas Hartzel,
32 William Drumhardt,
33 Josiah Nagel,
34 Reuben Osmann,
35 Samuel Brinker,
36 Charles Ritter,
37 David Scheetz,
38 Charles Seip,
39 Henry Gumpert,
40 John Young.

Females.

1 Mary Ginkinger,
2 Alavesta Ruhe,
3 Mary Raub,
4 Lydia Fetzer,
5 Leah Ueberroth,
6 Elizabeth Colver,
7 Mary Bast,
8 Lavinia Hoffert,
9 Mary Nagel,
10 Matilda Daniel,
11 Hetty Roth,
12 Mary Gabel,
13 Lydia Litzenberger,
14 Rebecca Roth,
15 Mary Hartzell,
16 Hannah Leibensperger,
17 Mary Bacher,
18 Susanna Ellender,
19 Mary Ludwig,
20 Elizabeth Laudenschlager,
21 Juliana Ginkinger,
22 Mary Horn,
23 Polly Gabel,
24 Matilda Ritter,
25 Sarah Bauer,
26 Polly Hunsberger,
27 Sarah Hunsberger,
28 Caroline M. Fetzer,
29 Hannah Seip,
30 Sarah Egge,
31 Henrietta Ueberroth,
32 Rebecca Mester,
33 Emmelina Scholl,
34 Sarah Stahr,

35 Cecilia Gold,
36 Catharine Stem,
37 Margaretha Nagel,
38 Mary Heckman,
39 Mary Gutekunst,

40 Susanna Gangawer,
41 Henrietta Seip,
42 Matilda Seip,
43 Elizabeth Sager.

APRIL 26th, 1840.

Males.

1 Franklin Sager,
2 William Balliet,
3 George Stein,
4 James Geidner,
5 Edwin Keck,
6 Solomon Keck,
7 Edward Quier,
8 Joseph Glase,
9 Charles Kemmerer,
10 Edwin Ritter,
11 Nathan Ritter,
12 John Hoffert,
13 James Bush,
14 Andrew Hoffert,
15 William Haupt,
16 Thomas Ginkinger,
17 George Ruhe,
18 Charles Ginkinger,
19 Nelson Weiser,
20 Edward Remmel,
21 John Kratzer,

22 Charles Rieb,
23 William Newhard,
24 William Rieb,
25 Hiram Brobst,
26 Joseph Reichart,
27 Simon Keck,
28 Henry Zuber,
29 Josiah Strauss,
30 Levi Stahr,
31 Jacob Sendel,
32 John Ruth,
33 Thomas Hoffert,
34 Daniel Geisler,
35 Amandus Hoffert,
36 Peter Ueberroth,
37 Charles Nunnemacher,
38 Moses Kramer,
39 Owen Gutekunst,
40 Solomon Blank,
41 Edward Schnear,
42 Joseph Scott.

Females.

1 Amelia Ruhe,
2 Susanna Stein,
3 Eleminda Martin,
4 Sarah Haberacker,
5 Matilda Keck,
6 Sophia Ginkinger,

7 Anna J. Scherer,
8 Laura Keck,
9 Matilda Ihrig,
10 Mary Hoffert,
11 Mary Trexler,
12 Susanna Laury,

13 Carolina Reinhard,
14 Carolina Trexler,
15 Sarah Geister,
16 Anna Leibensperger,
17 Henrietta Waltmann,
18 Mary Edelman,
19 Mary Seip,
20 Elizabeth Fusselman,
21 Sophia Young,
22 Ellen Raub,
23 Catharina Shick,
24 Abigail Acker,

25 Hannah Hartzel,
26 Susanna Beidler,
27 Eliza Eshenbach,
28 Judith Fetzer,
29 Mary Schmetzer,
30 Anna J. Ginget,
31 Sabina Sigfried,
32 Catharina Keiter,
33 Sarah Kratzer,
34 Lydia Ueberroth,
35 Eliza Keck.

MARCH 27, 1842.

Males.

1 John Newhard,
2 Charles Bachman,
3 Charles Gangawere,
4 Aaron Frankenfield,
5 Tilghman Eisenhard,
6 Edward Kratzer,
7 William Young,
8 Charles Young,
9 Thomas Seip,
10 William Roth,
11 Reuben Roth,
12 Gideon Roth,
13 Francis Schmelzer,

14 William Kuntz,
15 Charles Ritter,
16 Martin Ritter,
17 John Eschenbach,
18 Joseph Deily,
19 Jonas Hartzell,
20 Henry Egge,
21 Philip Nagel,
22 Francis Gold,
23 Henry Kleckner,
24 George Nagel,
25 Harry A. Nagel,
26 Abraham Himmelberger.

Females.

1 Mary Hagenbuch,
2 Louisa Giess,
3 Catharine Yeager,
4 Hannah Hunt,
5 Caroline Ludwig,
6 Mary Eisenbrown,
7 Marianna Sager,

8 Sarah Rieb,
9 Susanna Waldman,
10 Matilda Stein,
11 Mary Leibensperger,
12 Henrietta Balliet,
13 Mary A. Horn,
14 Elemina Horn,

15 Elemina Trexler,
16 Mary Albright,
17 Mary Geister,
18 Anna Kuhlmann,
19 Rosina Kiehe,
20 Mary Erig,
21 Catharine Kratzer,
22 Sarah Osman,
23 Mary Ritter,
24 Anna Ritter,
25 Elizabeth Kemmerer,

26 Lucy Ann Fuselman,
27 Christianna Deily,
28 Elemina Ruhe,
29 Sarah Eschenbach,
30 Lavinia Reichenbach,
31 Elemina Bauder,
32 Sarah Beitler,
33 Sarah Reichert,
34 Lucy Brobst,
35 Wilhelmina Lazarus,
36 Elizabeth Kech.

APRIL 21, 1844.
Males.

1 William Geidner,
2 Charles Halbach,
3 William Getz,
4 Samuel Roth,
5 Solomon Ihrig,
6 Charles H. Trexler,
7 Joel Sterner,
8 William Sterner,
9 John Yost,
10 William Scholl,
11 Charles Hagenbach,
12 David Diefenderfer,
13 Henry Seip,
14 Benjamin Knauss,
15 Josiah Lucas,
16 Harrison Young,
17 Charles Ihrig,

18 John Beidler,
19 Reuben Nagel,
20 Albert Newhard,
21 James A. Kramer,
22 Henry J. Ruhe,
23 Silas H. Newhard,
24 Josiah Wieser,
25 Francis Lehr,
26 Levi Frankenfield,
27 Kosmos Scott,
28 Jacob F. Bacher,
29 Edmund P. Kuntz,
30 Charles M. Stuber,
31 Walter F. Scholl,
32 Charles Fetzer,
33 John Sterner.

Females.

1 Elizabeth Rinker,
2 Mary Kuntz,
3 Fyetta Yoder,
4 Dianna Sterner,
5 Sarah Wagner,

6 Isabella Seip,
7 Matilda Totlen,
8 Sarah Schmelzer,
9 Lovina Klein,
10 Sarah Lautenschlager,

11 Charlotte Eisenbrown,
12 Mary Kramer,
13 Mary Ruhe,
14 Sarah Roth,
15 Louisa Seip,
16 Selina Moyer,
17 Sarah A. Leiser,
18 Mary Walter,
19 Rebecca Hartzel,
20 Abigail Ludwig,
21 Elizabeth Kratzer,
22 Anna Kuhns,
23 Mary Steinberger,
24 Ansenetta Nagel,
25 Christianna A. Kneller,
26 Lydia Keiter,
27 Hettie Ruhf,
28 Elizabeth Kistler,
29 Cath. Fusselman,
30 Maria Kemmerer.

April 19, 1846.

Males.

1 Charles L. Keck,
2 Andrew Keck,
3 Walter Miller,
4 Tilghman Roth,
5 Henry Reichard,
6 Solomon Roth,
7 Monroe Trexler,
8 Solomon Bacher,
9 Jonas Lowry,
10 Tilghman H. Ibach,
11 David Wieser,
12 Ephraim Yost,
13 Henry Nagel,
14 Henry A. Scholl,
15 Charles L. Hohlman,
16 William J. Stein,
17 Henry J. Horn,
18 Ephraim Roth.

Females.

1 Eliza Geidner,
2 Rebecca Bacher,
3 Dianna Walter,
4 Sarah A. Hoffert,
5 Isabella Kramer,
6 Adeline Schmauk,
7 Eliza A. Ludwig,
8 Mary A. Wetzel,
9 Rebecca Klein,
10 Mary Keck,
11 Mary Johanna Gangwer,
12 Mary Acker,
13 Leah Keck,
14 Eliza Kemmerer,
15 Rebecca Leibensperger,
16 Mary A. G. Schantz,
17 Mary A. Scholl,
18 Eliza Yohn,
19 Leah Lazarus,
20 Matilda Fatzinger,
21 Hettie Keiter,
22 Elemina Strauss,
23 Caroline Mahn,
24 Elizabeth Straly.

April 16, 1848.

Males.

1 Ephraim Brobst,
2 Franklin Ihrig,
3 Franklin Balliet,
4 Tilghman Kramer,
5 Henry Lautenschlager,
6 John Hallman,
7 Depew Ueberroth,
8 David Sendel,
9 William Weil,
10 James Weil,
11 Edward Ruhe,
12 Daniel Miller,
13 Daniel Kemmerer,
14 Joseph Sterner,
15 William Ritz,
16 Benjamin Roth,
17 Edwin Behrenkopf,
18 Eli Kratzer,
19 Peter Albright,
20 Jonathan Sterner,
21 George Sterner,
22 David Sterner,
23 Daniel Brobst,
24 Jeremiah Strahly,
25 Daniel Scholl,
26 Moses Wuchter,
27 Reuben Trexler,
28 Abner Trexler,
29 Thomas Reichard,
30 Thomas Diehm,
31 Daniel Schafer,
32 Solomon Ludwig,
33 George Miller,
34 James Trexler,
35 William Halteman,
36 Edward Ueberroth,
37 Aaron Raub,
38 Tilghman Kleckner,
39 Edwin Strauss,
40 George Roth,
41 Jonas Raub,
42 Daniel Young,
43 P. F. Eisenbrown.

Females.

1 Mary A. Lazarus,
2 Sarah Hauser,
3 Catharine Gougler,
4 Lovina Gougler,
5 Christianna Reichard,
6 Eliza Yeager,
7 Mary Miller,
8 Lovina Kemmerer,
9 Lovina Schweitzer,
10 Mary A. Reichard,
11 Angelina Huff,
12 Caroline Ihrich,
13 Matilda Kratzer,
14 Hetty Roth,
15 Catharine Hiltebeitel,
16 Eliza Wieser,
17 Ellen Kramer,
18 Rebecca Ruhe,
19 Cecilia Bader,
20 Caroline Miller,
21 Catharine Schaefer,
22 Catharine Bachman,

23 Cordelia Nagel,
24 Mary Geidner,
25 Ann Moser,
26 Mary A. Stein,

27 Sarah Stein,
28 Anna M. Fretz,
29 Catharine Kistler.

Confirmed in Solomon's Church, Macungie Boro.

April 10, 1857.

Males.

1 Hiram H. Danner,
2 James Miller,
3 William Stattler.

Females.

1 Lucinda Stattler,
2 Emmaline Stattler,
3 Emelia Koch,
4 Hannah E. Desch,
5 Susanna Baer,
6 Lydia Ann Lacy,
7 Catharine Miller.

May 1, 1859.

Males.

1 Harrison Jarret,
2 Charles Gorr,
3 James Gaumer,
4 James Neumeyer.

Females.

1 Mary Dilgert,
2 Emmeline Mohr,
3 Eliza Gorr,
4 Elizabeth Desch,
5 Josephine Gaumer,
6 Sarah Sieger.

April 28, 1861.

Males.

1 Benjamin F. Jarret,
2 William Acker,
3 William F. Danner,
4 Edwin H. Fritz.

Females.

1 Lydia Ann Gorr,
2 Caroline Knedler,
3 Sarah G. Gaumer,
4 Caroline Gaumer,
5 Catharine Reinhard,
6 Sarah A. Reiter,
7 Sarah J. Danner,
8 Catharine Baer.

APRIL 19, 1863.
Males.

1 Nelson C. Shankweiler,
2 Benjamin E. Reinhard,
3 Solomon A. Steininger,
4 Llewellyn A. Henninger,
5 Edwin G. Gross,
6 James F. Knedler,
7 William Bauer,
8 John D. Neumeyer.

Females.

1 Louisa C. Knauss,
2 Sophia Gaumer,
3 Mary Kock,
4 Mary Muth,
5 Mary Bauer,
6 Mary Gorr,
7 Mary A. Gaukler,
8 Anna C. Traub.

APRIL 13, 1865.
Males.

1 Daniel Desch,
2 John L. Reinhard,
3 John G. Bauer,
4 John J. Gaumer,
5 Morris A. Gaumer.

Females.

1 Mary J. Arner,
2 Tuvillia J. Henninger,
3 Lovina M. Gorr,
4 Caroline J. Shankweiler,
5 Sarah Heilig.

Confirmed at Friedensville.

SECOND SUNDAY AFTER EASTER, 1830.
Males.

1 Thomas Scotlen,
2 Isaac Hartman,
3 Charles Steinberger,
4 Renadus Quier,

FRIEDENSVILLE CHURCH.

5 Herman Yost,
6 Solomon Giess,
7 Michael Stuber,
8 David Thron,
9 Nathan Flexer,
10 George Miller,
11 Paul Gross,
12 Henry Cope,
13 Samuel Beidelman,
14 Solomon Lestny,
15 Joseph Scotlen.

Females.

1 Catharine Gauf,
2 Sarah Gauf,
3 Mary Shiffert,
4 Hannah Scotlen,
5 Juliana Reinhart,
6 Nellie Miller,
7 Christina Gangawere,
8 Sarah Martin,
9 Sarah Giess,
10 Sarah Quier,
11 Mary Gernert,
12 Elizabeth Alshaus,
13 Elizabeth Lukas,
14 Mary Hoffert,
15 Mary Gangawere,
16 Rebecca Quier,
17 Fanny Gross,
18 Catharine Hinkle.

April 21, 1832.

Males.

1 Jacob Cope,
2 Jacob Merkel,
3 David Ueberroth,
4 Joseph Deily,
5 Felix Seifert,
6 Samuel Busch,
7 Joseph Marsteller,
8 Charles Rickert,
9 Jacob Gernert,
10 August Gross,
11 Henry Miller,
12 Joseph Rickert,
13 Adam Gauf,
14 Joseph Gernet,
15 Israel Trone,
16 Owen Weber,
17 Lewis Quier,
18 Charles Hinkel,
19 Michael Stuber,
20 George Smith,
21 Tilghman Hartman,
22 Peter Weber,
23 Jacob Groman.

Females.

1 Carolina Grim,
2 Sarah Ueberroth,
3 Maria Gauf,
4 Juliana Hoffert,
5 Anna Steinberger,
6 Anna Hoffert,

7 Louisa Quier,
8 Rela Lein,
9 Hetty Rumfield,
10 Carolina Opp,
11 Elizabeth Wind,

12 Maria Seifert.
13 Catharine Groman,
14 Maria Stahl,
15 Leah Wentz.

APRIL 20, 1834.
Males.

1 Samuel Marsteller,
2 Joseph Quier,
3 Aaron Leibold,
4 William Bush,
5 Joel Benner,
6 Joshua Benner,
7 Alexander Moritz,
8 Reuben Kleckner,

9 Nicholas Fatzinger,
10 Michael Ziegenfuss,
11 William Stuber,
12 Jacob Diehl,
13 David Yost,
14 Nathan Dillgart,
15 Edward Miller.

Females.

1 Magdalena Stahl,
2 Hannah Stahl,
3 Juliana Merkel,
4 Lovina Moritz,
5 Lovina Steinberger,
6 Carolina Kaucher,
7 Hannah Wind,
8 Elizabeth Hauf,
9 Elizabeth Nagel,
10 Alavesta Ronkel,
11 Rachel Weber,

12 Maria Ziegenfuss,
13 Maria Martin,
14 Lovina Quier,
15 Anna Juliana Lucas,
16 Maria Anna Yaeger,
17 Henrietta Stuber,
18 Elizabeth Fatzinger,
19 Lucy Ann Lukes,
20 Lydia Rumfeld,
21 Elizabeth Marsteller.

APRIL 17, 1836.
Males.

1 Charles Funk,
2 John Yost,
3 Jacob Hoffman,
4 John Rickert,
5 Joshua Harwi,
6 Elias Elinger,

7 William Ehrig,
8 John Bachman,
9 Aaron Mory,
10 Peter Martin,
11 Jesse Rumfeld.

Females.

1 Lusetta Quier,
2 Leah Leibfried,
3 Maria Cope,
4 Lucy Hoffert,
5 Judith Scotlan,
6 Leah Harwi,
7 Elizabeth Wind,
8 Susanna Gernet,
9 Maria Hoffman,
10 Sarah Marsteller,
11 Sarah Ehrig,
12 Sarah Yost,
13 Henrietta Steinberger,
14 Mary Merkel,
15 Hannah Erdman,
16 Esther Erdman,
17 Veronica Rickert,
18 Mary Miller,
19 Judith Wind.

April 12, 1839.

Males.

1 Samuel Yaeger,
2 Aaron Ihrig,
3 Daniel Yost,
4 Charles Yaeger,
5 Reuben Merkel,
6 James Giess,
7 Samuel Marsteller,
8 William Wind,
9 Jacob Mory,
10 George Blank,
11 Nathan Gernet,
12 Jacob Miller,
13 Solomon Waldman,
14 Mandes Berkenstock,
15 Jacob Harwi,
16 Simon Fatzinger,
17 Solomon Fatzinger,
18 Charles Miller,
19 Napoleon Gauf,
20 Daniel Hoffert,
21 David Fatzinger,
22 Reuben Leibfried,
23 Henry Marsteller,
24 Jacob Ehrig,
25 Elias Erdman,
26 Jacob Stuber,
27 Edward Rufe,
28 Joshua Rumfeld,
29 Jacob Ueberroth.

Females.

1 Louisa Moerder,
2 Louisa Weil,
3 Elizabeth Bachman,
4 Sarah Schleider,
5 Elizabeth Harris,
6 Rebecca Yost,
7 Lucinda Berkenstock,
8 Fyanna Gartan,
9 Mary A. Ihrig,
10 Lovina Siegfried.

April 10, 1842.

Males.

1 Robert Yost,
2 Edward Weber,
3 Levi Emory,
4 Peter Bader,
5 Charles Thron,
6 Edward Yost,
7 Eli Eshbach,
8 Levi Weber,
9 William Reichard,
10 John Reichard,
11 Francis Marsteller,
12 William Billiard,
13 Abraham Harwi,
14 Thomas Billiard,
15 William Heckman.

Females.

1 Elizabeth Schaffer,
2 Matilda Steinberger,
3 Mary Yost,
4 Matilda Bachman,
5 Mary Hellener,
6 Louisa Mohry.
7 Elizabeth Schlosser,
8 Juliana Giess,
9 Sibylla Deily,
10 Elizabeth Bergenstock,
11 Christianna Gangewere,
12 Anna F. Mill,
13 Carolina Stuber,
14 Catharine Yost,
15 Abigail Deily,
16 Elizabeth Deily,
17 Carolina Mack.

April 5, 1846.

Males.

1 Daniel Bernt,
2 Charles G. Blank,
3 Herman Yeager,
4 Jacob Harres,
5 Henry Reichard,
6 James Harwig,
7 Joseph Clemmer,
8 John Croman,
9 Adam Merkel,
10 Charles Clewell,
11 William Reinhard,
12 Daniel Ihrig,
13 Edmund Weinland.

Females.

1 Catharine Rath,
2 Matilda Blank,
3 Catharine Hellener,
4 Dianna Deily,
5 Elizabeth Heckman,
6 Sarah A. Hopper.
7 Mary Benner.
8 Carolina Derr,
9 Sarah Benner,
10 Dianna Fatzinger,
11 Susanna Ihrig.

October 17, 1847.

Males.

1. William Moritz,
2. William Mill,
3. Owen Miller,
4. Joseph Groman,
5. William Ziegenfuss,
6. George Gangaware,
7. James Rau,
8. Levi Cope,
9. Lewis Benner,
10. George Berger,
11. Joseph Schlosser.

Females.

1. Judith Mill,
2. Mary Yost,
3. Eliza A. Blank,
4. Dianna Merkel,
5. Sarah Detterer,
6. Mary Weil,
7. Matilda Gangaware,
8. Sarah Ihrig,
9. Lovina Snyder,
10. Dianna Reichard,
11. Sarah Reichard,
12. Matilda Hartman,
13. Mary Stuber,
14. Henrietta Thron,
15. Ansenetta Wind,
16. Matilda Moritz,
17. Elizabeth Laziar,
18. Sarah A. Bader,
19. Juliana Benner,
20. Matilda Cope,
21. Eliza Hopper,
22. Emmalinda Deily,
23. Serena Laury,
24. Helena Sterner,
25. Susanna Yaeger,
26. Cecilia Wolbach,
27. Catharine Ihrig,
28. Eliza Ankel,
29. Mary Fister,
30. Sarah A. Pflueger.

November 11, 1849.

Males.

1. Cornelius R. Sterner,
2. Owen Harwi,
3. Reuben Weber,
4. John Elias Hellener,
5. Reuben C. Marsteller,
6. Jacob F. Marsteller,
7. Jacob M. Weber,
8. Levi Miller,
9. Edwin H. Blank,
10. Levi M. Billiard,
11. Owen Billiard,
12. Israel Harris,
13. Walter Clewell,
14. William Herman,
15. Charles Laziar,
16. Jacob Rath,
17. Thomas Nace.

Females.

1 Susanna M. Reichard,
2 Mary N. Diehl,
3 Justina Hartman,
4 Mary M. Hartman,
5 Catharine Schneider,
6 Matilda Nace,
7 Lucy A. Hermann,
8 Susanna C. Marsteller,
9 Elizabeth Sterner,
10 Maria Sterner,
11 Emeline Schleiter,
12 Hannah Deis,
13 Mary A. Weber,
14 Elizabeth Yaeger.

NOVEMBER 9, 1851.

Males.

1 Jacob Rath,
2 Edmund J. Reinhard,
3 Morgan Mory,
4 Joseph Hermany,
5 Frederic Gangawere,
6 John R. Cope,
7 Edwin Quier,
8 Henry Deily,
9 Daniel F. Weil,
10 Solomon Ueberroth,
11 Joseph H. Lerch,
12 Reuben F. Benner,
13 Charles F. Pflueger,
14 George K. Lerch,
15 David W. Marsteller,
16 William Laury,
17 George Harwi,
18 Henry Ankel,
19 Martin L. Yost,
20 John J. Yost,
21 Obadjah Ueberroth,
22 John W. Leidy,
23 Edward Schafer,
24 Solomon Kroman,
25 Tilghman Weil,
26 Henry Billiard.

Females.

1 Matilda Hermany,
2 Mary Nace,
3 Ellen W. Bader,
4 Matilda Ziegenfuss,
5 Hannah Diehl,
6 Mary Fretz,
7 Lydia A. Herman,
8 Adelina E. Laury,
9 Sarah Laury,
10 Diana Tillich,
11 Anna M. Wind,
12 Susanna C. Clewell,
13 Sarah A. Blank,
14 Mary L. Geyer,
15 Mary A. Moritz,
16 Lydia A. Trohn,
17 Elizabeth Mack,
18 Lovina Bilgart,
19 Elemina Blank,
20 Sarah A. Wind,

21 Mary A. Cope,
22 Elizabeth Weber,
23 Susanna Weil,
24 Eliza H. Nunnemacher,
25 Catharine Nunnemacher,
26 Lovina Bilgard.

NOVEMBER 6, 1853.

Males.

1 Addison Wint,
2 Edwin Pflueger,
3 Ephraim Walter,
4 Thomas Reichard,
5 David Reichard,
6 Thomas W. Moyer,
7 Jacob F. Diehl,
8 George Quier,
9 Henry Ueberroth,
10 Henry Schleiter,
11 Jacob F. Schleiter,
12 Samuel Groman,
13 Thomas M. Weber,
14 Jacob Ihrig,
15 Edwin Sterner,
16 Amos Ziegenfuss,
17 Theodore C. Yaeger,
18 Edwin Benner.

Females.

1 Mary C. Doerle,
2 Sarah Marsteller,
3 Hannah Marsteller,
4 Matilda E. Romig,
5 Sarah A. Hartman,
6 Elizabeth Nace,
7 Elizabeth Thron,
8 Sarah A. Moyer,
9 Lovina Harmony,
10 Fyette E. Bader,
11 Elenora A. Halbach,
12 Elizabeth Harwi,
13 Matilda Geyer,
14 Sarah A. Tice,
15 Matilda Sterner,
16 Lovina Kuntzman,
17 Susanna Mertz,
18 Matilda Heckman,
19 Elemina Ihrig,
20 Catharine Laziar,
21 Matilda Yost,
22 Anna E. S. Weber,
23 Anna M. C. Seibert,
24 Marietta Hartman,
25 Elizabeth A. Hartman.

NOVEMBER 4, 1855.

Males.

1 Charles Bilgert,
2 Benjamin Weil,
3 Stephen H. Weil,
4 James O. Knauss,
5 John W. Laury,
6 James Seigfried,

7 George W. Horning,
8 David Ihrig,
9 Jacob Groman,
10 Jacob Reichart,
11 Mannassa Wint,
12 William Wint,
13 Lewis Reinbold,

14 Franklin Wint,
15 Amos Harris,
16 Frederick Pflueger,
17 Charles Weil,
18 William Hartman,
19 William Koch.

Females.

1 Carolina Geyer,
2 Mary E. Billiard,
3 Dianna Benner,
4 Josephine Billiard,
5 Matilda Ueberroth,
6 Alavesta G. Moritz,
7 Emmalinda G. Ruth,

8 Lovina F. Harmony,
9 Araminda Cope,
10 Catharine Gangawere,
11 Sarah C. Carl,
12 Henrietta Reichard,
13 Henrietta Seigfried,
14 Elenora H. Weis.

NOVEMBER 1, 1857.

Males.

1 William Hartman,
2 Jacob Hartman,
3 John G. Blank,
4 Wm. G. Wind,
5 Benjamin Y. Wimmer,
6 Alfred Wind,
7 Alexander Ehrig,
8 Chas. G. Ziegenfuss,
9 Abr. J. Benner,

10 Edwin R. Y. Ueberroth,
11 Wm. A. Doerle,
12 Josiah Laury,
13 Stephen H. Diehl,
14 Jacob Grimm,
15 Morgan P. Weaver,
16 George G. J. Reinhard,
17 Amos J. Quier.

Females.

1 Julia C. Ueberroth,
2 Amanda W. Rumfield,
3 May M. Rumfield,
4 Susanna E. Rumfield,
5 Emma H. Seifert,
6 Amanda M. Jerret,
7 Sarah A. Harwi,
8 Catharine Groman,

9 Jacobine E. Pflueger,
10 Emelia H. Smith,
11 Sarah M. Smith,
12 Sarah A. Diehl,
13 Alavesta C. Weil,
14 Emeline Ziegenfuss,
15 Paulina V. Bilgert,
16 Ansanette H. Bilgert.

October 29th, 1859.

Males.

1 Solomon Shiffert,
2 William Ortt,
3 Reuben Transue,
4 Alfred S. Lerch,
5 William H. Knauss,
6 Martin R. Frey,
7 Phaon Laury,
8 Daniel I. Hartman,
9 James S. Lerch,
10 Aaron Seigfried,
11 Amos Harmony.

Females.

1 Anna Knerr,
2 Matilda A. Laury,
3 Emeline M. Hartman,
4 Celinda M. Pflueger,
5 Mary Wint,
6 Susanna Bader,
7 Sarah A. Thron,
8 Eliza A. Bader,
9 Susanna Stuber,
10 Amanda S. Geyer,
11 Eliza Mertz,
12 Mary Gernet,
13 Julia Ann Roth,
14 Mary Lerch,
15 Aravesta E. Mertz,
16 Anna Sterner,
17 Fyetta Frey.

October 27, 1861.

Males.

1 Jeremiah G. Gangawere,
2 Franklin Gangawere,
3 James A. Benner,
4 James Ehrig,
5 Andrew Wint.
6 Tilghman Gangawere,
7 Theophilus Pflueger,
8 Adam F. Schaeffer,
9 Henry Ritter,
10 Asher P. Bader,
11 Tilghman Mertz,
12 Joseph U. Weber,
13 Charles Geyer.

Females.

1 Lucy Ann Billiard,
2 Amanda E. Reinbold,
3 Emma J. Rumfield,
4 Emma C. Rumfield,
5 Sarah Schwenker,
6 Elemina Quier,
7 Araminta C. Ueberroth,
8 Emmalinda Ehrig,
9 Sarah A. Ache,
10 Christiana Laury,
11 Elizabeth Scherer,
12 Elemina Groman,
13 Matilda Frey.

OCTOBER 25, 1863.

Males.

1 Jeremiah A. Sigfried,
2 David C. Reinhard,
3 Asher E. Benner,
4 William R. Ueberroth,
5 John Scherer,
6 Theodore E. Schmidt,
7 Adaman G. Schmidt,
8 Ananam G. Ueberroth,
9 James A. Laury,
10 Abraham Blank,
11 William Mock,
12 Franklin L. Hartman,
13 Alfred M. Ritter,
14 William F. Walter,
15 Frederick Grossman,
16 Theodore Petzholz.

Females.

1 Ellen Scherer,
2 Amanda M. Laury,
3 Emma C. Miller,
4 Ellen E. Cope,
5 Leanna M. Kramm,
6 Eliza J. Knauss,
7 Annie M. Weikel,
8 Valeria C. Gangewere,
9 Eliza E. Ehrig,
10 Ellen H. Ehrig,
11 Amanda Ehrig,
12 Elenora H. Torns,
13 Amanda C. Mertz,
14 Sarah Ann Mertz.

OCTOBER 22, 1865.

Males.

1 George W. Blacker,
2 Sylvanus Wittman,
3 Peter Isaac Sigfried,
4 Marcus Gernet,
5 Harvey E. Miller,
6 John H. Holtzerman,
7 Nathan M. Ziegenfuss.

Females.

1 Urcilla C. Seibert,
2 Ellen Louisa Warmkessel,
3 Aravesta Amanda Yost,
4 Amelia C. Sherer,
5 Maria Cath. Yost,
6 Cordelia Weiss,
7 Elizabeth Kuhns,
8 Amanda C. Diehl,
9 Ellen Weil.

NOVEMBER 17, 1867.

Males.

1 Oliver W. Merkle,
2 Edward B. Hartman,
3 Henry F. Brinker,
4 Solomon J. Hartman,

5 Henry Wittman,
6 Wilson C. Fatzinger,
7 Henry Keeler,
8 Peter Kunz,
9 Benjamin F. Reichard,
10 Theodore F. Kunz,
11 Adams S. Ueberroth,
12 Robert J. Eschbach,
13 Morgan Wint,
14 William Roth,
15 Wilson Roth,
16 Ephraim Meyer.

Females.

1 Amanda F. Bilgard,
2 Mary Ehrig,
3 Amanda Gangawere,
4 Sarah Young,
5 Emma F. Geyer,
6 Catharine Henrich,
7 Adeline L. Bader,
8 Amanda Young,
9 Emma M. Gangawere,
10 Matilda M. Rumfeld,
11 Christianna M. Ueberroth,
12 Mary A. Rufe,
13 Mary A. Lachleder,
14 Sarah N. Keeler,
15 Victoria Rumfeld,
16 Christianna E. Reinhard,
17 Adrianna A. Ehrig,
18 Juliana Weaver,
19 Susan S. Weaver,
20 Eliza Reinbold,
21 Sarah Wint,
22 Elamina Weaver.

OCTOBER 17, 1869.

Males.

1 John Olpp,
2 Amandus Mertz,
3 Henry Missimer,
4 Jonathan Weil,
5 William J. Ritter,
6 Milton Ritter,
7 Theodore W. Knauss,
8 Reuben R. Weidner,
9 Levere O. F. Gangaware,
10 Edwin T. Fatzinger,
11 George W. H. Reinbold,
12 Wilson J. Ueberroth,
13 Augustus H. Keenan,
14 George Kessler,
15 Henry H. Miller,
16 Wm. H. Miller,
17 Francis Grupe.

Females.

1 Mary J. Kiehler,
2 Matilda Sigfried,
3 Christianna Yost,
4 Juliana E. Markle,
5 Sarah A. Reichard,
6 Jane Diehl,
7 Ella J. Yost,
8 Mary Arnold,

9 Pauline A. Holtzward,
10 Mollie C. Harwi,
11 Rebecca Ziegenfuss.

OCTOBER 15, 1871.

Males.

1 Sylvester F. Smith,
2 Sylvester F. Weaver,
3 Richard C. Trohn,
4 Quintus P. Kreidler,
5 Allen L. Rumfeld,
6 Amos H. Klein,
7 James H. Bleam,
8 William H. Mohr,
9 Daniel F. Hittinger,
10 William H. Hittinger,
11 Henry A. Hartlein,
12 Peter F. Weaver,
13 George A. Schlosser,
14 Francis Miller,
15 William Ehrig,
16 Jacob Beick,
17 Henry W. Leibley,
18 Josiah Muth,
19 Henry Cressman,
20 William Apple,
21 Thomas J. Apple,
22 Milton H. Clewell,
23 Reuben J. Benner,
24 Levi J. Benner,
25 Anaman J. Gangaware,
26 Oscar J. Roth,
27 Erwin H. Weidner.

Females.

1 Mary J. Young,
2 Mary J. Reichard,
3 Sarah L. Doney,
4 Louisa M. Doney,
5 Sarah J. Yeager,
6 Emma J. Marsteller,
7 Susanna M. Markle,
8 Angelina E. Kunzman,
9 Elenora C. Knauss,
10 Sarah N. Knecht,
11 Catharine Lachleder,
12 Amena Ambrunn,
13 Sarah N. Klinker,
14 Elenora E. Ambrunn,
15 Anna E. Yeager,
16 Elemina Weaver,
17 Mary Mack.

OCTOBER 12, 1873.

Males.

1 Henry G. Herman,
2 Jacob G. Yost,
3 Marcus D. Rice,
4 Morris D. Neisser,
5 Chas. W. Finady,
6 John E. Mertz,
7 Benjamin V. Billiard,
8 Oliver A. Wagner,
9 Allen S. Heller,
10 Wm. H. Reinbold,

11 Alfred Reichard,
12 Peter D. Harris,
13 Joshua Miller,
14 George Kuhn,
15 Herman Brisser,
16 Joseph B. Rohr,
17 Israel A. Rudolph,

18 Chas. Reichard,
19 Adam Schlosser,
20 John Kutz,
21 Joseph Lachleder,
22 Jacob D. Harwi,
23 Samuel Torence,
24 Charles Lambert.

Females.

1 Amelia Harwi,
2 Emma L. Reinhard,
3 Amanda M. Nace,
4 Alice E. Clewell,
5 Isadora E. Yost,
6 Laura D. Schitz,
7 Louisa M. Berger,
8 Alavesta Kuhn,
9 Mary A. Hittinger,
10 Ellen V. Eisenhard.
11 Emma M. Cope,
12 Elamina L. Harwi,

13 Cecilia S. Gangaware,
14 Catharine E. Adams,
15 Elizabeth W. Kerner,
16 Dianna F. Veater,
17 Charlotte C. Horning,
18 Elvina Breiser,
19 Mary Emlich,
20 Amanda L. Bears,
21 Anna M. Heller,
22 Mary M. Hillegass,
23 Jennie Schiffert.

NOVEMBER 7, 1875.

Males.

1 Cocen Wagner,
2 Asmus H. Mack,
3 Wm. Blacker,
4 Edwin Leibly,
5 Alfred J. Cope,
6 Theodore W. Clewell,
7 Chauncey W. Diehl,
8 David J. Weidner,
9 Ambrose S. Cope,

10 Wm. D. Heist,
11 Preston Schantzbach,
12 Henry C. Yeager,
13 Orville O. Marsteller,
14 Reuben Deily,
15 George W. Roth,
16 Charles J. Roth,
17 Wm. H. Gehman.

Females.

1 Isadora Miller,
2 Emma Roth,

3 Emma J. Hittinger,
4 Mary D. Markle,

5 Emma S. Yeager,
6 Ellen C. Yeager,
7 Emma P. Leibly,
8 Elamina Giess,
9 Emalinda Harwi,
10 Sarah A. Licht,
11 Ellen S. Weidner,
12 Sarah A. Christ,
13 Mary Blacker,

14 Agnes I. Diehl,
15 Emma M. Young,
16 Sedonie Ambrunn,
17 Mary A. E. Miller,
18 Marietta Weinland,
19 Marietta Horning,
20 Christianna Ehrig,
21 Mary J. Weaver.

NOVEMBER 4, 1877.

Males.

1 Hiram Reichard,
2 Thomas H. E. Yeager,
3 Henry J. Harwi,
4 John F. Wittman,
5 James F. Marsteller,
6 Thomas F. Young,
7 Quintus H. Cope,
8 Andrew S. Clewell,
9 Charles H. Heil,
10 George M. Strauss,
11 Alfred S. Kemerer,

12 Jerome Christman,
13 Alfred T. Ebbert,
14 William H. Zentner,
15 George H. Reily,
16 Alfred Harwi,
17 John Harwi,
18 Josiah W. Harwi,
19 Henry B. Wagner,
20 William H. Quier,
21 Chas. F. Zentner.

Females.

1 Emma A. Reichard,
2 Mary A. Harwi,
3 Helena Ehrig,
4 Sarah A. M. Hoh,
5 Lizzie S. Weaver,
6 Ida A. Marsteller,
7 Wilhelmina C. Ginder,
8 Elizabeth S. Siegfried,
9 Mary F. Mack,
10 Alice S. A. Cope,
11 Catharine Trapp,
12 Elizabeth Minich,

13 Anna M. Wint,
14 Lucinda Snyder,
15 Ellen C. Sell,
16 Elmira E. Marsteller,
17 Eliza J. Lachleder,
18 Mary J. Harwi,
19 Amelia R. Lambert,
20 Matilda W. Dietzel,
21 Alice M. Herman,
22 Mary S. Minich,
23 Emma M. Torrence,
24 Ellen S. Young.

November 2, 1879.

Males.

1 James F. Lambert,
2 Oscar P. Hartman,
3 Joseph S. Boyer,
4 Jacob J. Clewell,
5 George E. Laury,
6 William A. Schlosser,
7 Oliver W. H. Marsteller,
8 Calvin D. Clauser,
9 William F. Haun,
10 William C. Dietzel.

Females.

1 Mary Kramer,
2 Mary N. Rice,
3 Sarah E. Weaver,
4 Mary A. Reinhard,
5 Alice M. Reinhard,
6 Amanda A. Gebhard,
7 Mary M. Reinbold,
8 Amelia Wagner,
9 Mary M. Cope,
10 Emma S. Nace,
11 Emma E. Seifert,
12 Louisa E. Gross,
13 Montana Bower,
14 Maria M. Weaver,
15 Mary S. Billiard.

October 30, 1881.

Males.

1 Solomon Harwi,
2 Isaac Marsteller,
3 Milton Harmony,
4 Sylvanus Lambert,
5 George Laury,
6 John Quier,
7 George Harmon,
8 Henry Ebert,
9 Myras Quier,
10 Henry Weidner,
11 Oscar Schlosser,
12 Charles Diehl,
13 William Ambrunn,
14 Charles Ambrunn,
15 William Shiffert,
16 John Sell,
17 George Ueberroth,
18 Eugene Benner,
19 George Rudolph.

Females.

1 Clara J. Nace,
2 Alice A. Flexer,
3 Emma Ebert,
4 Alice C. Souders,
5 Ellen L. Gangawere
6 Sarah C. Hittinger,
7 Amanda Stern,
8 Elemina Hillegass,
9 Aliene Wagner,
10 Louisa Wagner,

11 Emma Kuhn,
12 Mary Moll,
13 Mary Miller,
14 Ellen Rudolph,
15 Emma Harmon,
16 Laura Quier,

17 Nietta Heil,
18 Julia Schlosser,
19 Hannah Dice,
20 Theresa Hellener,
21 Catharine R. Harwi.

OCTOBER 28, 1883.

Males.

1 William Weidner,
2 George Quier,
3 Edwin Quier,
4 Wilson Keiper,
5 Howard Ritter,
6 Erwin Fatzinger,
7 Alfred Quier,

8 Morris Heil,
9 Oscar Eisenhart,
10 William Trapp,
11 Daniel Torrence,
12 Charles Minnich,
13 Mr. Funk,
14 Mr. Dietzel.

Females.

1 Emma Laury,
2 Ida Clewell,
3 Katie A. Hartman,
4 Amanda Hittinger,
5 Alice Stern,
6 Minnie Dietzel,
7 Sarah Harwi,
8 Caroline Minnich,
9 Kate Heil,
10 Amanda Heil,
11 Maria Trapp,

12 Ellen Christ,
13 Sarah Gross,
14 Agnes Moll,
15 Emma Zandeler,
16 Emma Schlosser,
17 Emma Henn.
18 Julia Zentner,
19 Miss Herman,
20 Eliza Henn,
21 Kate Lant.

Confirmed in Salisbury Church (Jerusalem's).

NOVEMBER 20, 1853.

Males.

1 Thomas Ihrig,
2 Lewis Weber,

3 Edwin Moritz,
4 Levin Giess,

·215

5 Henry Moritz,
6 George M. Finly,
7 Henry M. Schlosser,

8 William H. Diehl,
9 John Coyne,
10 John Nunnemacher.

Females.

1 Catharine A. Schmidt,
2 Catharine Ihrig,
3 Sarah Ihrig,
4 Louisa S. Nunnemacher,
5 Tuvillia E. Lynn,

6 Helena Moritz,
7 Marsiriam Gram,
8 Eliza A. Gram,
9 Sarah Messer,
10 Livy Schlosser.

NOVEMBER 11, 1855.

Males.

1 Solomon Giess,
2 Tilghman M. Ritter,
3 Henry M. Miller,

4 Augustus G. Ibach,
5 John German,
6 Edwin Ueberroth.

Females.

1 Catharine Schlosser,
2 Sarah Schlosser,
3 Alavesta Deily,
4 Matilda Miller,
5 Mary Moritz,
6 Marlierum Giess,

7 Alavesta Weiss,
8 Sarah A. Yost,
9 Mary Deily,
10 Mary Stuber,
11 Mary Schmidt,
12 Amru Linsenbilger.

NOVEMBER 8, 1887.

Males.

1 Jacob D. Appel,
2 Edward Bauer,
3 Josiah Fallstich,
4 Henry Diehl,

5 John Frantz,
6 Milton Rufe,
7 Jonas Amey.

Females.

1 Lovina Meschter,
2 Amanda Brinker,
3 Tuvillia Lautenschlager,

4 Matilda Ueberroth,
5 Rebecca Diehl,
6 Sophia Sterner,

7 Adeline Moritz,
8 Mary A. Trone,
9 Salome Nunnemacher,
10 Christiana Fallstich,
11 Elizabeth Funk,
12 Sarah Funk,
13 Sarah Giess,
14 Elizabeth Rufe.

November 6, 1859.
Males.

1 William Lautenschlager,
2 Alfred Romig,
3 James Moritz,
4 Henry Emery,
5 William Stuber,
6 Daniel Leibensperger,
7 Charles Bauer,
8 Lewis Rufe.

Females.

1 Tuvillia Giess,
2 Cornelia Stuber,
3 Mary Sterner,
4 Sarah A. Mangle,
5 Amanda Yost,
6 Araminda Siegfried,
7 Mary A. Romig,
8 Anna M. Ritter,
9 Lydia N. Reichenbach,
10 Susanna Marsteller,
11 Anna Deily.

November 3, 1861.
Males.

1 Charles A. Nunnemacher,
2 Milton Nunnemacher,
3 Alfred Moritz,
4 William Bauer,
5 Henry Miller,
6 Joseph Kincaid,
7 Edwin Deily.

Females.

1 Fannie Leibensperger,
2 Caroline A. Hoffert,
3 Amanda Ueberroth,
4 Estalinda Eppit,
5 Ellen Stuber,
6 Lovina Berger,
7 Margaret Horning.

November 8, 1863.
Males.

1 Thomas A. Cope,
2 Jacob Leibensperger,
3 Milton H. Clees,
4 Ambrose Giess,

217

5 Milton Kerschner,
6 John L. Schrank,
7 George Stuber,
8 Frank Ueberroth.

Females.

1 Eliza Ueberroth,
2 Mary A. Giess,
3 Martha A. Lacey,
4 Marietta Giess,
5 Sarah Schmidt,
6 Amanda Lacey,
7 Sarah Nunnemacher,
8 Emma Leibensperger,
9 Catharine A. Schmidt,
10 Eliza Schlosser,
11 Sarah A. Reinbold,
12 Fyanna Kramm,
13 Sarah M. K. Lautenschlager,
14 Elamanda J. Ritter.

OCTOBER 29, 1865.

Males.

1 Morris R. Benner,
2 Philip Reichard,
3 Manoah Diehl,
4 Jeremiah I. Stuber,
5 Wilson Robert,
6 William H. Berger,
7 Harrison Ritter,
8 Henry M. Berger,
9 Charles F. Ihrig.

Females.

1 Eliza A. Romig,
2 Rebecca M. Barner,
3 Henrietta J. Moritz,
4 Mary A. Bauer,
5 Sarah A. Deily,
6 Ellen J. Rufe,
7 Eliza Leibensperger,
8 Eliza Groman,
9 Catharine Kessler,
10 Aurelia Deily,
11 Eliza Meyer,
12 Emma Ohl,
13 Catharine E. Minich,
14 Alice Newhard,
15 Hannah Ernst,
16 William Catharine Degli,
17 Cecilia Schmoll,
18 Mary A. Moyer,
19 Mary A. Pellit,
20 Anna M. Segel,
21 Mary Frank.

NOVEMBER 10, 1867.

Males.

1 Levi J. Rufe,
2 George Reinbold,
3 William Funk,
4 Joseph Torrence,

5 Tilghman Trapp,
6 William Cope,
7 George H. Bauer,
8 Henry Hess,
9 Martin B. Wagner,
10 Tilghman H. Ihrig,
11 Henry Stahlender,
12 William Eichelberger.

Females.

1 Sibylla Lerch,
2 Anna M. Leibensperger,
3 Juliana Springer,
4 Emma Newhard,
5 Alice Berger,
6 Amanda Cope,
7 Emma Moritz.

OCTOBER 17, 1869.

Males.

1 Joshua Nagel,
2 Peter Leschter,
3 Frank Brinker,
4 Clinton Mohr,
5 Owen Stuber,
6 John Brick,
7 Conrad Cope,
8 Sylvanus Ritter,
9 Frank Torrence.

Females.

1 Tuvillia Schmidt,
2 Rebecca Ulrich,
3 Mary Funk,
4 Amanda Schneider,
5 Catharine Kuhn,
6 Mary Trapp,
7 Matilda Trapp.

OCTOBER 22, 1871.

Males.

1 Albert Stuber,
2 George Springer,
3 Eugene Stahlnecker,
4 John Hess,
5 Walter Ueberroth,
6 Milton Nagel,
7 Samuel Moyer,
8 John P. Hansen,
9 Henry Traub,
10 Morris Berger,
11 Morris Benner.

Females.

1 Aravesta Grove,
2 Caroline Gebhart,
3 Sarah Benner,
4 Minnie Holzword,

5 Matilda Hess,
6 Amanda M. Schlosser,
7 Elvina Trapp,
8 Mary Weil,
9 Anna M. Stein,
10 Matilda Holzword,

11 Ellen Brinker,
12 Mary Ann Moll,
13 Anna Stuber,
14 Mary Stuber,
15 Mary Lest,
16 Helena Cope.

November 9, 1873.
Males.

1 Alfred H. Knauss,
2 James Grampy,

3 Henry R. Deifer,
4 John Edward Miller.

Females.

1 Isadora M. Ueberroth,
2 Sarah A. Stahlnecker,
3 Emma Markle,
4 Mary Deily,
5 Emma Grampy,
6 Maria Graff,
7 Elenora Light,

8 Mary Frank,
9 Carolina W. Snyder,
10 Lilly Deifer,
11 Alavesta Ritter,
12 Senia Nagel,
13 Emma Weil,
14 Mary Springer.

December 5, 1875.
Males.

1 David J. Moritz,
2 Josiah Berger,
3 George A. Ueberroth,
4 Levan Brinker,
5 Josiah Laubach,

6 William Mertz,
7 Lewis Deifer,
8 Alfred Ueberroth,
9 David Leibensperger.

Females.

1 Catharine Fetter,

2 Augusta Cope.

November 18, 1877.
Males.

1 Augustus H. Scholl,
2 George M. Berger,
3 George W. Weil,

4 Charles A. Auer,
5 Marcus G. Gauf,
6 Alfred Miller.

Females.

1 Araminda Grampy,
2 Ida R. Ueberroth,
3 Sarah R. Lehr,
4 Francis A. Hoffman,
5 Ida J. Deifer,
6 Pruella A. Brinker,
7 Emma J. Sperling,
8 Joséphine A. Hoffman,
9 Alice A. Ueberroth,
10 Alavesta S. Weil,
11 Amanda C. Licht.

NOVEMBER 30, 1879.

Males.

1 Stephen H. Benner,
2 William H. Hoffman,
3 Lorenz Kramer.

Females.

1 Isadora Schlosser,
2 Sarah H. E. Burger,
3 Juliana S. Burger,
4 Isadora M. Groman,
5 Mary E. Fetter,
6 Elenora E. M. Cope.

NOVEMBER 27, 1881.

Males.

1 Ambrose J. Cope,
2 Harvey M. Ueberroth,
3 Noah A. Cope,
4 Ferdinand J. Snyder,
5 William W. Snyder,
6 John W. Springer,
7 Alfred L. Deifer,
8 George H. Stahlnecker,
9 John W. Scholl,
10 James H. Moritz,
11 John M. Ueberroth,
12 John H. Sperling,
13 William W. Ueberroth,
14 C. Albert Groman.

Females.

1 Annie C. Scholl,
2 Ida J. Markle,
3 Mary A. Snyder,
4 Sarah A. Sperling,
5 Truxilia L. Cope,
6 Lizzie J. Stahlnecker,
7 Mary C. Becker,
8 Mary A. Ueberroth.

Rittersville Church.

Confirmations at Rittersville.

December 25, 1844.

Males.

1 Charles Hower,
2 Franklin Ritter,
3 Henry Moyer,
4 Paul Reichard,
5 Charles Dickson,
6 Paul Fatzinger,
7 Charles Harvey,
8 Henry Eberhard.

Females.

1 Mary Beidler,
2 Mary Ritter,
3 Dianna Knauss,
4 Rebecca Beidler,
5 Sarah Bauer,
6 Lucy Ann Kramer,
7 Dianna Florey,
8 Sarah Moll,
9 Mary Sterner,
10 Amelia Ritter.

May 8, 1846.

Males.

1 Charles Bader,
2 Jonas Huber,
3 Franklin Reichenbach,
4 Levi Fenner,
5 Levin Hunsicker,
6 Herman Ginkinger,
7 William Fusselman,
8 Richard Mellen,
9 Tilghman Reichard,
10 Franklin Miller,
11 Walter Mull.

Females.

1 Matilda Hauer,
2 Fyetta Ritter,
3 Matilda Knauss,
4 Louisa Frey,
5 Rebecca Herz,
6 Lydia Ann Billiard,
7 Caroline Ihrig,
8 Dianna Fatzinger,
9 Eliza Bernz,
10 Isabella Nagel,
11 Mary Alm,
12 Susanna Clauss,
13 Catharine Clauss,
14 Rebecca Anthony,
15 Phœbe Ann Koenig.

NOVEMBER 24, 1850.
Males.

1 Oliver A. Ritter,
2 William S. Hoehle,
3 James Oliver Nagle,
4 John Beidler,
5 Thomas J. Baumgartner,
6 Asher J. Ritter,
7 Adam Luckenbach,
8 James Yaeger.

Females.

1 Elizabeth Reichard,
2 Sarah E. Beidler,
3 Sabina Moyer,
4 Catharine Reitenour,
5 Fyetta Colver,
6 Alavesta R. Halteman,
7 Isabella Fasbenner,
8 Fyetta Fatzinger,
9 Matilda M. Moshlitz,
10 Anna M. Cath. Swain,
11 Catharine Wendel.

NOVEMBER 21, 1852.
Males.

1 Thomas Boyer,
2 Samuel Horn,
3 Edwin Ritter,
4 John J. Paul,
5 Tilghman Ihrig,
6 Aaron H. Fatzinger,
7 Nathan Bader,
8 Samuel F. Hower,
9 Edwin Oliver Reichard,
10 Joseph Aaron Frey,
11 Henry William Ihrig,
12 George H. Lautenschlager,
13 Jacob H. Schell.

Females.

1 Sibylla Horn,
2 Caroline M. Moyer,
3 Paulina Eberhard,
4 Sarah A. Sterner,
5 Emelina Sterner,
6 Eliza J. Hower,
7 Mary S. Stump,
8 Anna M. Hower,
9 Susanna J. Frey,
10 Dianna J. Beidler,
11 Maria Acker.

NOVEMBER 19, 1854.
Males.

1 Franklin Ritter,
2 Charles W. Colver,
3 Alfred C. Roth,
4 William J. Groman,
5 Peter H. Steltzer.

Females.

1 Mary A. Stuber,
2 Susanna M. Ihrig,
3 Clarissa A. Stump,
4 Amelia A. Walter,
5 Mary A. Groman,
6 Angelina Ritter,
7 Sarah Dewald,
8 Mary Dewald.

NOVEMBER 16, 1856.
Males.

1 Oliver Zellner,
2 John Trexler,
3 James Beidler,
4 Cornelius Acker,
5 Oliver Nagel,
6 Tilghman Dickson,
7 Charles Lautenschlager,
8 Oliver Gibens.

Females.

1 Dianna Moyer,
2 Dianna Sterner,
3 Sophia Walter,
4 Eliza Ritter,
5 Sophia Stump,
6 Amanda Fatzinger,
7 Sarah A. Zellner,
8 Amelia Acker,
9 Elizabeth Emmerich.

DECEMBER 6, 1858.
Males.

1 Asher Gruber,
2 John Acker,
3 James Sterner,
4 Charles Ihrig.

Females.

1 Mary Diehm,
2 Emmaline Ihrig,
3 Mary A. Baumgartner,
4 Hettie Schneider,
5 Fyanna Dickson.

NOVEMBER 11, 1860.
Males.

1 Theodore A. Eberhard,
2 Charles F. Moyer,
3 Oliver F. Walter,
4 Charles F. Wonderly,
5 Edwin F. Osenbach,
6 Edwin Deily,
7 Osler Schweikoffer,
8 Daniel Fatzinger,
9 Wm. H. Hower,
10 Henry Fatzinger,
11 Levi Beidler.

Females.

1 Sarah R. Eckerd,
2 Mary A. Hoehle,
3 Sarah A. Stump,
4 Alavesta Sterner,
5 Sophia Hower,
6 Lovina Diehm,
7 Mary Singer,
8 Elenora Nagel,
9 Sophia Nagel.

NOVEMBER 9, 1862.
Males.

1 Tilghman Osenbach,
2 Hiram Roth.

Females.

1 Amanda Ihrig.
2 Augusta Walter,
3 Ellen Fatzinger,
4 Amanda Beidler,
5 Matilda Frey.

APRIL 16, 1865.
Males.

1 Daniel A. Butz,
2 Samuel A. Roth,
3 Alfred C. Osenbach,
4 William B. Walter,
5 James Remmel,
6 Samuel S. Stump,
7 Eli G. Deily,
8 Richard F. Nagel,
9 Josiah Deily,
10 Alfred Nagel.

Females.

1 Sarah L. Schmoykeffer,
2 Marietta M. Diehl,
3 Amanda L. Eberhard,
4 Martha S. J. Fatzinger,
5 Josephine Frey,
6 Alavesta L. Nolf.

MAY 12, 1867.
Males.

1 David Sterner,
2 William Schlosser,
3 Thomas Hoehle,
4 Harrison Miller.

Females.

1 Ellen S. Osenbach,
2 Elmira Gross,
3 Mary J. Osenbach,
4 Matilda J. Albrecht,
5 Lucy J. Berger,
6 Catharine Nagel.

225

NOVEMBER 22, 1868.
Males.

1 Edmund A. Walter,
2 Amandus L. Fatzinger,
3 Michael Kidd,
4 William Harvey,
5 Ulrich Ritter,
6 Theodore E. Trexler,
7 Aaron Johnson,
8 George Tilgh. Fallstich.

Females.

1 Eliza A. Kidd,
2 Mary A. Reichard,
3 Mary A. Sterner,
4 Mary A. J. Mertz,
5 Matilda L. Stump,
6 Jane Schneider,
7 Eliza J. Deily.

OCTOBER 30, 1870.
Males.

1 William Osenbach,
2 Theodore W. Moyer,
3 Richard Schlegel,
4 Hiram C. Deily,
5 Jeremiah G. Moyer,
6 Oliver R. Moyer,
7 Peter Nagel,
8 John Ernst.

Females.

1 Catharine Ann Flores,
2 Lucetta Flores,
3 Ida Mary Fatzinger,
4 Mary Jane Fatzinger,
5 Margaret S. L. Moyer,
6 Amanda J. Sterner,
7 Isabella J. Wisser,
8 Fyetta Sterner.

OCTOBER 27, 1872.
Males.

1 Abraham Kreiss,
2 Thomas H. Bauer,
3 William H. Roller,
4 Thomas F. Reichard,
5 John F. Roller,
6 Monroe A. Reichard,
7 Milton C. Ritter,
8 Milton F. Reichard,
9 Alfred S. Hoehle,
10 James M. Smith,
11 Alfred W. Moyer,
12 Theodore Flores,
13 Amandus Nagel,
14 Sylvester Handschuh,

Females.

1 Camilla Osenbach,
2 Lizzie J. Moyer,
3 Alice F. Kichline,
4 Mary A. Donnecker,
5 Mary R. Bauer,
6 Emma Deily,
7 Emma Weimer,
8 Emma Layton,
9 Mary Miller,
10 Luella Trexler,
11 Jane Oswald.

NOVEMBER 15, 1874.
Males.

1 Wilson Jefferson Schmidt,
2 Theodore Nagel,
3 George Daniel Worman,
4 Levi Wenner,
5 Lovin Kramer,
6 Marcellus Frank Boyer,
7 Albert Moser,
8 George Kreiss,
9 Henry H. Fetter,
10 William Everhart,
11 William Stecher,
12 Charles Moser.

Females.

1 Montana Hoehle,
2 Amanda Reichert,
3 Laura Walter,
4 Jane Taylor,
5 Laura Weil,
6 Alavesta Weil,
7 Fyanna Ritter,
8 Alice Sterner,
9 Susan Werkheiser,
10 Camilla Boyer,
11 Emma Fatzinger,
12 Emma Osenbach.

NOVEMBER 12, 1876.
Males.

1 Samuel D. Deily,
2 Alfred C. Moyer,
3 Preston Dixon,
4 Orange D. Nagle,
5 William H. Weil,
6 Louis Worman,
7 Oliver C. Ritter,
8 John Q. Moyer.

Females.

1 Elenora Weil,
2 Mary C. Flores,
3 Elenora Roller,
4 Lucinda Schaffer,
5 Elizabeth Berry,
6 Mary A. Herman,
7 Jennie Flores,
8 Mary Deily,
9 Laura Sterner,
10 Theodora M. Swain.

November 17, 1878.

Males.

1 Harrison J. Werst,
2 Oliver Abner Souders,
3 Milton A. Miller,
4 William Franklin Fenchel,
5 Thomas Franklin Miller,
6 George Burnside Walter,
7 Robert I. Osenbach,
8 Elmer M. Osenbach,
9 Elmer Miller,
10 William Albert Berger,
11 Henry Robach.

Females.

1 Lucy Ann Berger,
2 Mary Jane Rape,
3 Alice P. Hoehle,
4 Laura Elizabeth Wisser,
5 Emma Ellen Brader,
6 Laura A. Snyder,
7 Alice Olivia Nagle,
8 Amelia Nagle,
9 Hannah Rebecca Wisser,
10 Emma A. Schlosser.

October 17, 1880.

Males.

1 Jacob F. Kreiss,
2 Edwin Kreiss,
3 Peter Butz,
4 John Deily,
5 Monroe Tice,
6 Tidel Robuck,
7 Erwin A. Weil,
8 John A. Reed,
9 Lewellyn E. Mosser,
10 William H. Deily,
11 Charles H. Harris,
12 William A. Acker,
13 Clinton L. Herst,
14 Charles Robuck.

Females.

1 Annie M. Kreiss,
2 Celesta M. Weil,
3 Mary E. Beitler,
4 Mary A. Ehret,
5 Ellen V. Nicholas.

November 12, 1882.

Males.

1 Monroe Flory,
2 Jeremiah Falstich,
3 Orange Miller,
4 Theodore Frey,
5 Stephen Wisser,
6 Jacob Donnecker,

7 Edwin Hoehle,   12 Elner Sterner,
8 Frank Walter,   13 Forrest Mill,
9 Jeremiah Butler,   14 Quinton Hendricks.
10 Frank Marsteller,   15 Frank Harris,
11 Preston Weil,   16 James Miller.

Females.

1 Ellen Kratzer,   5 Mary S. M. Deily,
2 Emma D. Flory,   6 Laura C. Nagle,
3 Ellen Wisser,   7 Lilly J. Sterner.
4 Ida R. Boyer,

NOVEMBER 9, 1884.

Males.

1 Albert C. Saeger,   5 Harry S. Mill,
2 George A. Ritter,   6 Lewis H. Texter,
3 Charles H. Kratzer, 7 Martin H. Falstich.
4 Thomas B. Wieser,

Females.

1 Emma J. Nagle,   5 Mary J. Harris,
2 Annie M. Brinker,   6 Mary E. Flores,
3 Lucinda C. Brinker, 7 Cora M. Sterner,
4 Ellen J. Acker,   8 Clara E. Roller.

REMARKS.

FATHER YEAGER usually added at the end of each list of names of those whom he confirmed: "It is my wish and prayer that these names may be recorded in the Book of Eternal Life." So may it be, and if any one has become unfaithful to God or his duty, may that one, when he sees his name in this book, be reminded of his duty and his solemn promises, and return penitent to his God and his Church.

Several of the photographs from which the engravings of this book have been made were taken by Mr. Francis Warmkessel, photographer, Allentown, Pa., whom Father Yeager confirmed in Lehigh Church in 1873.

The funds for engraving the excellent photograph of Father Yeager were contributed by J. B. Reeme, Esq., and Miss Minnie W. and Norton R. Yeager.

A. R. H.

Allentown, Pa., August 1, 1889.

www.ingramcontent.com/pod-product-compliance
Lightning Source LLC
Chambersburg PA
CBHW031748230426
43669CB00007B/537